IMAGES
of America

UPPER MISSISSIPPI RIVER AT WINONA

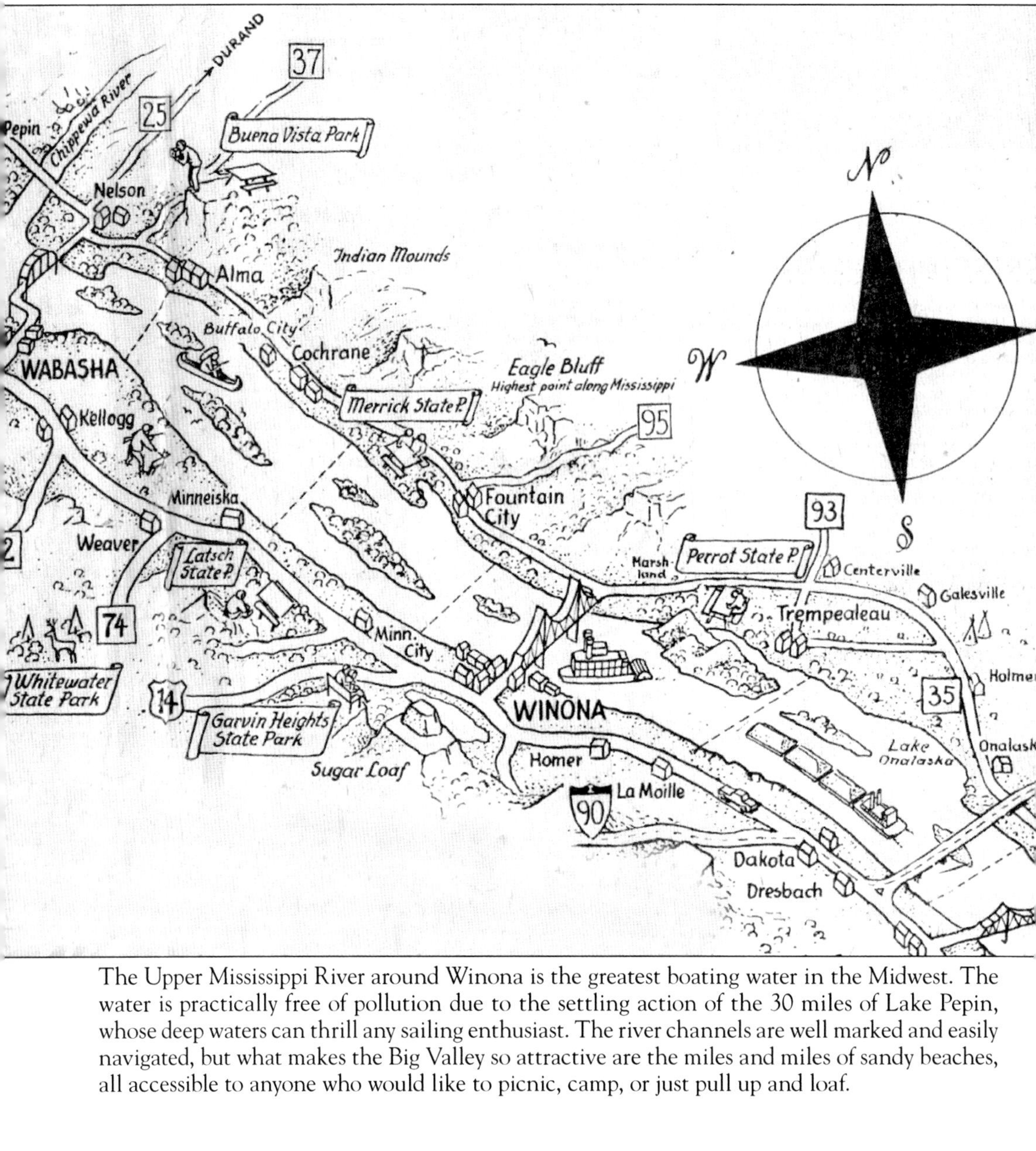

The Upper Mississippi River around Winona is the greatest boating water in the Midwest. The water is practically free of pollution due to the settling action of the 30 miles of Lake Pepin, whose deep waters can thrill any sailing enthusiast. The river channels are well marked and easily navigated, but what makes the Big Valley so attractive are the miles and miles of sandy beaches, all accessible to anyone who would like to picnic, camp, or just pull up and loaf.

On the Cover: On August 18, 1979, the *Delta Queen*, carrying Pres. Jimmy Carter and his family, steams past the Chicago & Northwestern Railroad swing bridge and toward Winona's Levee Park, where 6,000 local and area residents anxiously wait to get a glimpse. The boat stopped about 100 feet offshore, and with its sternwheel slowly churning to hold against the current, the president briefly spoke to the assembled crowd from the third deck.

IMAGES
of America

UPPER MISSISSIPPI RIVER AT WINONA

Walter Bennick

ARCADIA
PUBLISHING

ISBN 978-1-4671-1510-0

Published by Arcadia Publishing
Charleston, South Carolina

Printed in the United States of America

Library of Congress Control Number: 2015943997

For all general information, please contact Arcadia Publishing:
Telephone 843-853-2070
Fax 843-853-0044
E-mail sales@arcadiapublishing.com
For customer service and orders:
Toll-Free 1-888-313-2665

Visit us on the Internet at www.arcadiapublishing.com

To Bunny, my wife of 50 years.

Contents

ACKNOWLEDGMENTS

The photographs in this book were exclusively selected from the Winona County Historical Society's collection of photographs, lithographs, and albums—all of which have been donated to the society's archives. Many of these photographs were donated by the *Winona Daily News* and have appeared in print in the *Winona Daily Republican*, *Winona Republican-Herald*, *Winona Daily News*, or *Winona Post*. The remainder were donated by individuals, families, and community organizations. A number of photographs have been used in this book, including those by Angelyn de Groot, Charles A. Tenney, Merritt W. Kelley, Calvin R. Fremling, the US Fish and Wildlife Service, the US Army Corps of Engineers, and Kenneth M. Wright.

Much of the history here has been obtained from county history books in the Winona County Historical Society's collection and from the local newspapers, both on microfilm and courtesy of the *Winona Daily News*. Many were available online through Winona State University's Winona Newspaper Project, which covers the period from 1857 through 1976.

Thanks go to the Winona County Historical Society for the opportunity to utilize its collection of photographs for this project and to the staff for their encouragement. In addition, thank you Mark Peterson, society director, for assistance and direction.

INTRODUCTION

The Mississippi River at Winona is near the center of the 50 miles of the navigable portion of the river that flows from west to east. It is located about 125 miles from the head of navigation near Minneapolis. The navigable portion of the Upper Mississippi River is an 850-mile waterway connecting its ports to the world. Commercial navigation, recreation, and wildlife all flourish along this waterway. In addition, a larger region relies on river water for public and industrial supplies, power plant cooling, wastewater assimilation, and a variety of other uses.

The Mississippi River is an integral part of Winona's proud heritage. It once served as the nation's western border until 1851, when the Treaty of Mendota was signed, which allowed for settlement beyond. The Mississippi River is a unique resource, home to a diverse array of wildlife that find habitat in the river valley. It is a navigational corridor for waterfowl and provides habitat for breeding and wintering birds. In addition, recreational activities abound on the river, including boating, fishing, swimming, or simply enjoying its beauty.

The Upper Mississippi River probably originated as an ice-margin stream. At the end of the last glacial period, it was part of a now-extinct glacial river that carved its valley with water from the melting ice sheets. The Upper Mississippi River from below the Falls of St. Anthony to St. Paul is in a gorge carved by this meltwater. Downstream from St. Paul, the torrents of meltwater carved a channel to a depth of about a thousand feet and a width up to five miles. As the water subsided, much of the sediment being carried by the water was deposited, filling the valley. Later, water scoured out some of the deposited glacial debris, leaving the channels and terraces seen today.

In earlier times, the Mississippi River and its valley were swarming with life, and natives took advantage of this bounty by settling along both sides of the river. In the 1700s, white men began to invade the valley, exploring and filching its riches. The next three centuries witnessed the opening of the river and its valley to land-grabbers, squatters, loggers, trappers, steamboaters, and industrial barons who recognized the river as a highway on which to carry their goods to market.

Following settlement, canoes gave way to rafts, keelboats, and steamboats transporting soldiers, settlers, and freight into the new frontier. The earliest steamboat to travel the Upper Mississippi River was the *Virginia*, which carried supplies to Fort Snelling. It left St. Louis on April 21, 1823, and arrived at the fort 20 days later. The fort was later supplied by Capt. Orrin Smith, who traveled from Galena, Illinois. On his way to the fort, Captain Smith sailed past a large island in the river, and on October 15, 1851, he had Erwin Johnson claim the island for himself and Smith.

Paddle wheelers became the next mode of transportation on this inland waterway transporting freight and passengers. The river swarmed with them, especially as millions of logs were rafted downriver to the sawmills. At Winona in 1890, some 8,585 boats, barges, and rafts were counted stopping or passing by. After the forests were decimated, the rafts were phased out and used for excursions.

The days of show and excursion boats represented one of the most colorful eras on the river, and area cities played host to dozens on a regular basis. Capt. John Streckfus was the first to build a boat exclusively for excursion use. These boats were so popular that many had to be built to meet the demand.

The history of navigation on the Upper Mississippi River goes back to 1820, when Congress authorized the removal of obstructions to navigation on the river. As navigation on the river became more commonplace, modifications were made to create a maneuverable channel with such man-made features as wing dams. These dams directed the flow of water into the main channel to scour it of sediment. In 1878, Congress authorized a four-and-a-half-foot-deep channel, which was accomplished by the removal of snags and the scarping of sandbars.

In 1907, Congress authorized a six-foot-deep channel, which was accomplished with the use of wing dams. The wing dams did not help much, and for many of the larger packets, Winona became the head of navigation. At Winona, freight and passengers were transferred to smaller and lighter packets for the rest of their trip upriver.

Droughts in the 1920s reduced the flow of water in the Mississippi River, limiting navigation. Congress therefore authorized the creation a nine-foot-deep and 400-foot-wide navigation channel, which used a series of 27 locks and dams to create a series of pools. These locks and dams resulted in a sequence of steps designed to allow boats to climb or descend as they traveled the river. From the Twin Cities to Dam No. 27, the river drops 420 feet in a distance of 670 miles. The average drop is about 15 feet, and boats entering a lock from a lower pool are lifted by water flowing out of the upper level, thus raising the boat to the level of the upper pool.

Times of high water, primarily in the spring, cause the river to flood, sometimes with great damage. Following the flood of 1965, a system of levees was built to protect Winona from floods up to 22 feet. These levees have changed the character of Winona's connection with the river but have limited damage caused by periods of high water.

Modification and development in the valley have had a wide-ranging effect on the valley's ecosystem. Although the lock and dam system created a significant increase in the diversity of habitat, sedimentation has resulted in a significant decrease in habitat. It has filled in backwaters, increased turbidity, and carried excessive nutrients into the aquatic ecosystem.

The Mississippi River has been designated both a significant ecosystem and navigable river system, and Congress has directed that it be regulated and maintained in recognition of its main purpose. The river has been a source for food and other products for the local market, including sand for fill, clamshells for buttons, and ice for cooling. It has also been a place for recreation, including boating, swimming, and water skiing. Winona has celebrated the river with water carnivals and Steamboat Days. Riverside Park, later known as Levee Park, was developed to connect the city to the river and during the second half of the 20th century. Attempts were made to develop interpretive centers and river tours, and while most have gone by the wayside, new ways to celebrate the river continue to develop.

One

Untamed and Barely Navigable

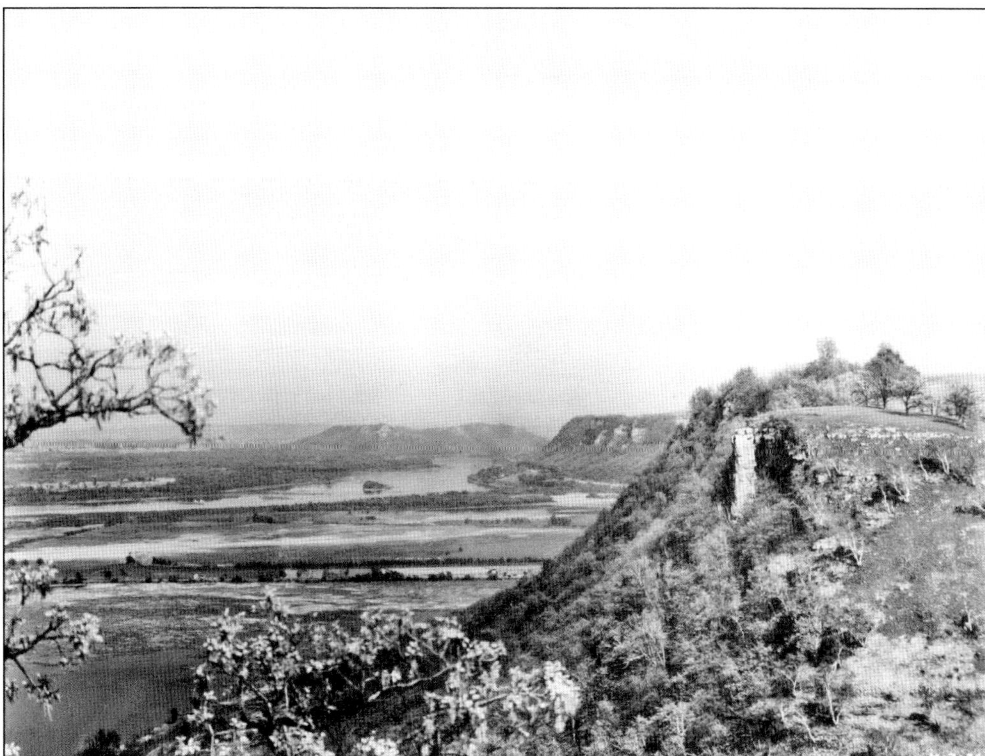

The Mississippi River Valley was carved by water from the melting glaciers at the end of the last ice age, resulting in a deep, wide valley. As melting subsided, the valley was halfway filled with glacial sediments, which formed the river's floodplain.

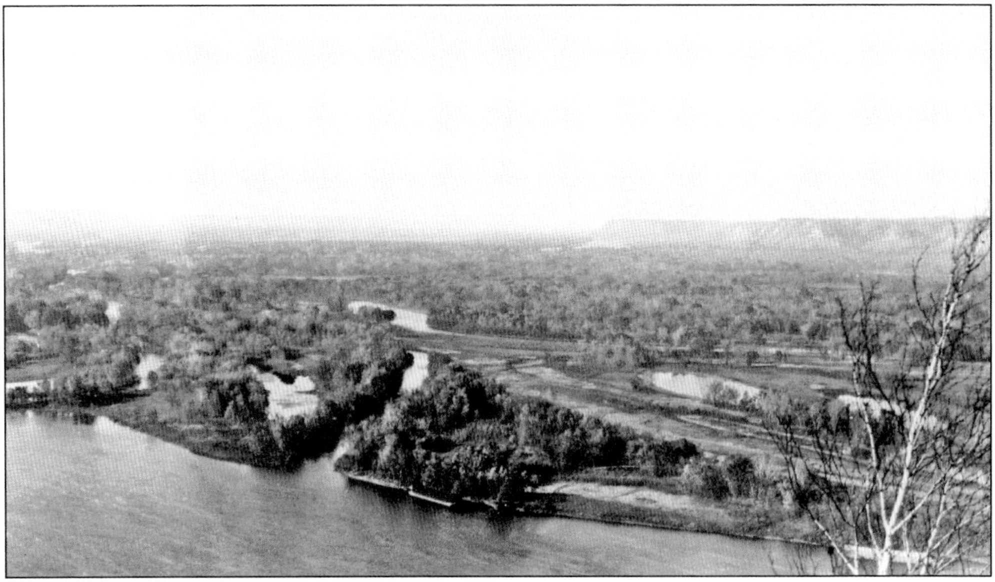

In some places, the Mississippi River Valley is over three miles wide and contains an underfit stream, which is now too small for its valley. Most of the river valley now contains numerous side channels, sloughs, lakes, and marshes. Many were caused by the meandering of the stream, with older channels being filled or plugged with sediments.

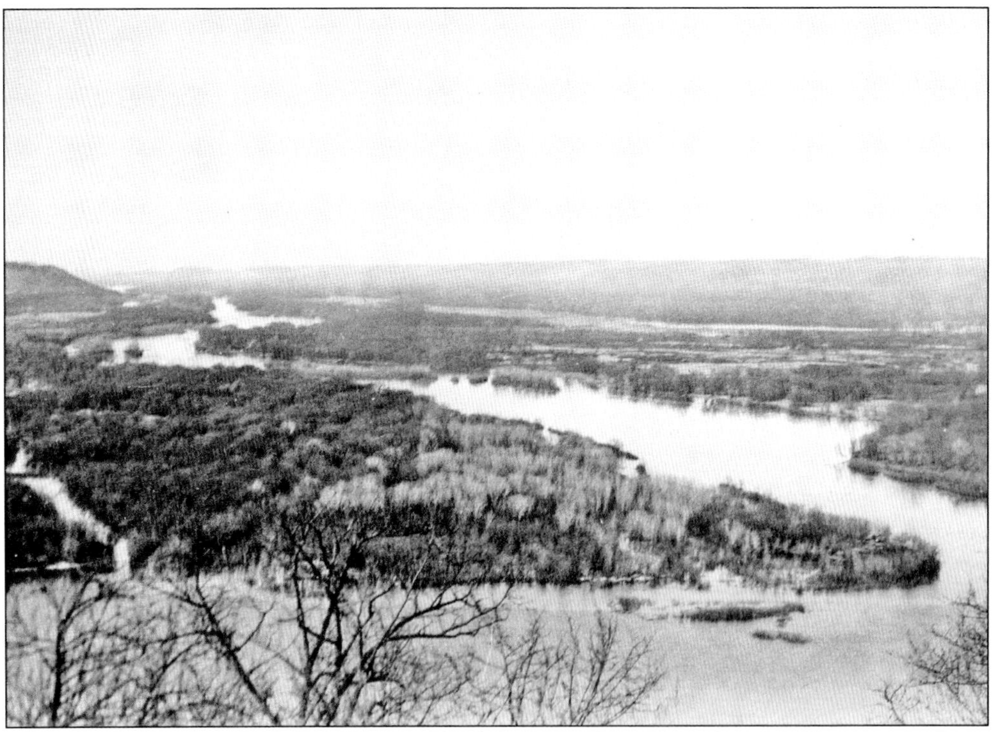

The Mississippi River was named by Fr. Claude Allouez from an Ojibwa word meaning "Great River." In the mid-1660s, Father Allouez, a Jesuit priest, was stationed at a mission near present-day Ashland, Wisconsin, when he was told by the Native Americans of the *Messippi*, the great central river of the continent. This word first appeared in print in the *Jesuit Relation* of 1666–1667.

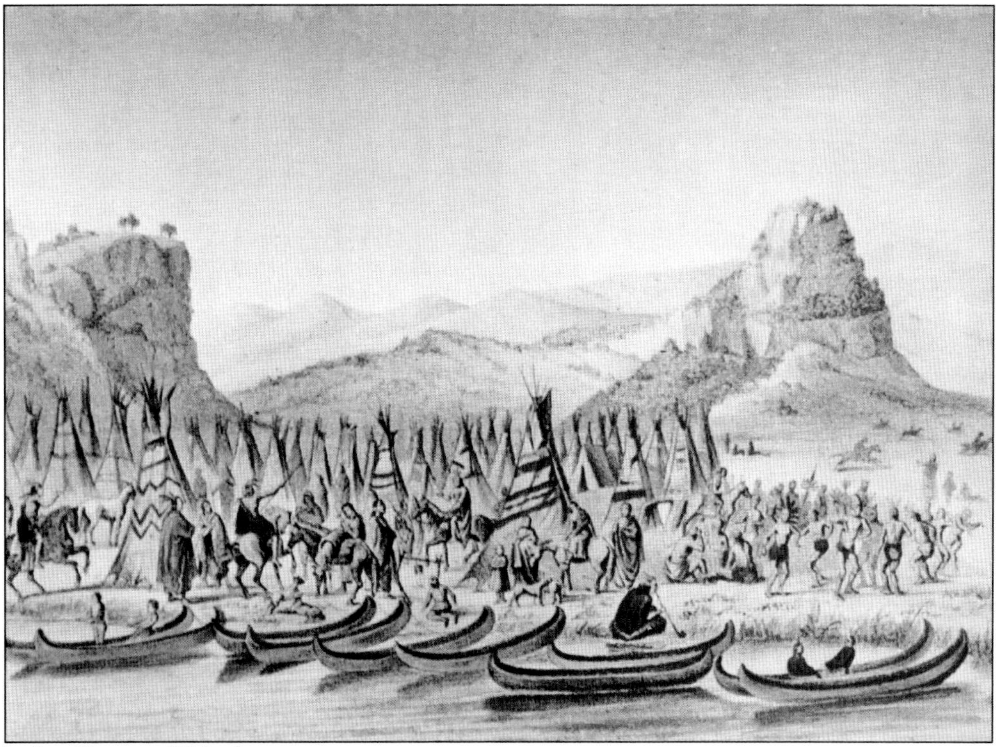

Indian Camp at Wabasha Prairie, a colored lithograph by Henry Lewis (1819–1904) from *Das Illustrirte Mississippithal* (1854–1858), presents a view of Chief Wabasha's camp just after the white settlers moved onto Wabasha's Prairie.

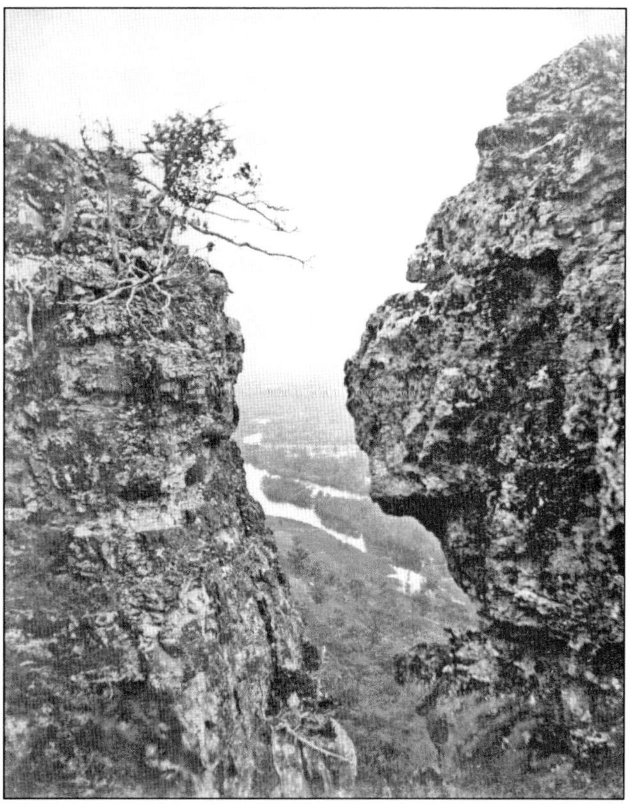

An early view of the Mississippi River Valley is seen through a break in the bluffs near Fountain City, Wisconsin.

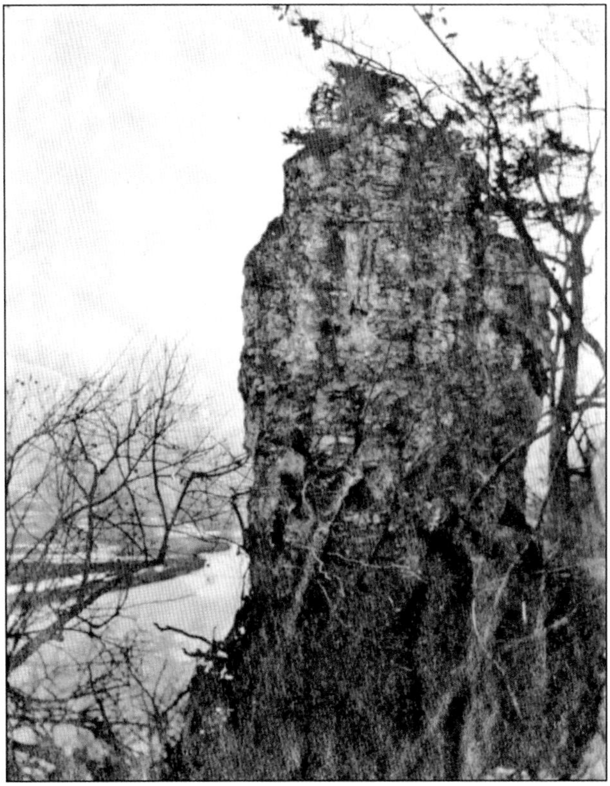

This craggy pinnacle is a part of the river valley bluffs near Winona. The river's backwaters and marshland can be seen encroaching onto the edge of the bluffs.

A keelboat was used to move men and materials on the unexplored inland river systems, such as the Mississippi River. The keelboat was of shallow draft and relatively narrow to allow navigation through and around shallow water, snags, and sawyers. It was propelled upstream by men pushing on poles or pulling it along from the stream bank.

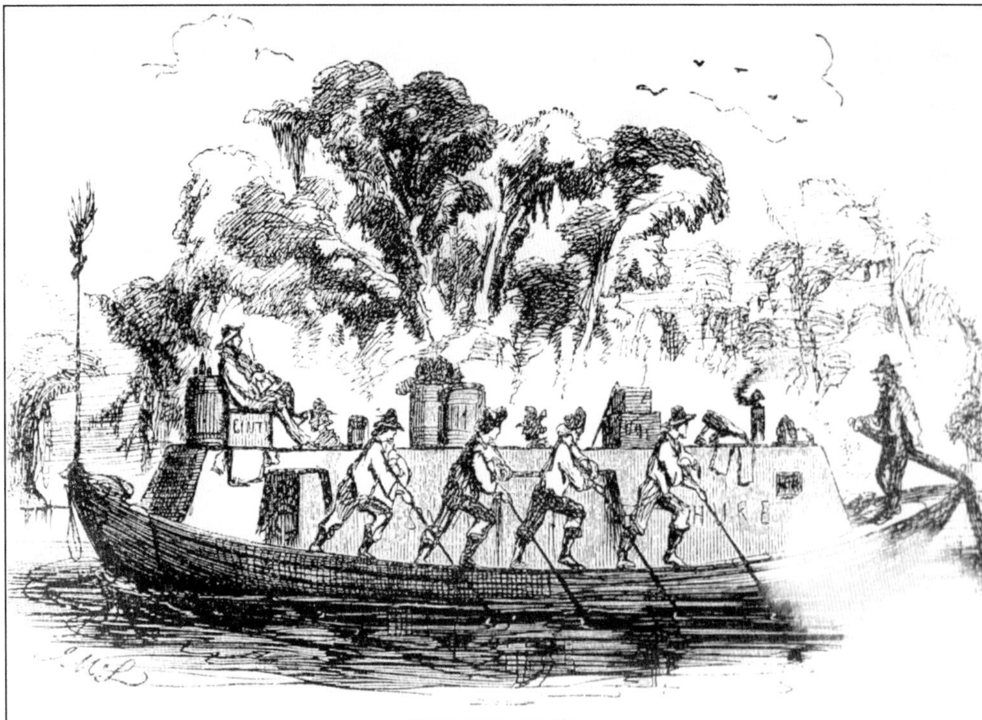

THE KEEL-BOAT.

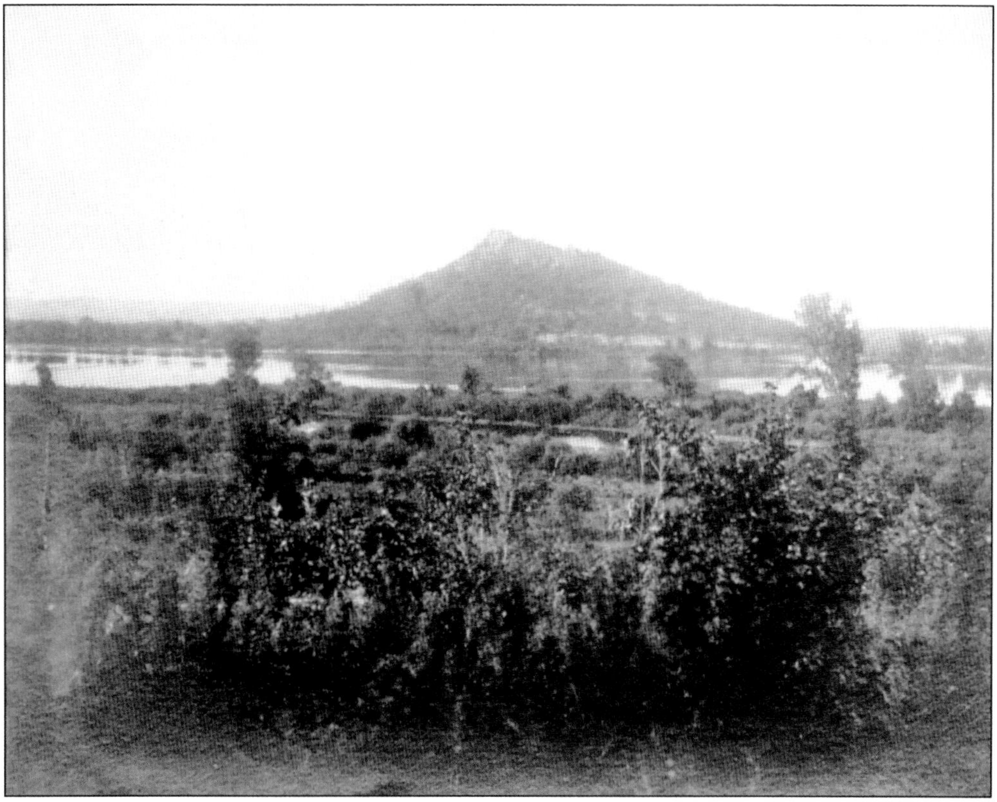

Hay-nee-ah-chah (Soaking Mountain), now known as Trempealeau Mountain, is pictured from the Minnesota side of the Mississippi River. This photograph shows effectively that it is isolated from the other bluffs—a mountain soaking in the river. Before white settlement, the mountain was completely surrounded by water and could only be reached by canoe. It was not a favorite place for Native Americans because of the rattlesnakes that lived on it. To the area Dakota, it was known as Maya-hin-ca-sin-ta-da (Rattlesnake Bluff).

Steamer *Anson Northup*, pictured in *Harper's Weekly*, was built in 1859 for use on the Red River of the North. It was similar to the *Virginia*, which became the first steamer to travel on the Upper Mississippi River in 1823. These early paddleboats were from 50 to 70 feet in length and 12 to 18 feet in width. Sleeping accommodations consisted of open bunks separated by curtains.

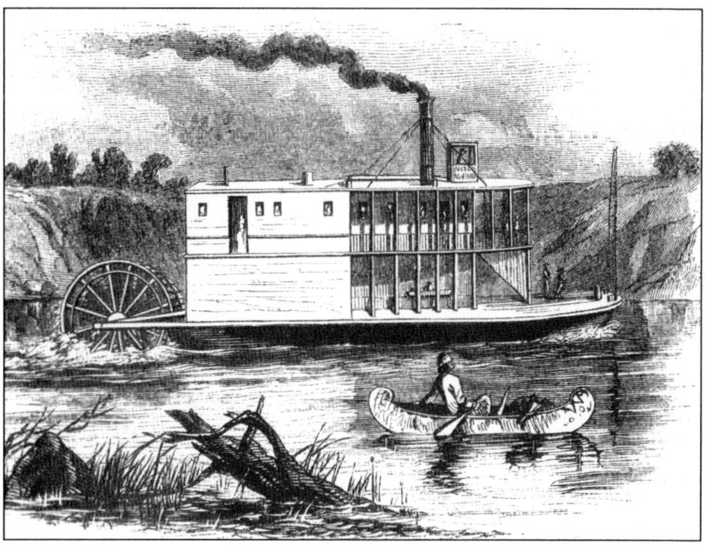

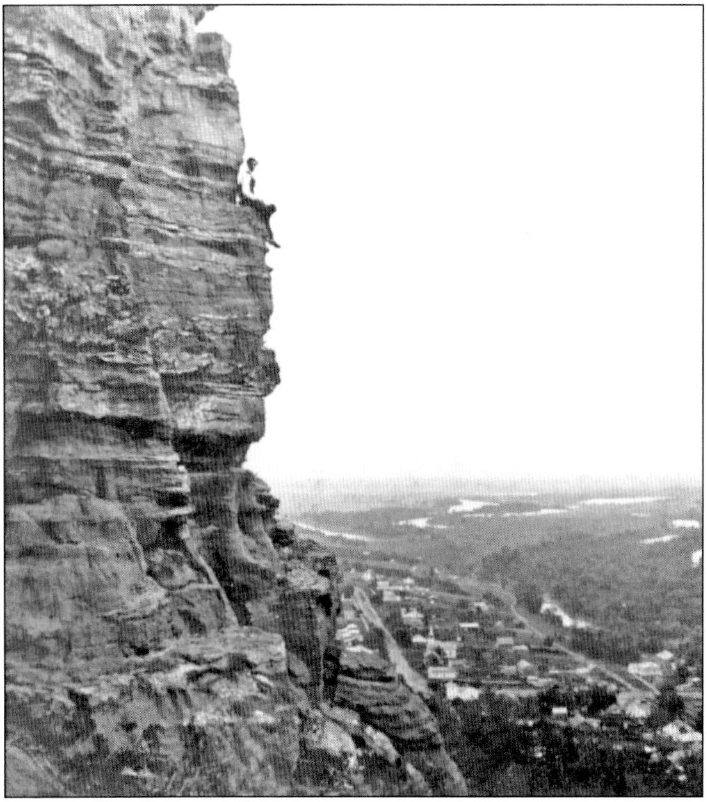

This 1875 view of the village of Trempealeau, Wisconsin, and the Mississippi River Valley was taken by Winona photographers E. Harry Hoard and Charles A. Tenney from the Wisconsin bluffs. A climber can be seen sitting on a narrow ledge on the side of the bluff.

Pictured is one of the numerous side channels or sloughs found in the Mississippi River Valley extending from the main channel toward the bluffs, which mark the limits of the valley.

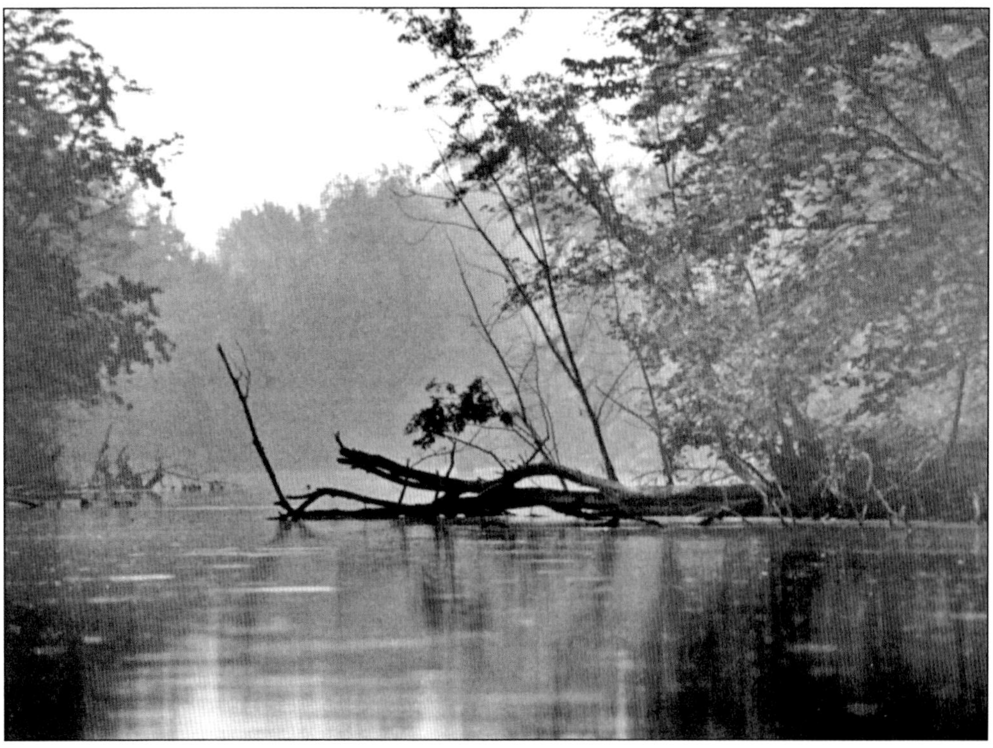

The Mississippi River and its valley are seen in this 1880s Charles A. Tenney photograph from Castle Rock, an isolated pinnacle in the Wisconsin bluffs near Winona. Castle Rock, known by tourists far and wide, is one of the most beautiful of the many natural landmarks found along the Upper Mississippi River. It has new splendors each time the nature lover visits its commanding position overlooking the river. Located on the Wisconsin bluffs, two miles upriver from Winona, it was often visited by local residents, including Prof. John M. Holzinger, who would bring his students from the Winona State Normal School to explore this rock formation. In this view, three individuals can be seen standing at the top of the pinnacle while studying a large expanse of the river valley.

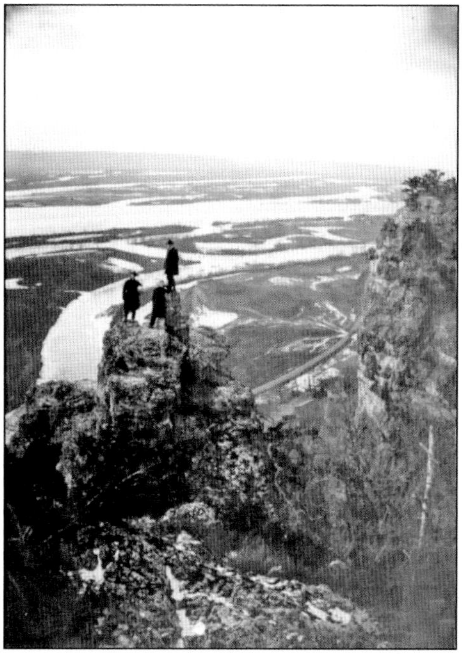

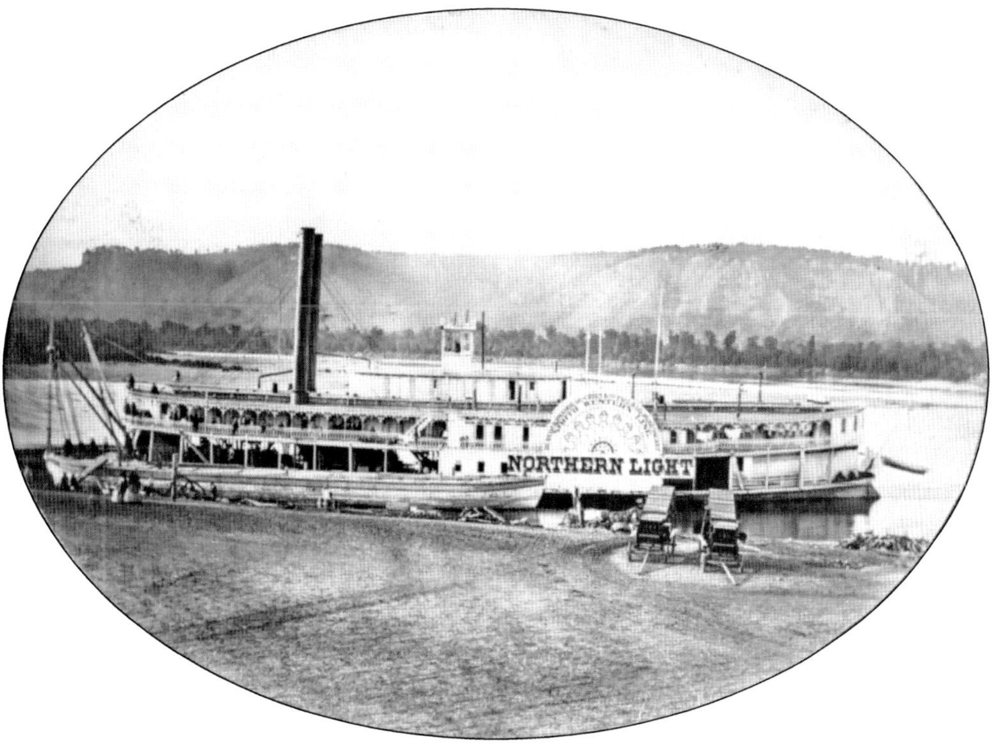

The *Northern Light*, docked at the Winona Levee, was a sidewheel packet steamboat that was built in 1847 in Madison, Indiana. The boat, owned by the Minnesota Packet Company, was under the command of Capt. Preston Lodwick and plied the waters of the Upper Mississippi River from 1848 until April 11, 1866, when it struck a pile of ice in Coon Slough near Brownsville, Minnesota, and sank in 30 feet of water.

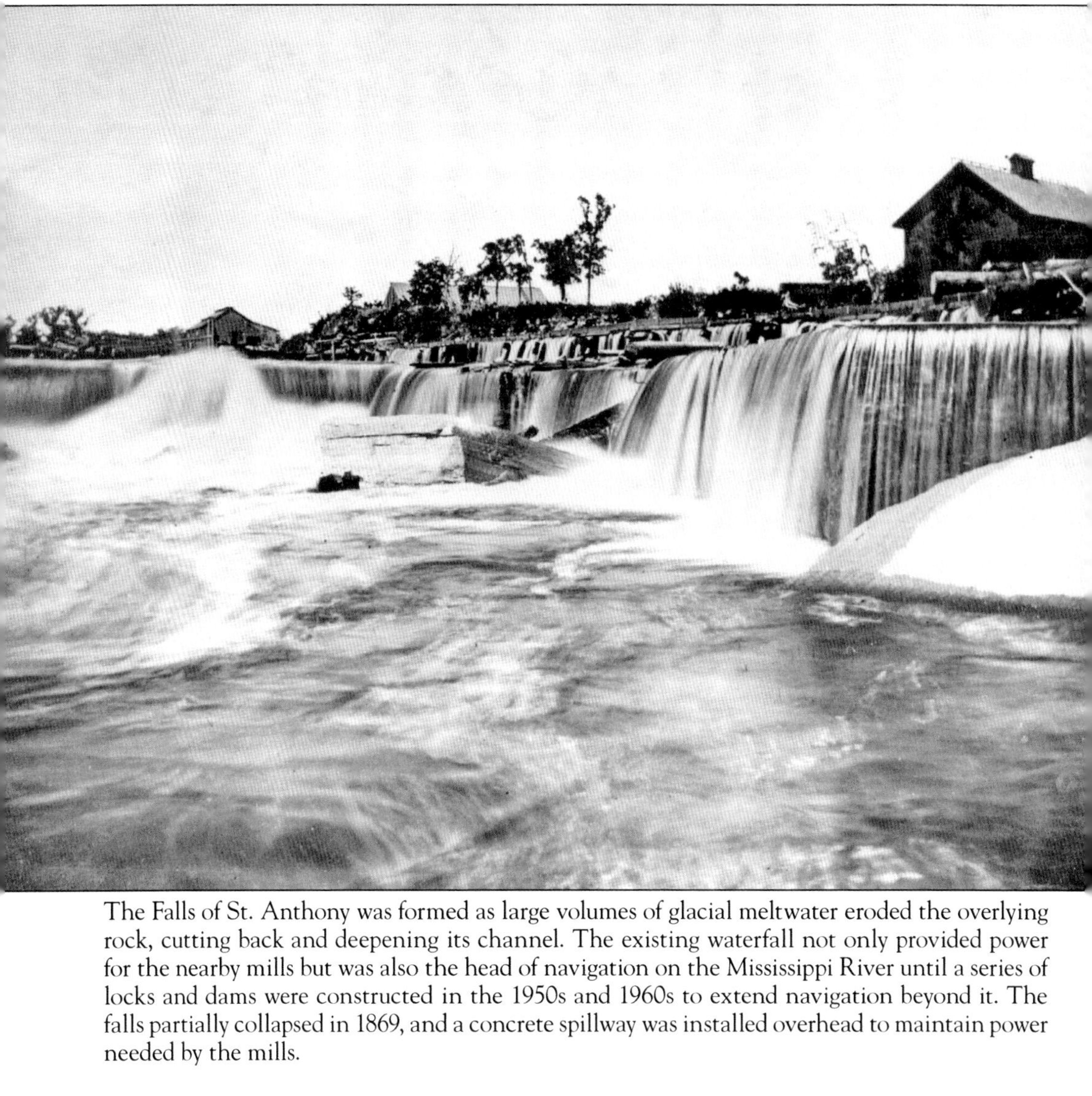

The Falls of St. Anthony was formed as large volumes of glacial meltwater eroded the overlying rock, cutting back and deepening its channel. The existing waterfall not only provided power for the nearby mills but was also the head of navigation on the Mississippi River until a series of locks and dams were constructed in the 1950s and 1960s to extend navigation beyond it. The falls partially collapsed in 1869, and a concrete spillway was installed overhead to maintain power needed by the mills.

Two

Taming the River

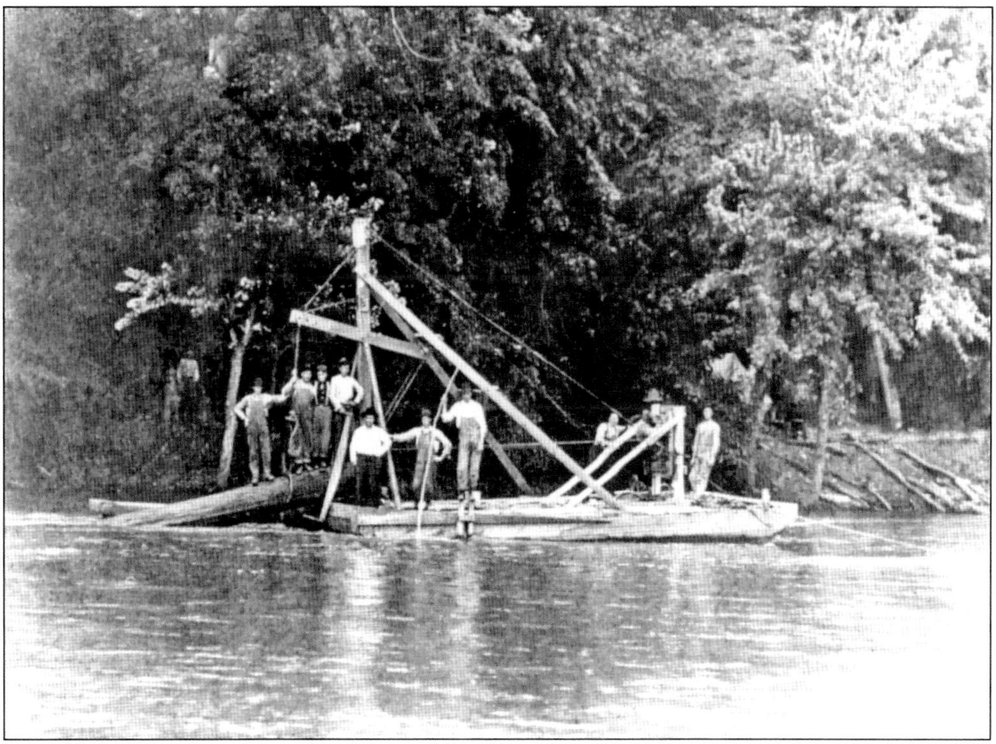

Early in our republic, Congress authorized that the War Department Corps of Engineers would maintain the inland waterways for safe navigation. One of the many hazards to navigation were tree trunks, on which boats would snag and become damaged. Boats were used by the Corps of Engineers to remove such snags, as shown in this photograph.

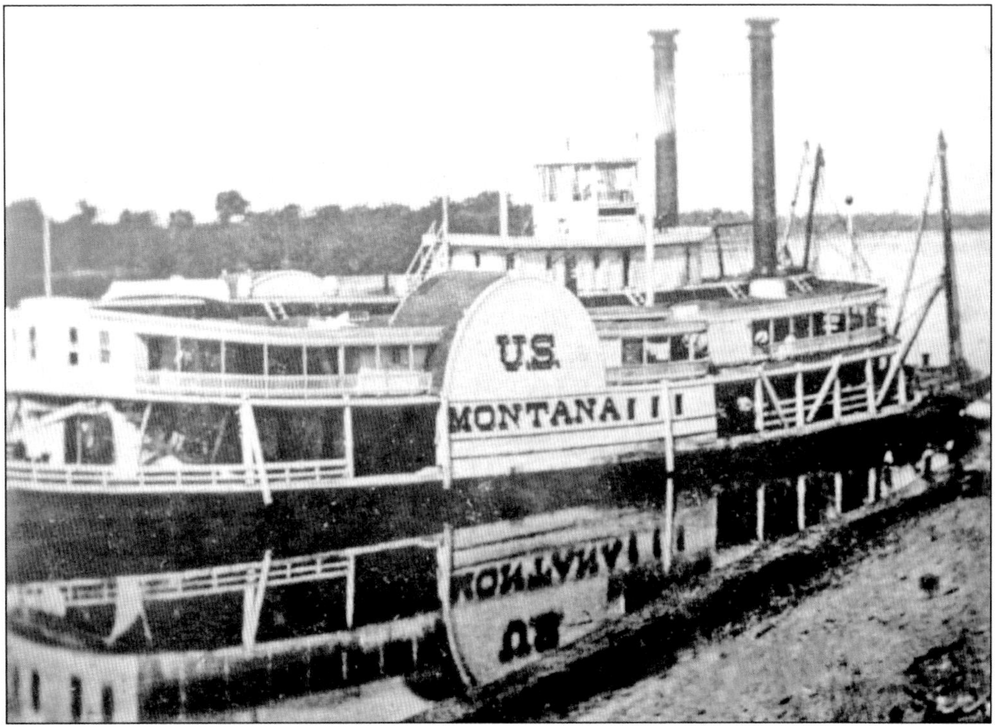

Government steamer *Montana* was used to clear the navigation channels of snags and sandbars in order to maintain a channel four feet in depth. To clear away the sandbars, it would literally scrape the sand away.

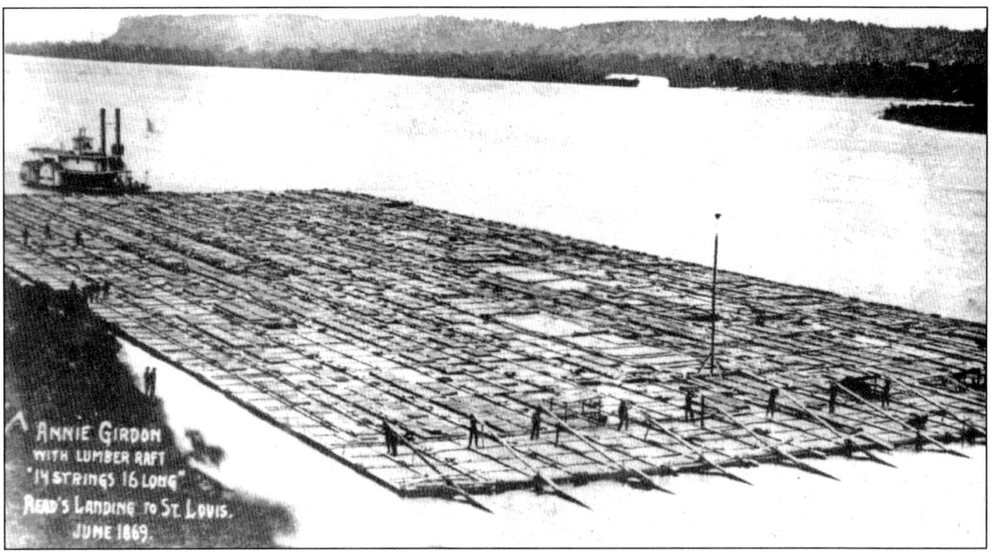

In June 1869, steamer *Annie Girdon* was pushing a fair-sized lumber raft from Reads Landing to St. Louis. The steamer did not have enough power to steer the raft around the bends in the river, so in order to guide the raft around these bends, long-bladed oars with long handles were attached to the front of the raft. These oars, manned by oarsmen, were moved in unison to swing the raft to the right or left through the river bends. The steamer's captain would blow the vessel's whistle to indicate the direction of the turn needed.

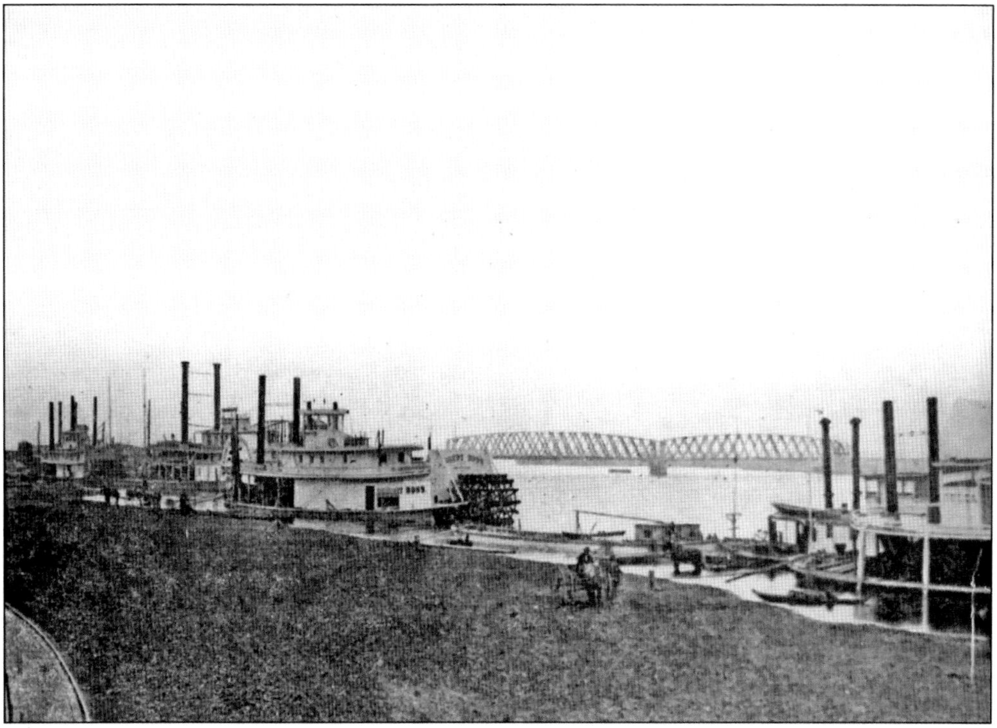

About six paddle wheelers are tied up at the Winona Levee in 1872, shortly after the Winona & St. Peter Railroad swing bridge was placed in operation. At the time, the steamboat was the most popular method of conveyance.

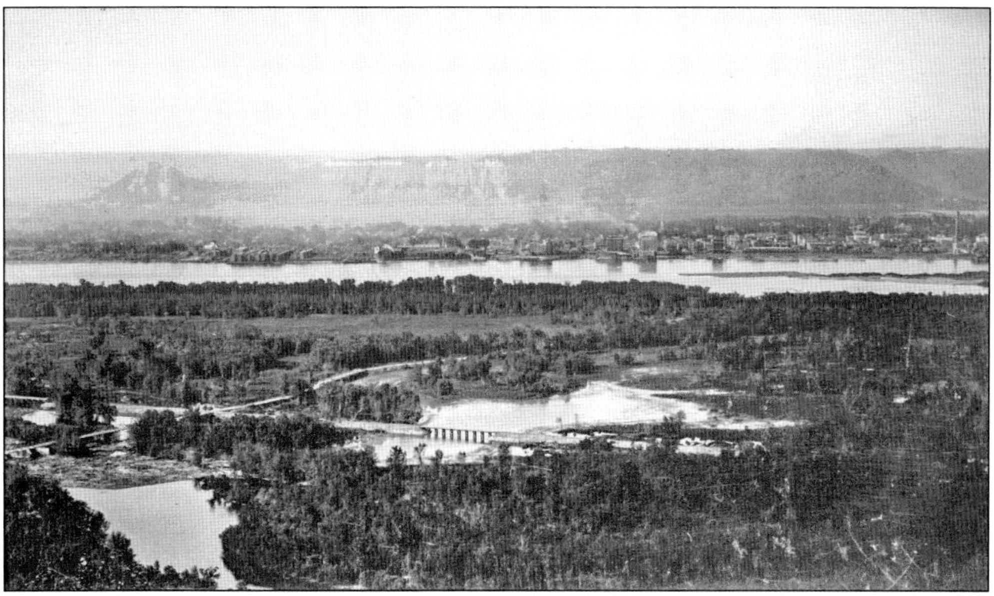

This photograph of Winona in the late 1870s was taken from the Wisconsin bluffs. The bridge in the foreground carries the Winona & St. Peter Railroad to the swing bridge, completed in 1872, which crosses the Mississippi River at far right. The roadway near the center led to the ferry landing near Bluff Siding, Wisconsin.

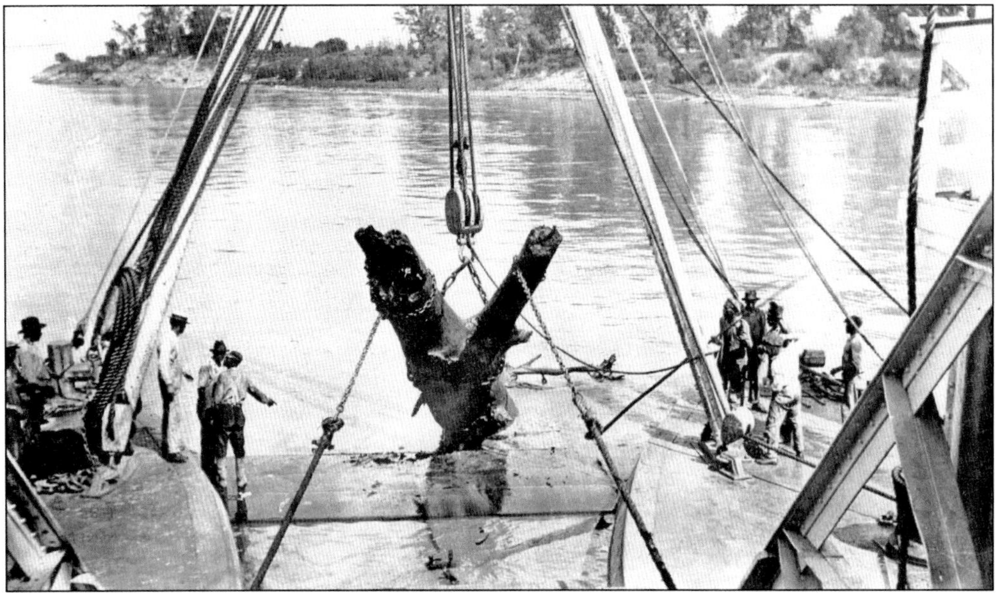

Later snagboats were equipped with a twin hull, strong windlasses, and steam-powered saws. The boat would ram into the snag with an iron-platted bow and pull the snag from the riverbed onto the boat with a strong windlass. With the steam-powered saw, the snag would be cut into harmless pieces before being tossed back into the river to float away.

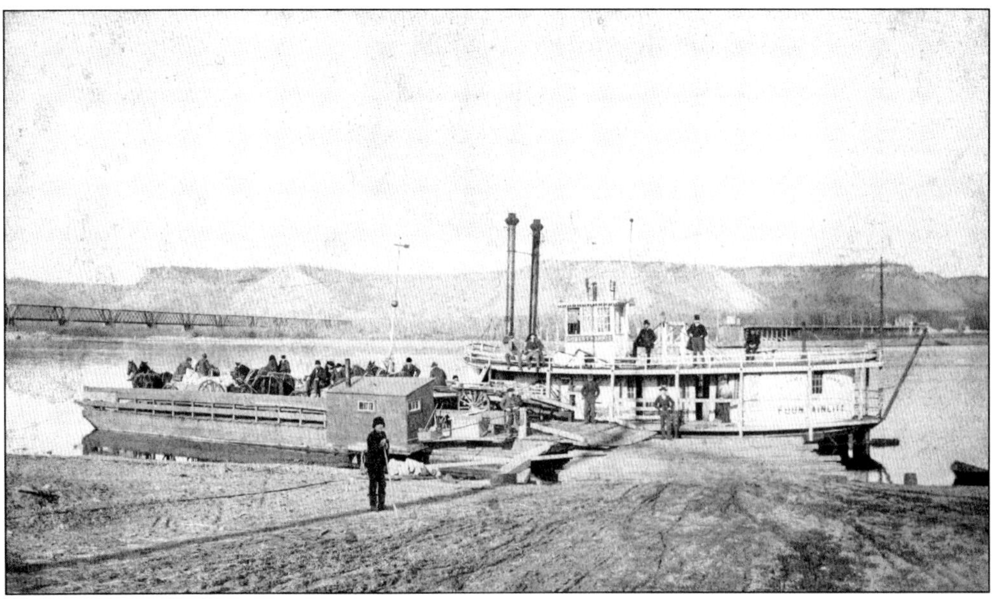

Steamer *Robert Harris*, a small short-line packet and excursion boat, was owned and operated by Capt. Peter Schneider and William Heck, engineer. It made regular runs between Fountain City, Wisconsin, and Winona between 1875 and 1905.

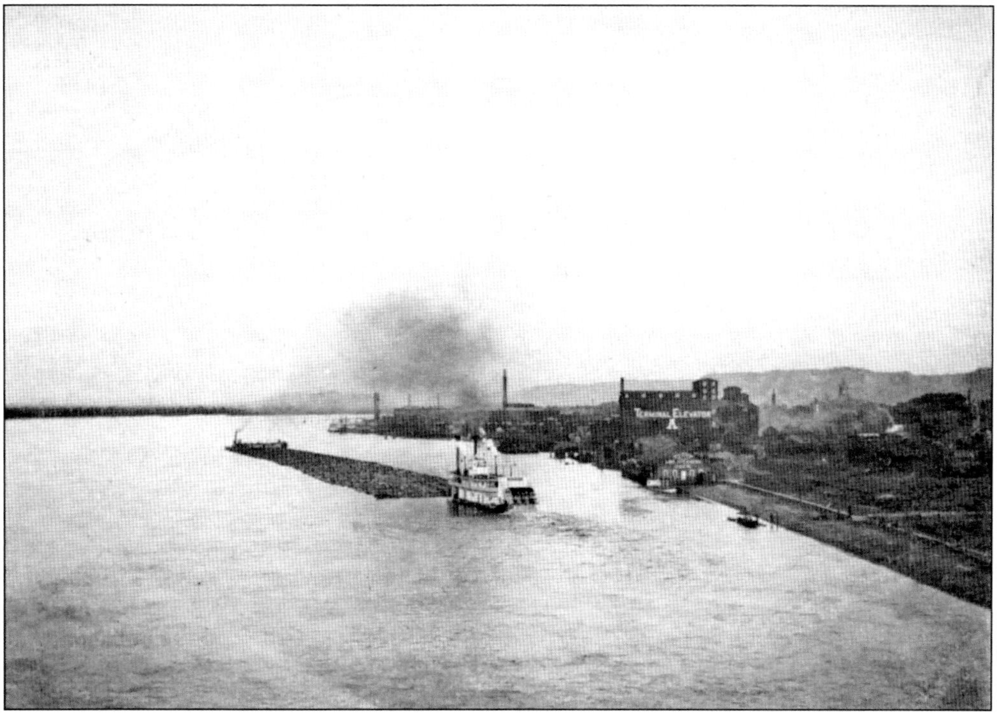

A log raft travels past Winona Levee in late 1890. In order to keep the raft in the navigation channel, a bow-boat is attached to the front of the raft, which can steer the raft to the left or right by changing the direction of its paddle wheel.

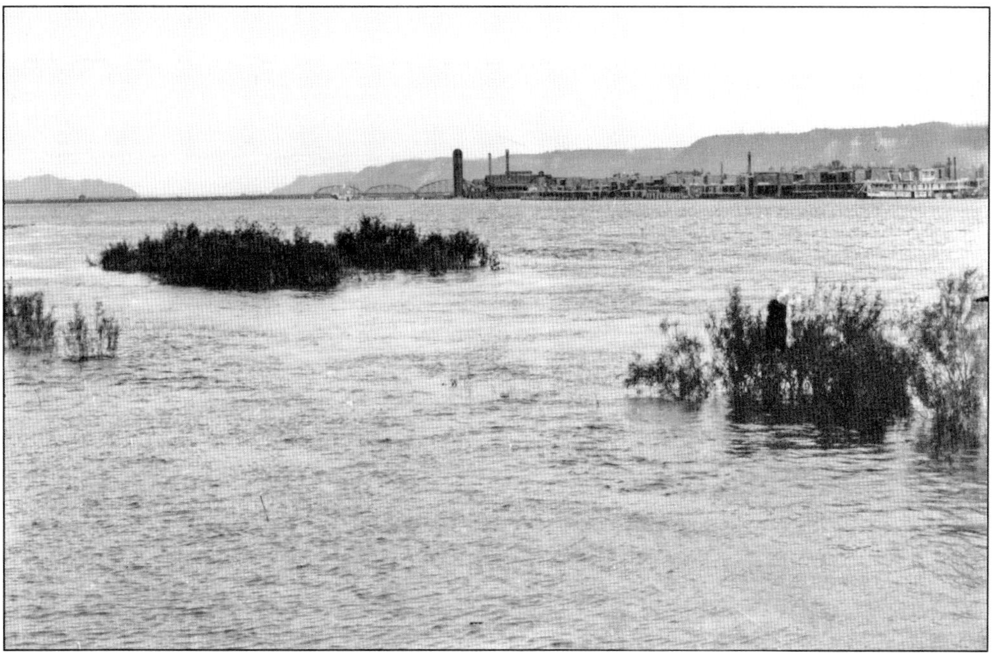

A springtime view across the flooded Mississippi River from Wisconsin toward Winona is pictured. In the distance, the large sawdust burners and smokestack at the sawmills are visible, as are the buildings near the water's edge.

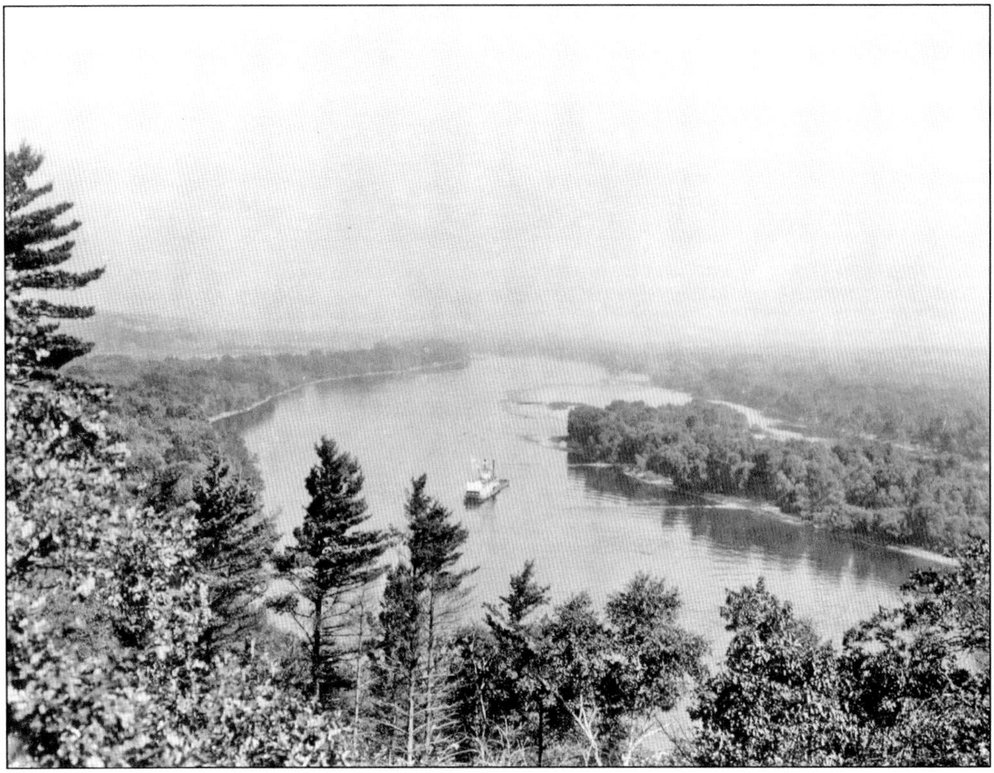

A paddle wheeler sails downstream through the mandated six-foot navigation channel, which was kept open with the use of wing dams, one of which is just visible to the right of the steamer. The six-foot channel mandate was described in the Rivers and Harbors Act of 1910, which was moved through Congress by the Hon. James A. Tawney of Minnesota's first district.

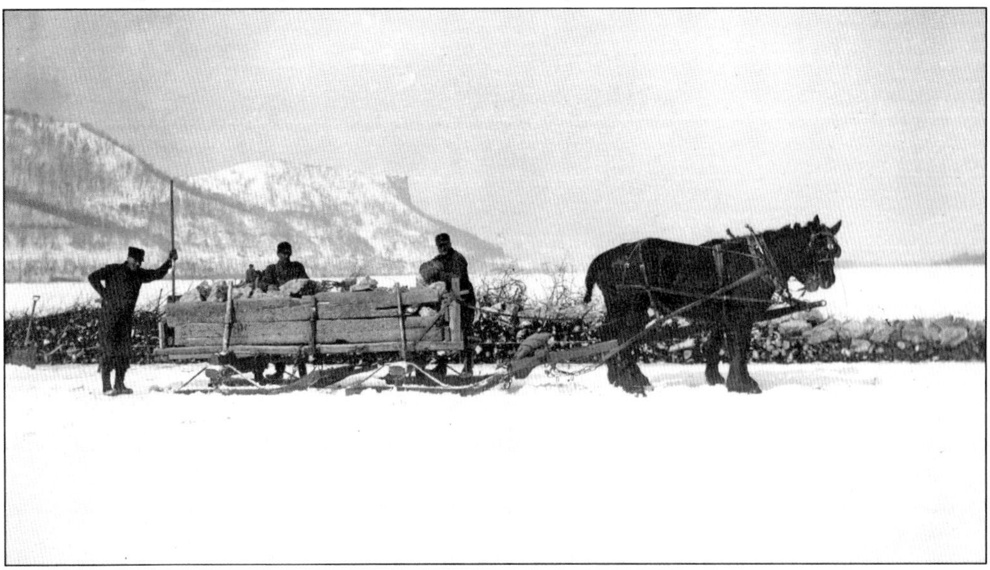

Limestone rock quarried from the nearby bluffs was hauled to the bundles of brush and laid on top. When the ice thawed in the spring, the heavy rock would settle onto the sinking brush and hold it in place.

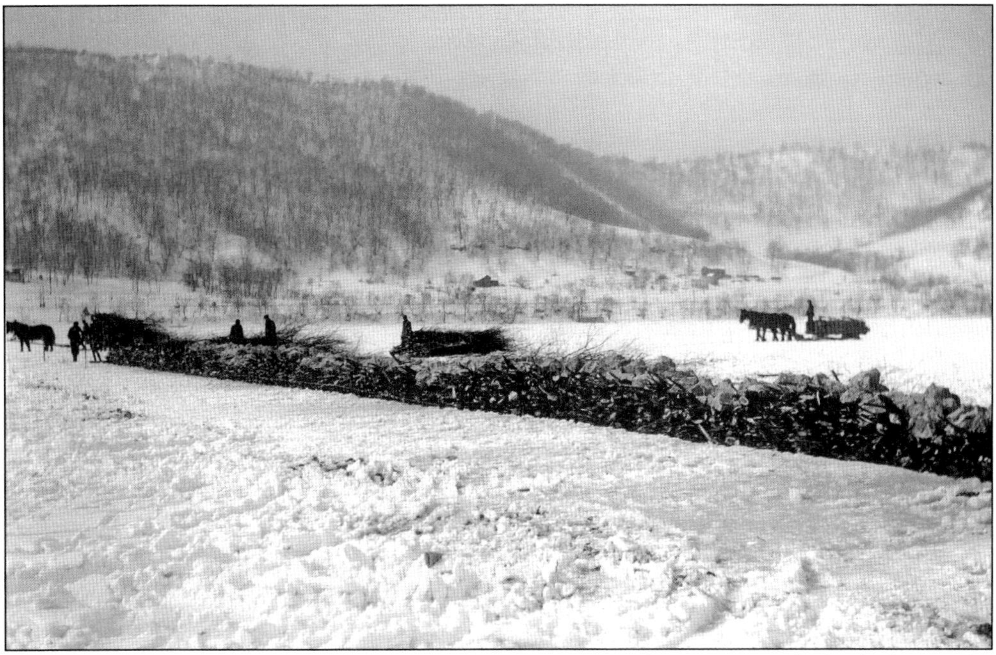

Wing dams that were used to maintain the six-foot channel were generally built during the winter months, when bundles of brush taken from the nearby bluffs could be laid out in a long row on the ice.

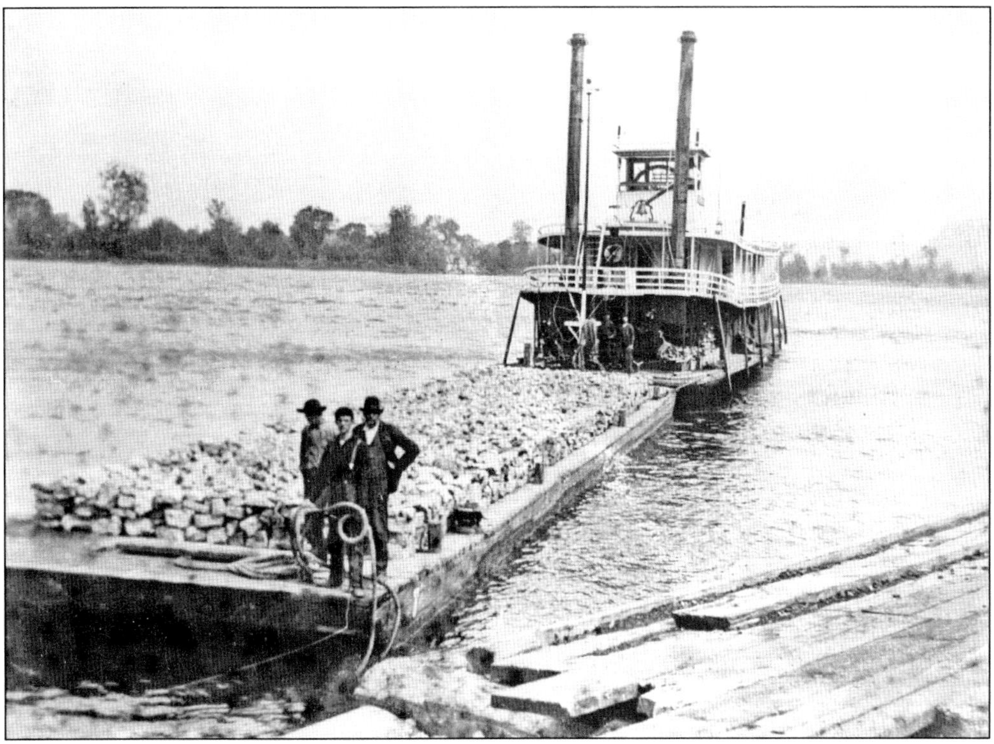

During the summer, barges would bring additional rocks to the wing dams to improve their performance in diverting the flow of water around them to scour out the navigation channel.

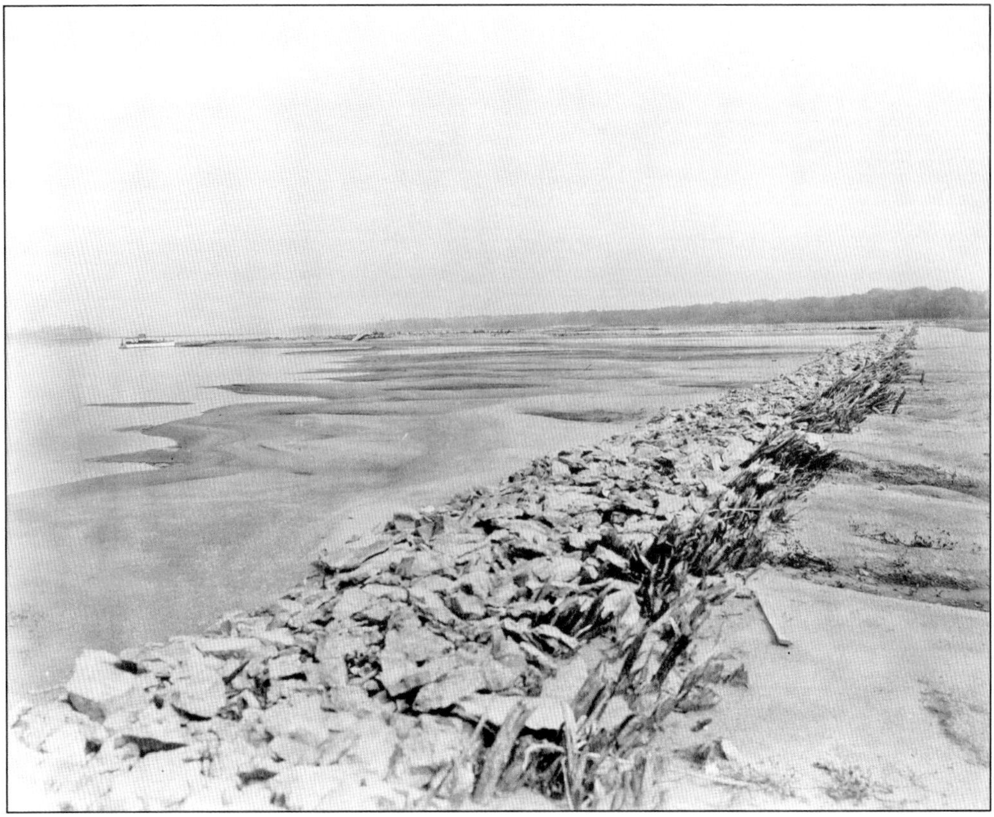

An exposed wing dam during a low water episode shows the layering of brush and overlying rock.

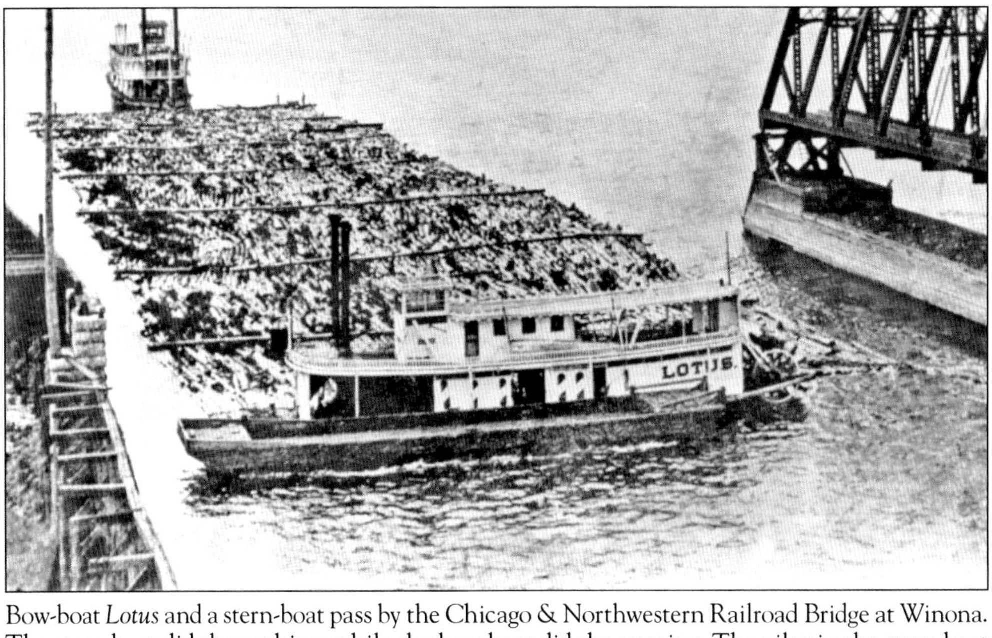

Bow-boat *Lotus* and a stern-boat pass by the Chicago & Northwestern Railroad Bridge at Winona. The stern-boat did the pushing, while the bow-boat did the steering. The pilot in the stern-boat would signal the bow-boat to come ahead, back up, or stop.

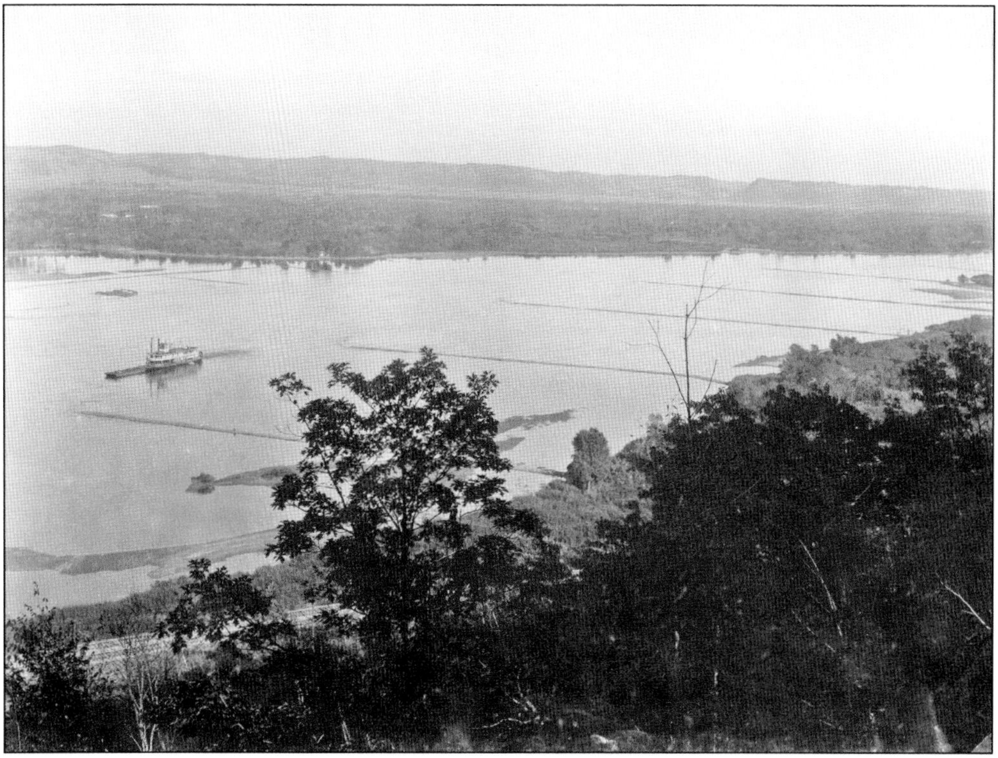

This photograph shows a better view of the numerous wing dams near La Moille, which help maintain the six-foot channel in the middle of the Mississippi River.

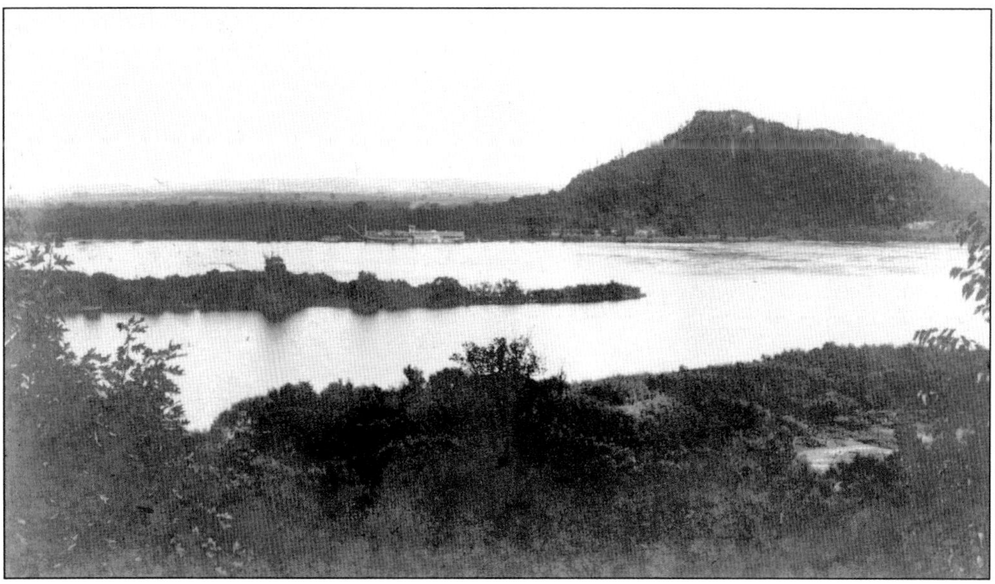

Looking across the Mississippi River near La Moille in 1906, steamer *Quincy* can be seen along the far shoreline near Trempealeau Mountain. The *Quincy*, a new steamer of the Diamond Jo Line that was designed for shallow water, was rebuilt in 1896 from the *Gem City*, an 1880s steamer. It was 266 feet in length and was equipped with 78 state rooms, with space for cargo and livestock. In 1919, it was rebuilt into an excursion steamer and renamed *JS* in honor of Capt. John Streckfus.

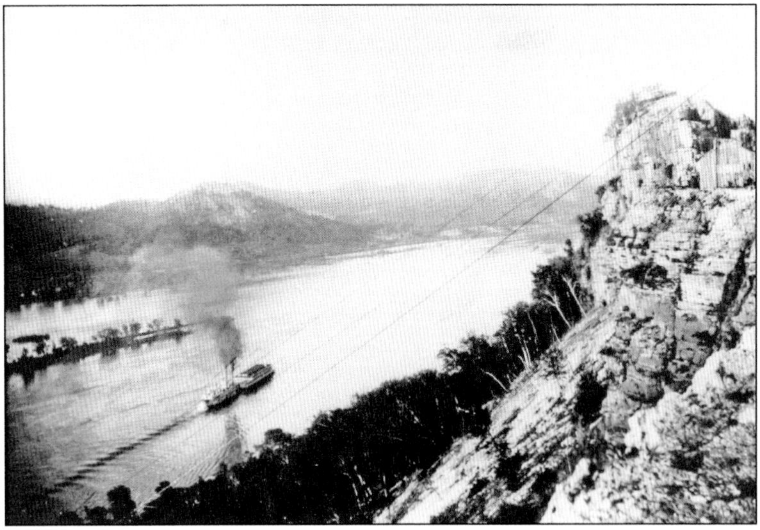

In the second decade of the 1900s, a river steamer pushing a barge can be seen from the government rock quarry above La Mollie, Minnesota.

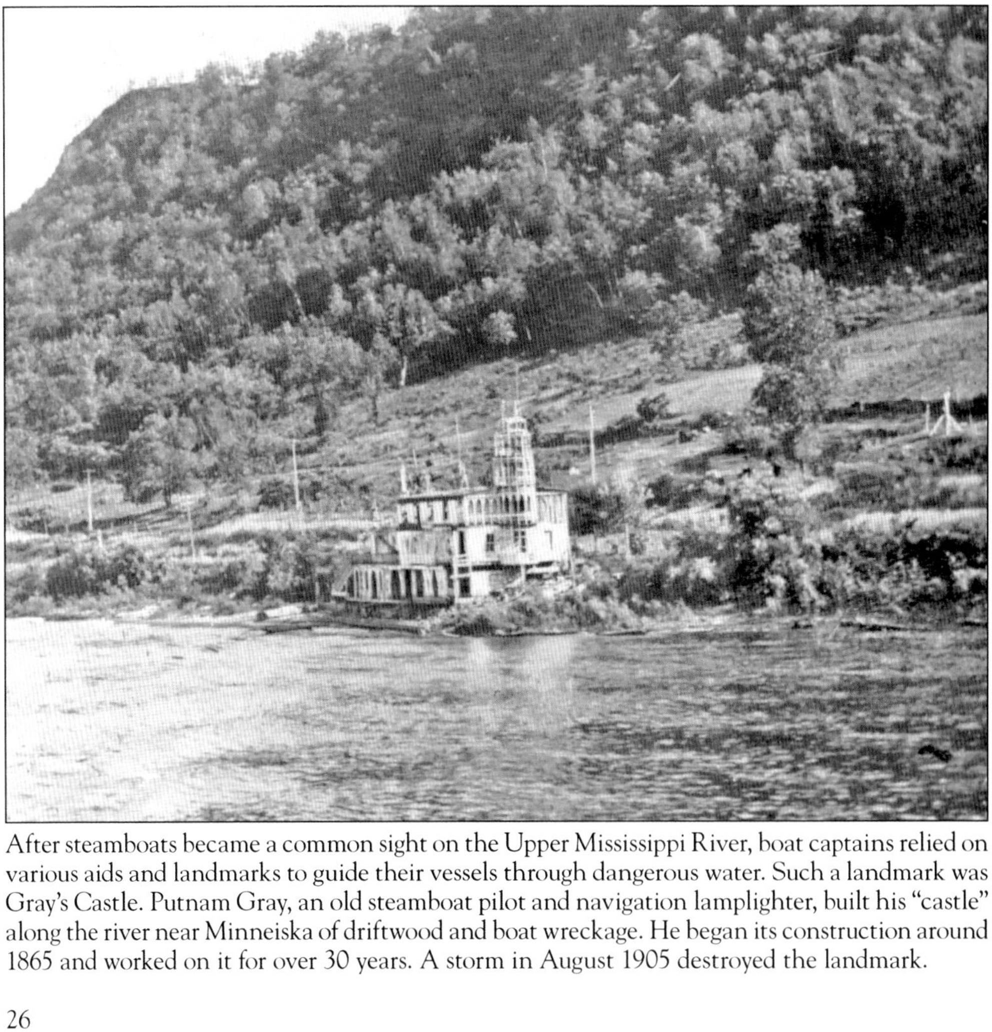

After steamboats became a common sight on the Upper Mississippi River, boat captains relied on various aids and landmarks to guide their vessels through dangerous water. Such a landmark was Gray's Castle. Putnam Gray, an old steamboat pilot and navigation lamplighter, built his "castle" along the river near Minneiska of driftwood and boat wreckage. He began its construction around 1865 and worked on it for over 30 years. A storm in August 1905 destroyed the landmark.

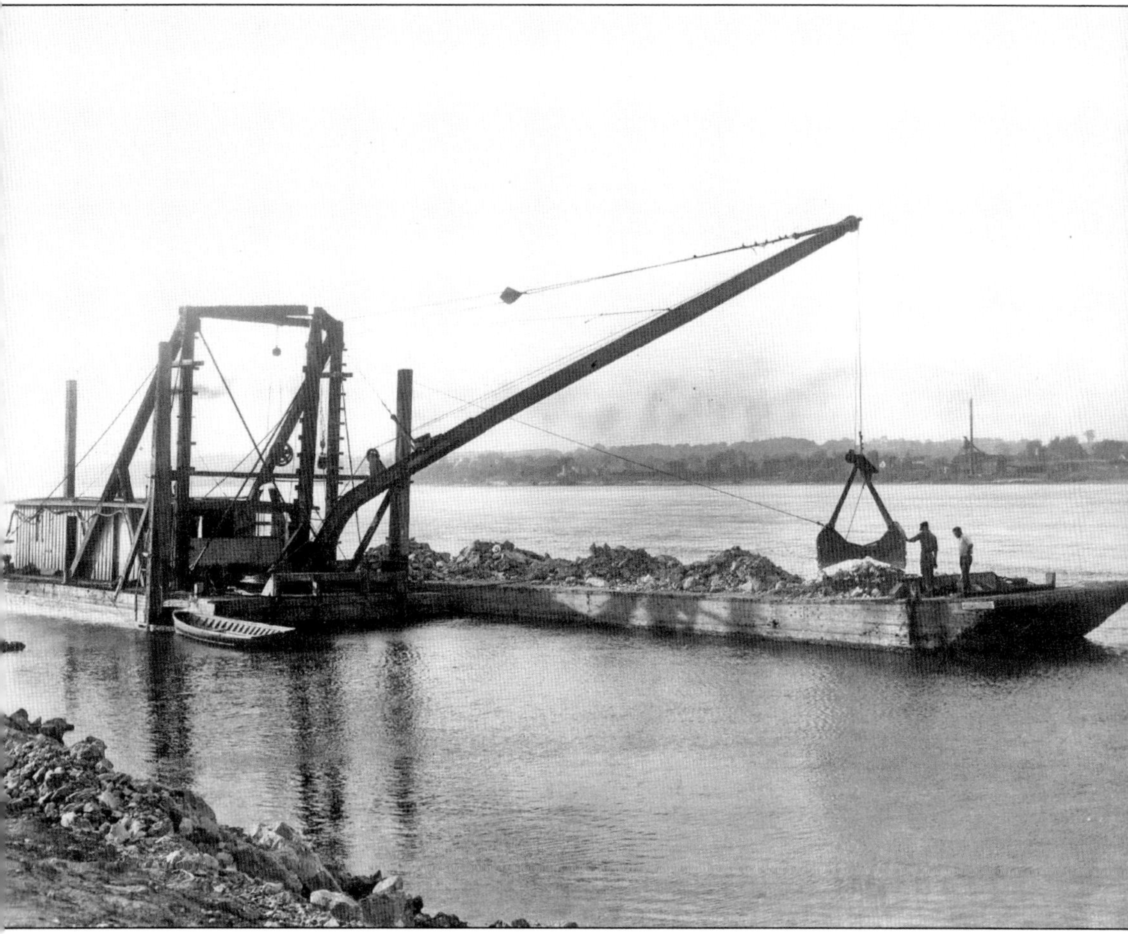

In order to maintain a safe navigation channel in the Mississippi River, it was necessary to constantly remove deposited sediment. To fund this effort, Congress, under the leadership of Sen. William Windom, passed the River and Harbor Bill in 1878. This legislation provided the funding to move sediments from the navigation channel by such means as steam-powered shovels.

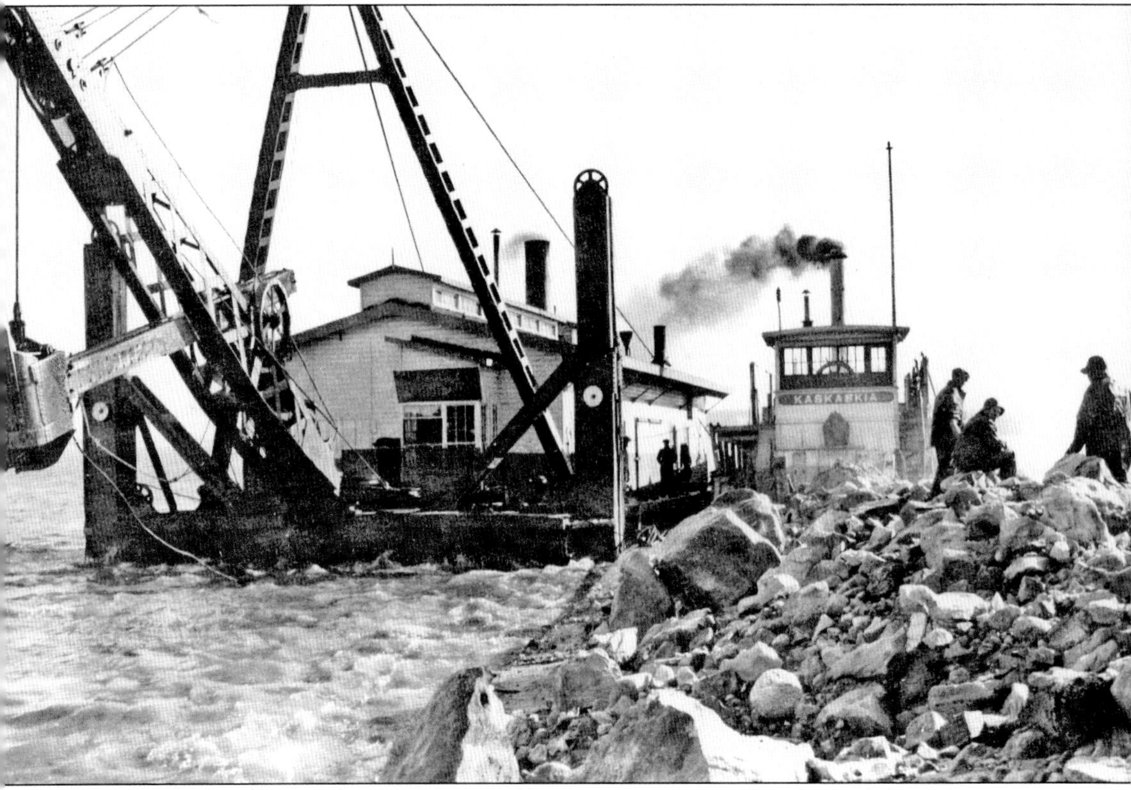

Later dredges became larger and were able to move more sand and gravel from the navigation channel with each scoop of their buckets.

Three

Conquering the River

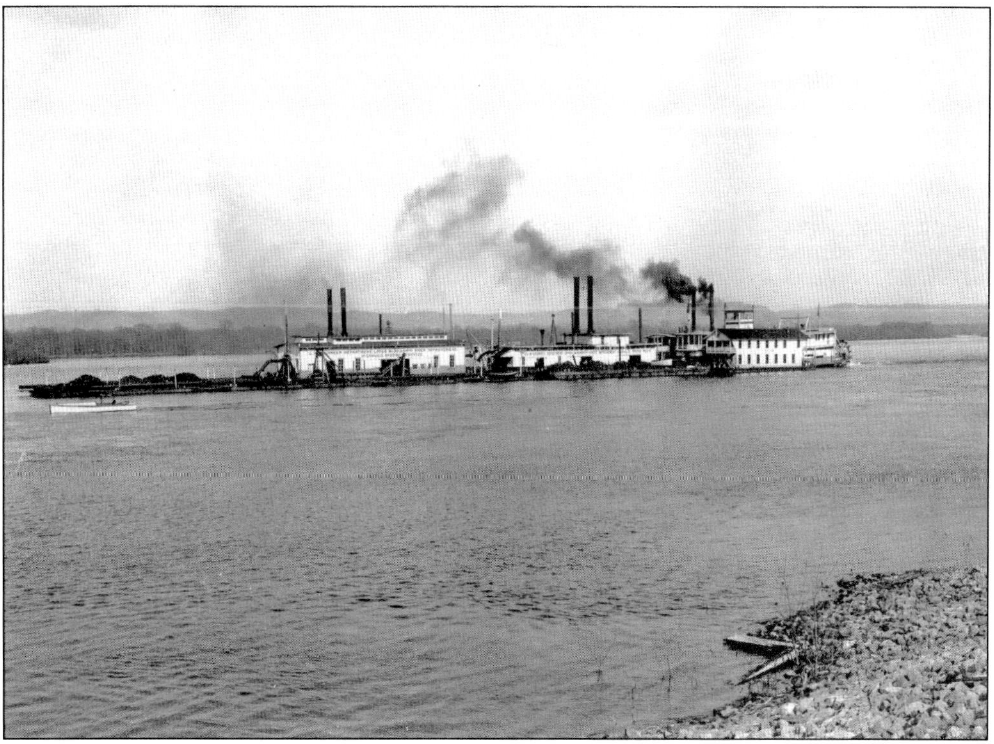

Hydraulic dredges *Vesuvius* and *Pelee*, pushed by government steamer *Vixen*, are moving upriver for dredging work on the Mississippi River. The *Vesuvius*, built around 1895, and the *Pelee*, built around 1910, both operated out of the Army Corps of Engineers Fountain City Boat Works. A dormitory barge is between the camera and the steamer, and a barge with a load of rocks leads the way.

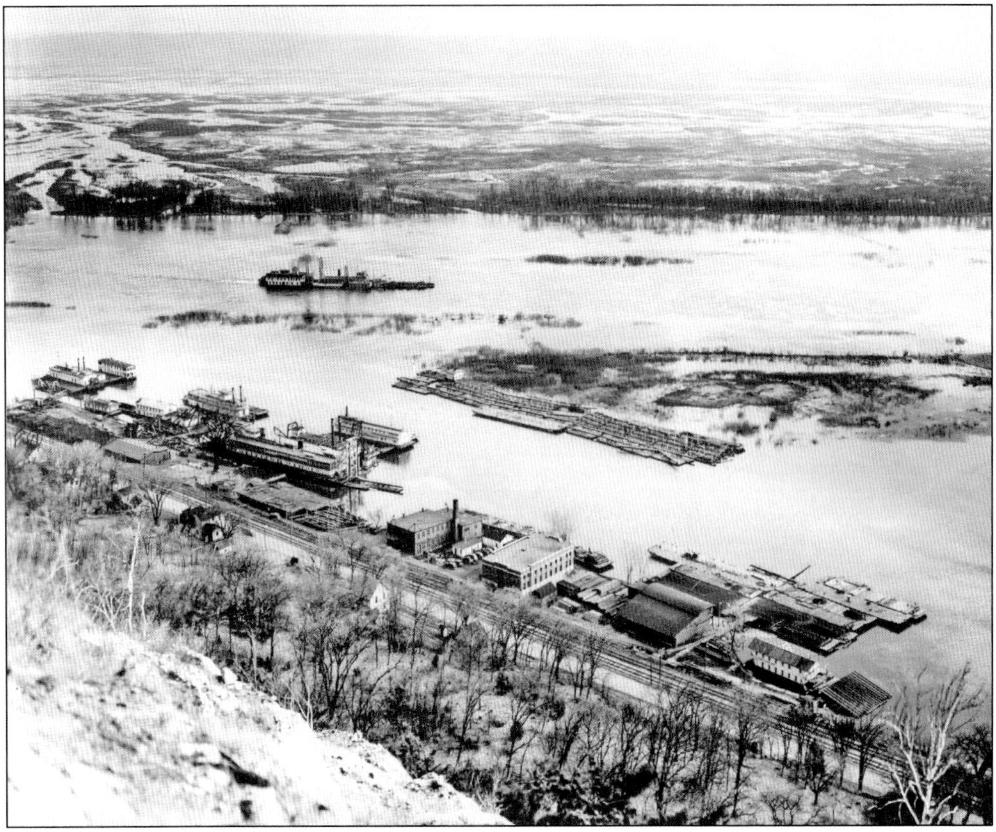

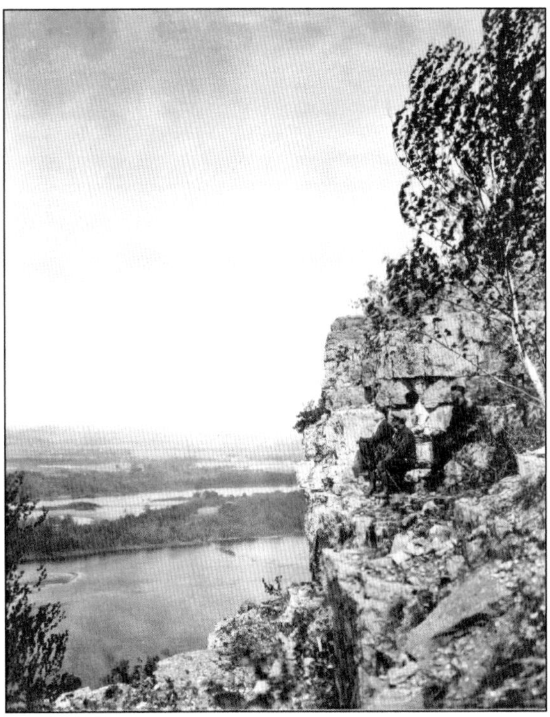

The US Army Corps of Engineers station and boat works at Fountain City, Wisconsin, is pictured during the spring flood of 1937. The location for the station was selected in 1894 because of the natural harbor. The station went into operation in 1895 as a service base for the corps fleet. Docked at the facility, from left to right, are the dredge *Vesuvius*, steamer *Elinor*, and dredge *Thompson*. The house located near the *Thompson* is the home of Capt. R.J. Karnath, a local river boat captain. In the main navigation channel is the *General Allen*, pushing a barge upriver.

The Mississippi River and its broad valley are pictured from the bluffs near Homer. From this vantage point, the wing dams, sloughs, and marshes can be seen.

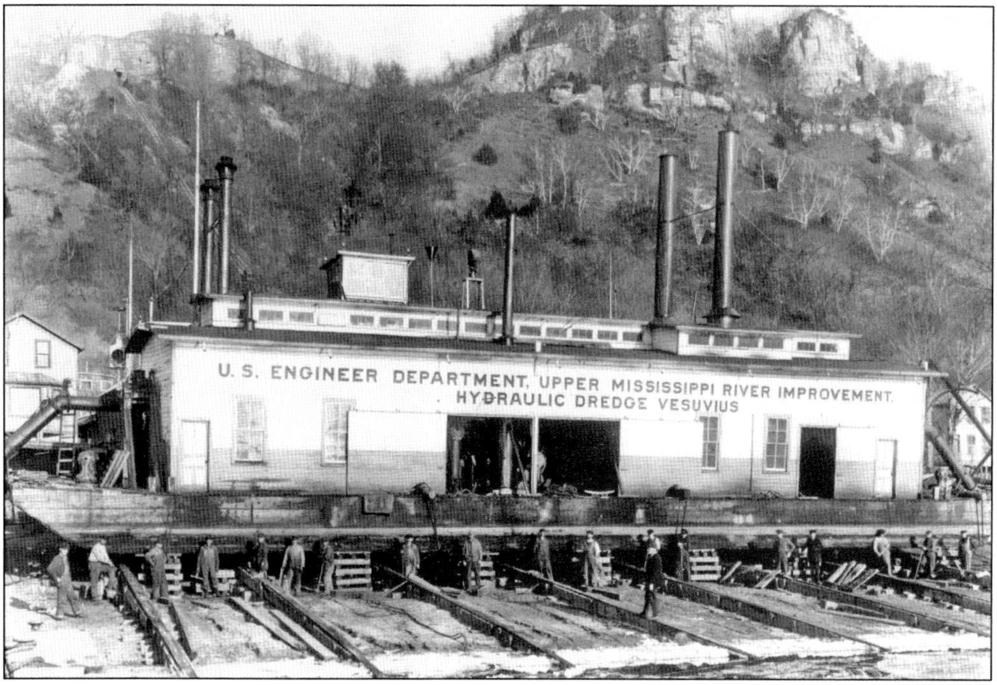

The Upper Mississippi River Improvement Association hydraulic dredge *Vesuvius* is pictured in dry dock at the Army Corps of Engineers Fountain City Boat Works for repairs. Block and tackle rigs powered by horses were used to pull the dredge onto the wooden skids called marine ways.

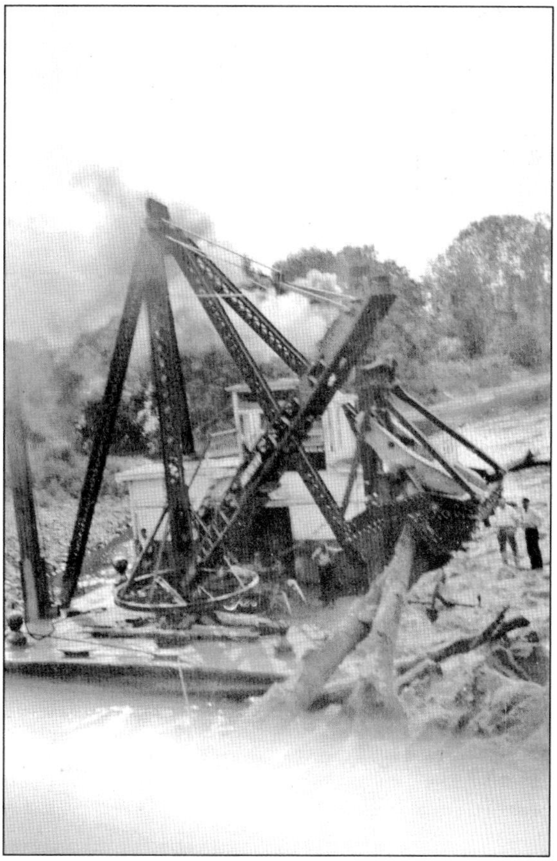

Sunken trees, or snags, continued to be problematic to navigation and had to be constantly removed from the channel.

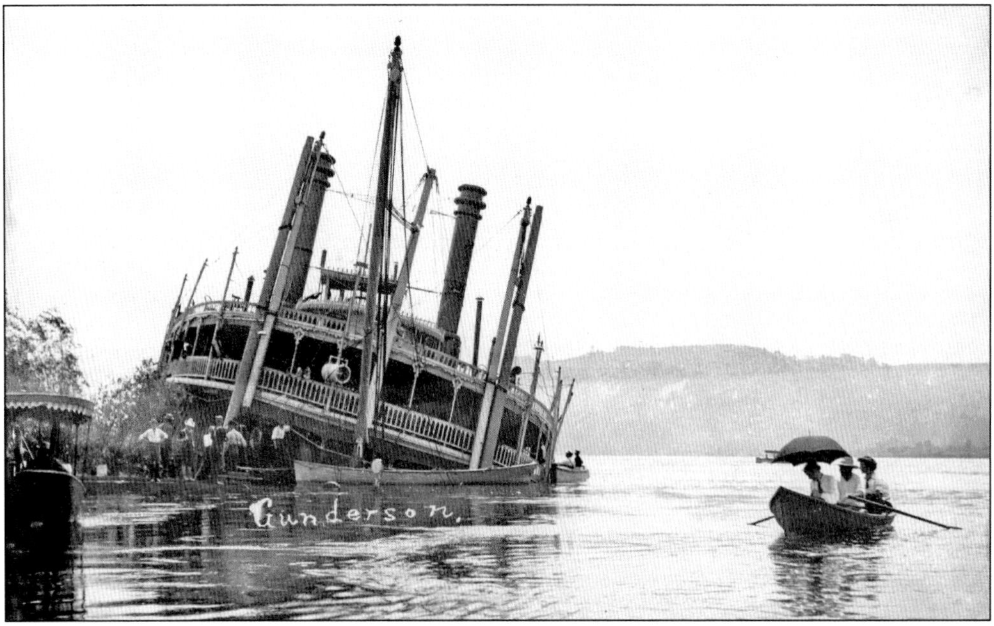

Steamer *Quincy* was sunk with no injuries on the evening of July 11, 1906, after striking a snag near Trempealeau Mountain. After striking the snag, it sank into 18 feet of water near the upriver end of the mountain. A hole, two-by-ten-feet in size, had been punched by a tree stump into the bow. The *Quincy* was repaired, improved, and back on the river the following year.

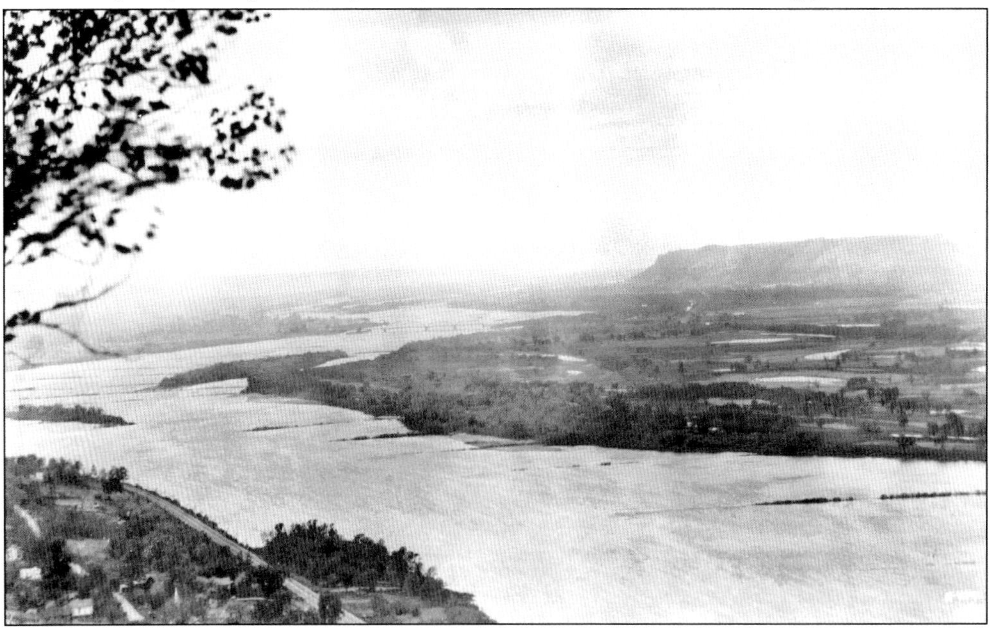

This photograph looks upriver in the Mississippi River Valley from Homer toward Winona. Wing dams can be seen extending from the riverbank toward the navigation channel. In the background is the city of Winona, with three bridges crossing the river. Toward the right is the flat delta of the Trempealeau River and the old Delta Fur Farm, now a part of the Upper Mississippi Fish and Wildlife Refuge. All these obstacles to navigation, including the visible wing dams, prompted shipping companies to lobby Congress for improvements to the river.

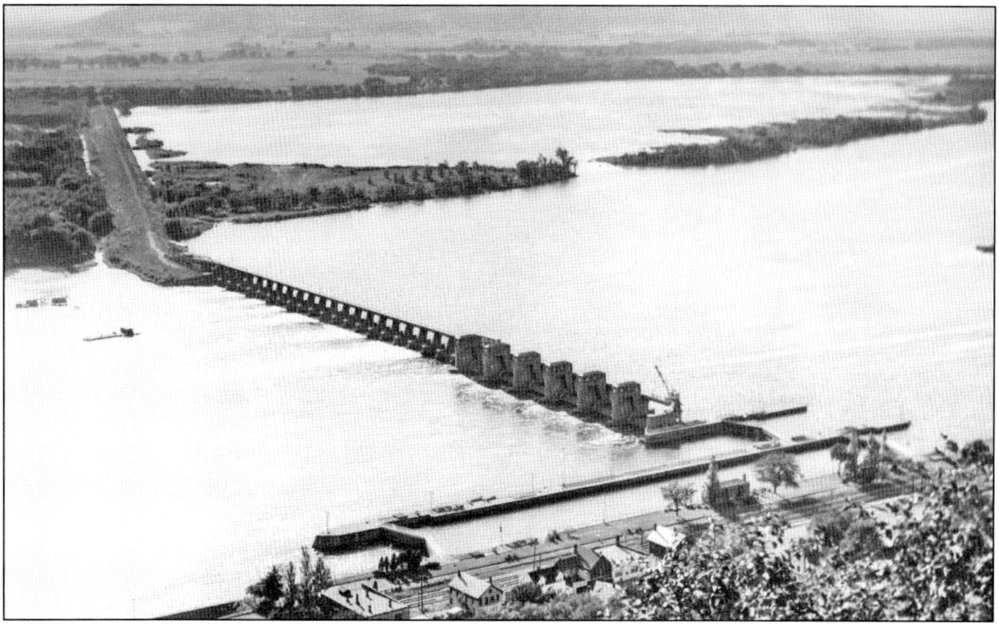

Dam 4, at Alma, Wisconsin, was the first of the 26 navigation dams to be built after legislation was passed authorizing the Upper Mississippi River's nine-foot channel. This dam was constructed to cut down on dredging due to sedimentation at the mouth of the Chippewa River. The 1,357-foot dam with its 28 gates was put into operation in May 1935. Tying the dam to high ground on the Minnesota side is an earthen levee over a mile long. The dam raises the water level by seven feet, which allows for more clearance when passing by the mouth of the Chippewa River.

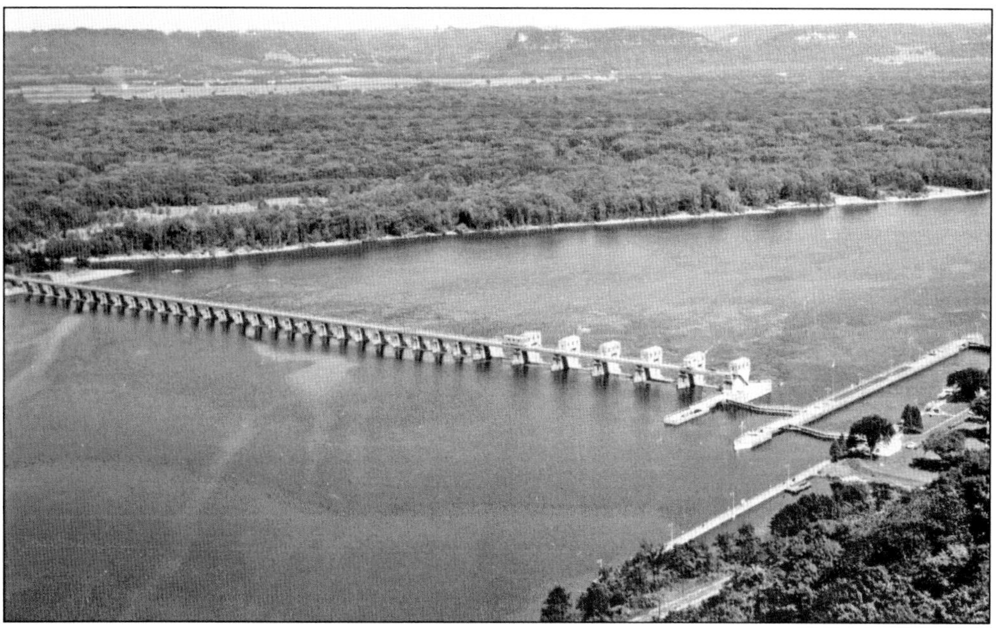

Dam 5, the Whitman Dam, near Weaver, Minnesota, was the second to be built and was also put into operation in May 1935. The lock is on the Minnesota side and has a vertical lift of nine feet. The dam is 1,619 feet long and connects to an earthen levee, some 18,500 feet long, located between the dam and high ground in Wisconsin. Pres. Franklin Roosevelt visited the dam in 1934.

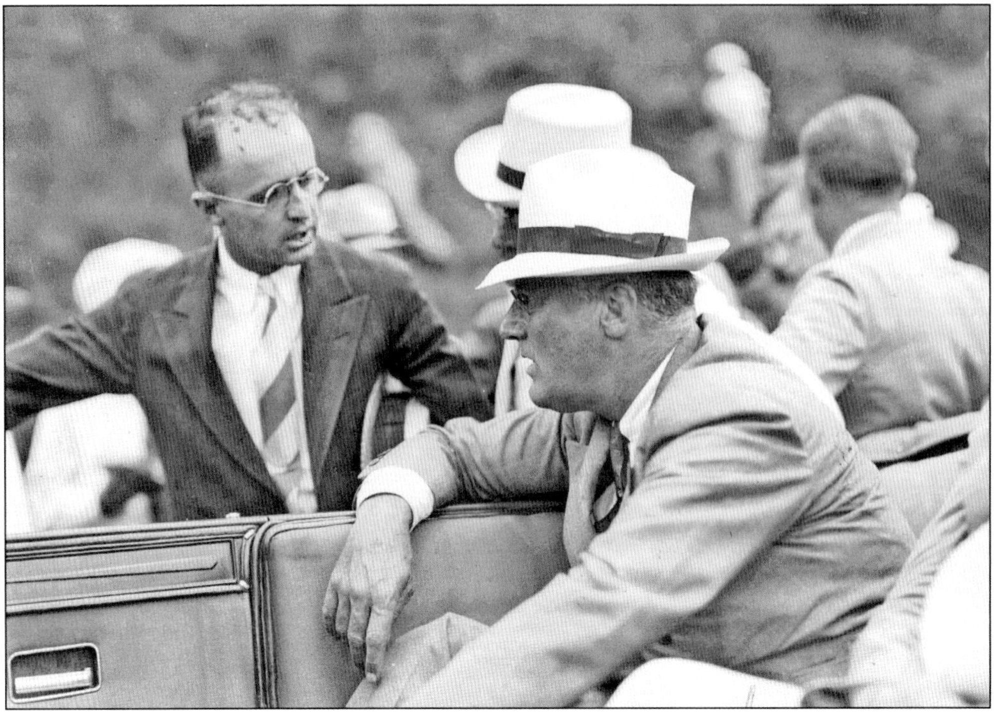

President Roosevelt is seen here on a visit to inspect the nine-foot Mississippi River channel project at the Whitman Dam on August 8, 1934. He is discussing the project with Lt. Colonel Edmund L Daley, the division engineer in charge of the project.

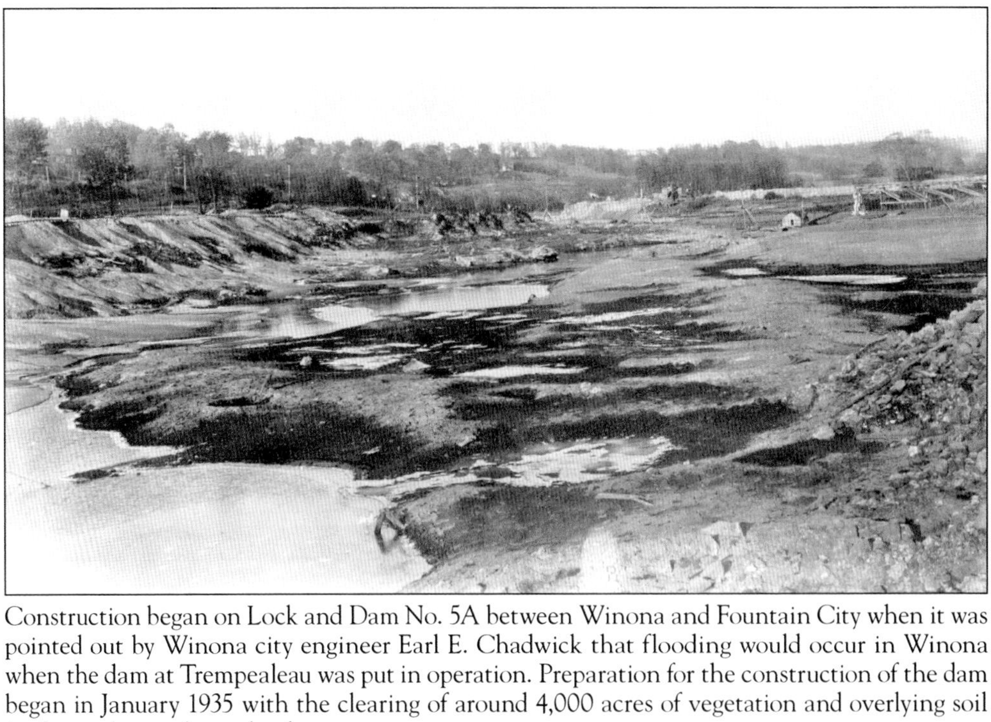

Construction began on Lock and Dam No. 5A between Winona and Fountain City when it was pointed out by Winona city engineer Earl E. Chadwick that flooding would occur in Winona when the dam at Trempealeau was put in operation. Preparation for the construction of the dam began in January 1935 with the clearing of around 4,000 acres of vegetation and overlying soil in the pool area above the dam.

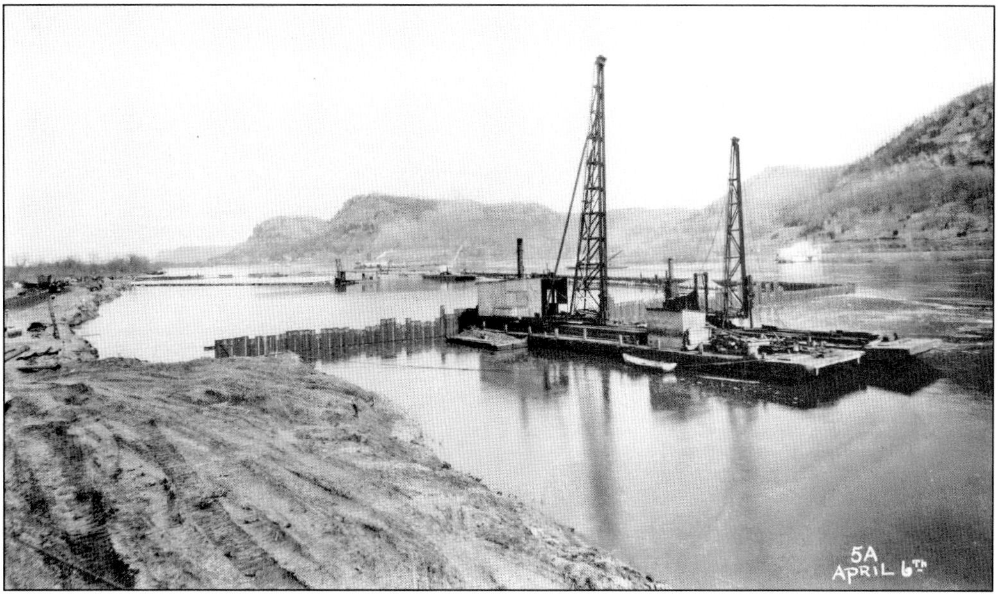

After the overlying soil was removed, cofferdams were put in place, and piling was driven into the ground to support the massive structure.

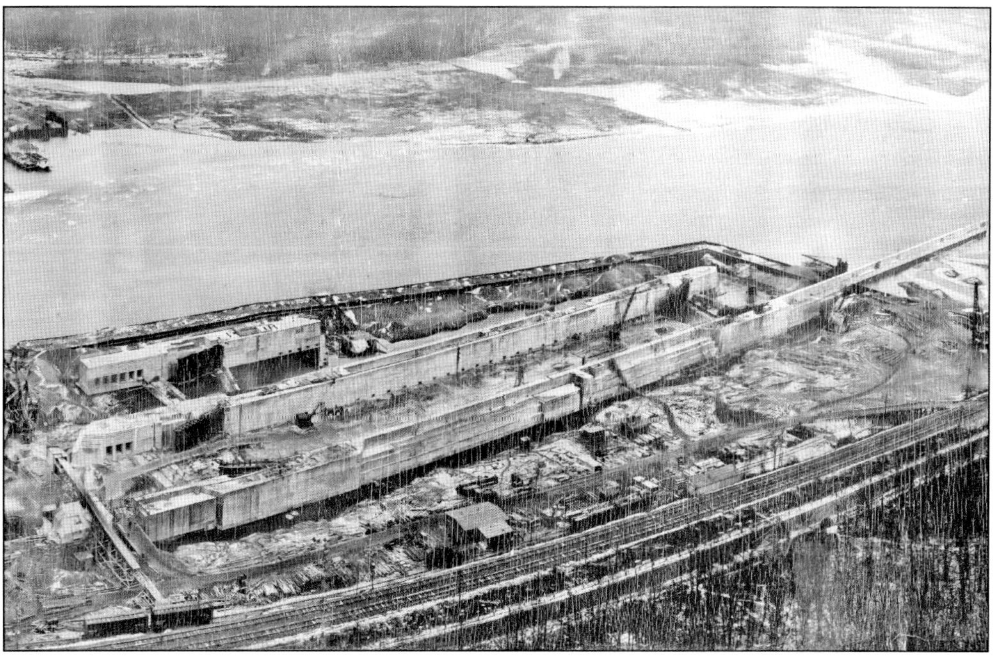

This photograph of the Whitman Dam Project taken from the bluff top in December 1933 shows the construction of the lock at Dam No. 5. The project began in April 1933 on the Minnesota side of the river by the Merritt, Chapman, and Whitney Corporation of Cleveland, Ohio. The lock chamber is 110 feet wide and 600 feet long and provides for a vertical lift of nine feet. The lock and dam went into operation in May 1935. The project included the building of a railroad spur from the Chicago, Milwaukee, St. Paul & Pacific Railroad line.

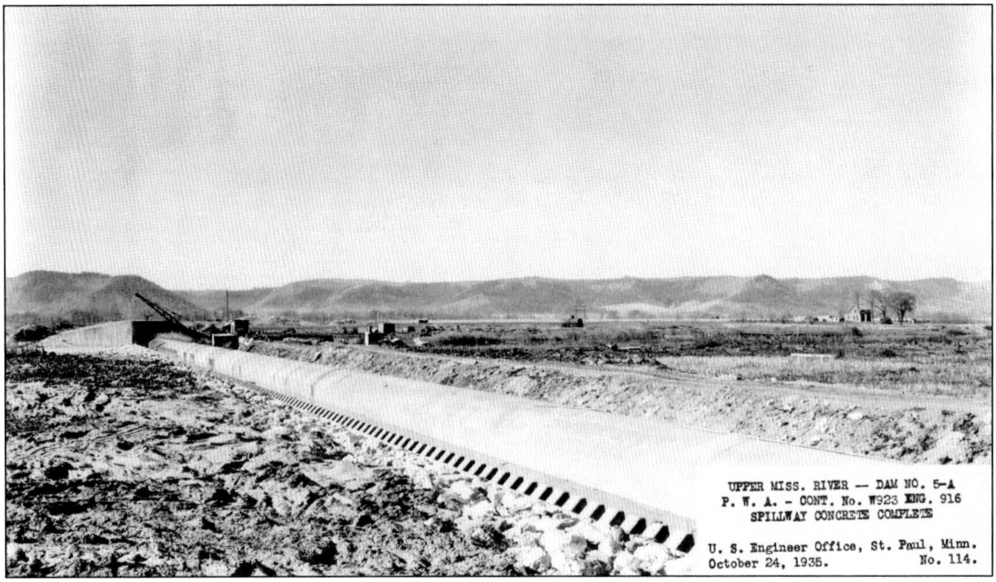

The 1,000-foot-long concrete spillway at Dam No. 5A was completed by the United Construction Company of Winona in October 1935. This spillway extends from the dam's main lock to high ground on the Minnesota side of the river valley. The bottomland above the spillway is nearly barren, as most of the vegetation has been removed.

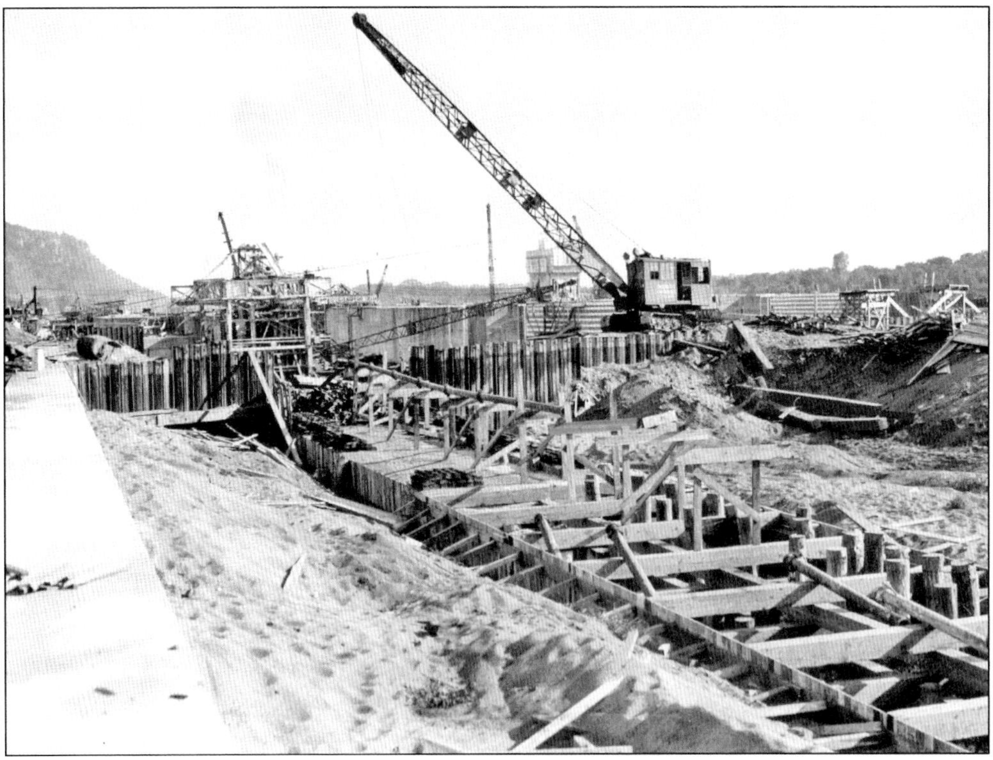

Piles are being driven within a cofferdam of the $2 million Winona dam. In front of the cofferdam are wood forms being placed, which hold concrete that will make up a portion of the auxiliary lock. Behind the cofferdam, the main wall of the dam is being built.

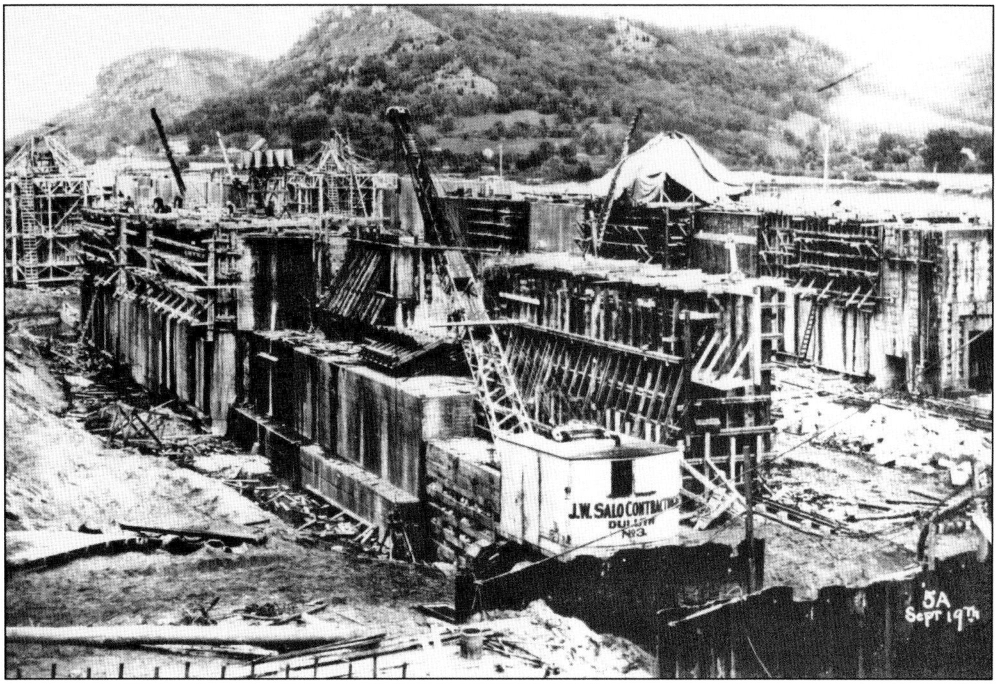

The pouring of concrete for the piers of the roller gate sections of Dam No. 5A is pictured. Around 500 men were employed in order to complete the concrete work before the cold weather set in.

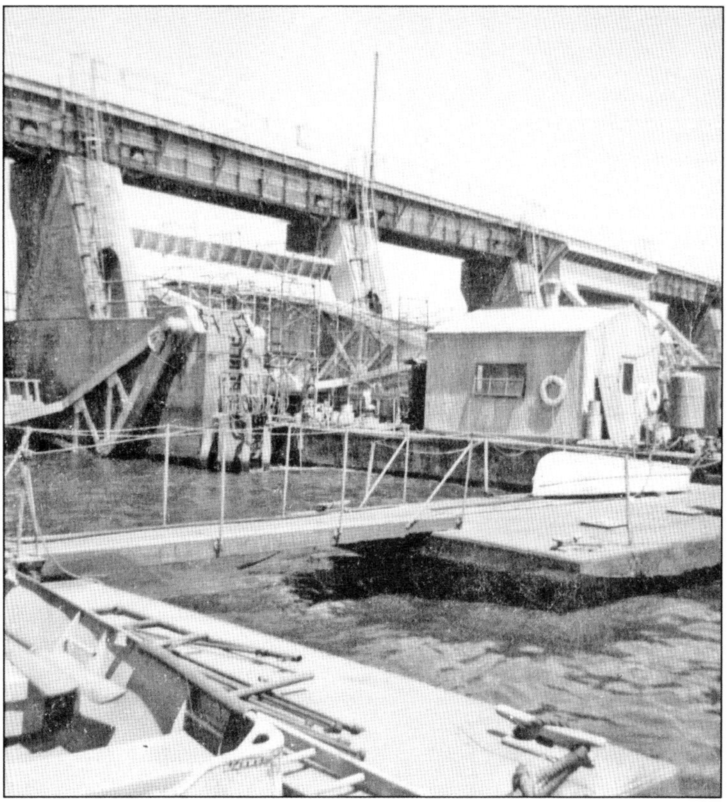

Tainter gates, which are used to control water flow through the dam, are being installed between concrete piers by workmen at Dam No. 5A.

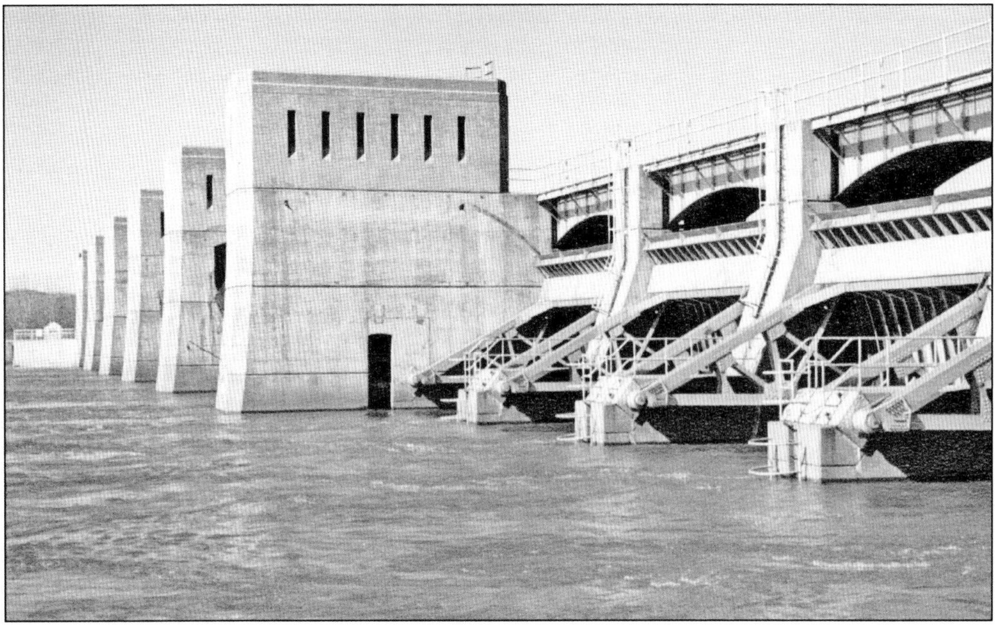

The Tainter gates are pictured from the downstream side of Dam No. 5A. Beyond the Tainter gates are the massive pierhouses of the roller gates, which allow water to flow continuously over their tops. The pierhouses have flat roofs and slit, three-pane windows. They house the equipment needed to operate the roller gates.

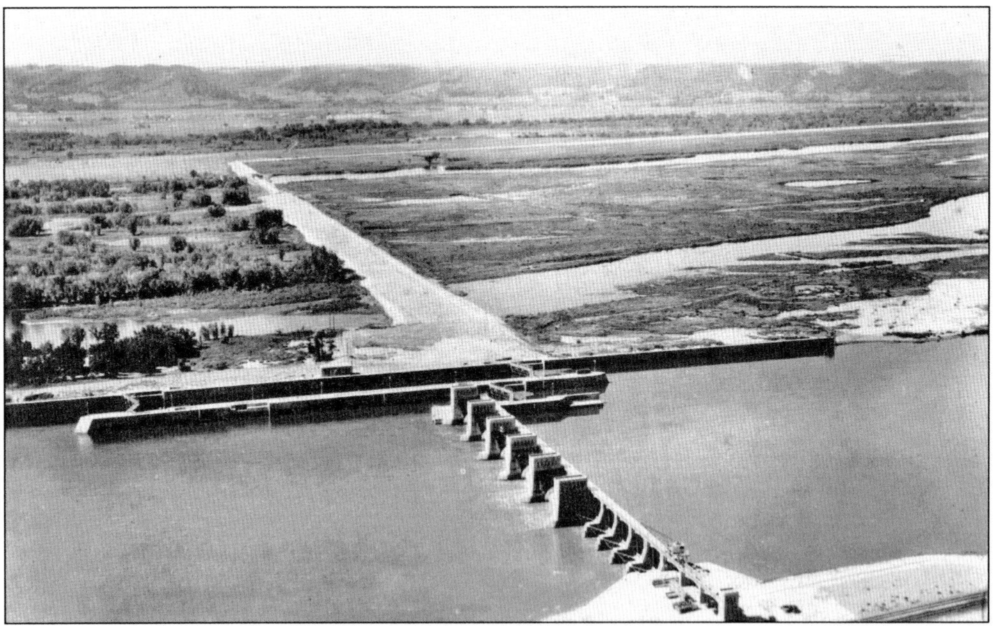

Dam No. 5A, photographed from the Wisconsin bluffs, nears completion on December 31, 1935. In the foreground is the Tainter gate section, followed by the huge roller gate section and the long lock walls. A dike and concrete spillway run beyond the locks across the Minnesota bottomlands, and another long dike in the distance runs parallel to the slough and upriver toward Minnesota City. Above the dam is a section of the area to be flooded, where all the trees have been removed. This dam was opened for business in July 1936.

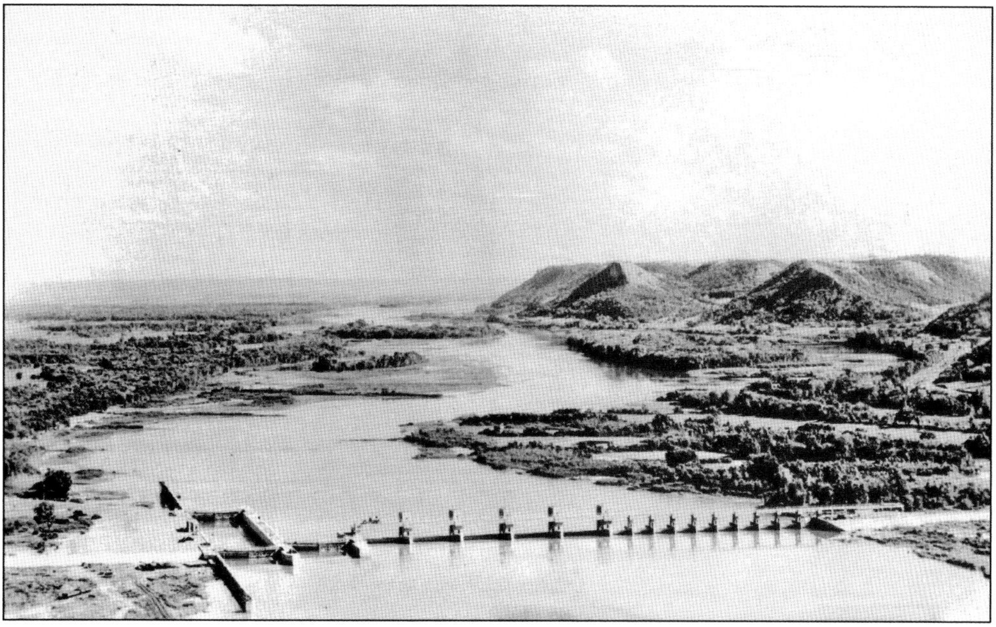

Dam No. 6 at Trempealeau, completed in June 1936, is one of 26 dams needed to control navigation and maintain the nine-foot channel. These dams brought new life to the Mississippi River with new commerce and better fishing.

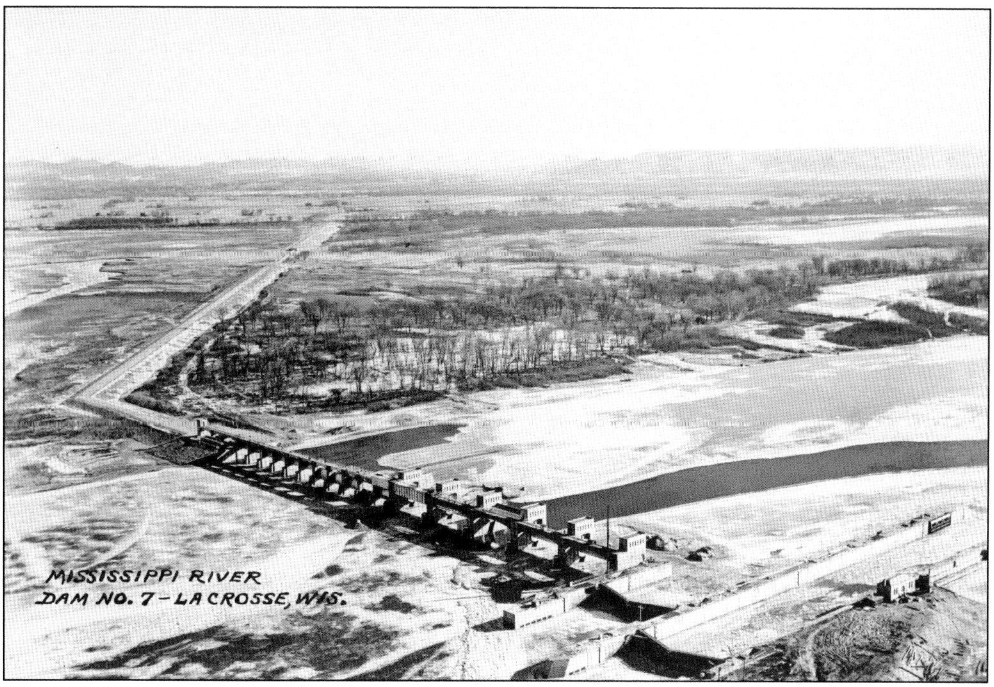

Dam No. 7 between Dresbach and La Crescent, Minnesota, became operational in April 1937. The dam consists of a 940-foot-long concrete structure with five roller gates and 11 Tainter gates. Two 8,100-foot-long earthen levees extend from the concrete dam toward the Wisconsin side of the river. These structures together form Lake Onalaska, which is a valuable environmental habitat and resting place for migrating waterfowl.

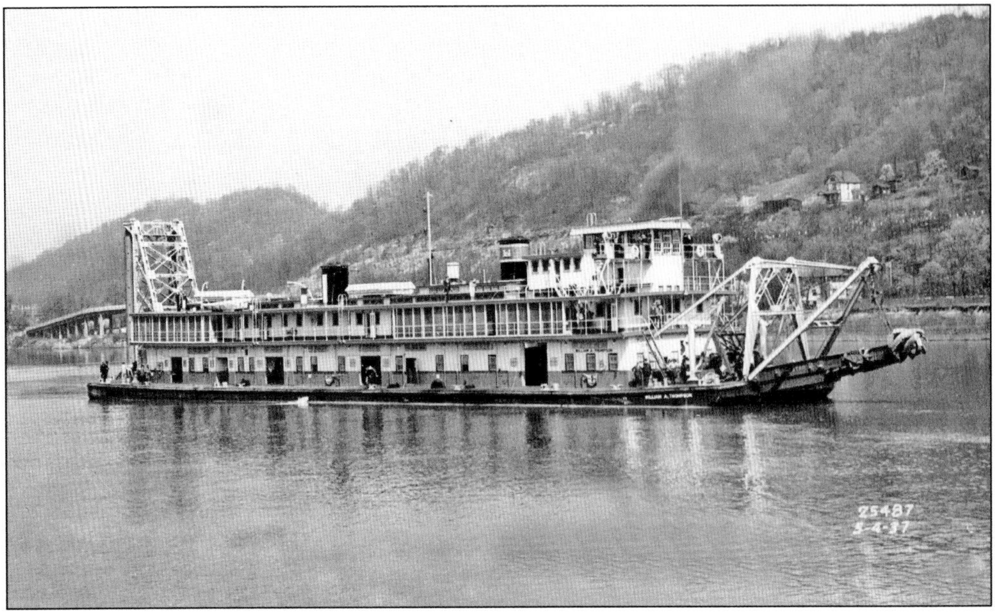

To maintain the channelized Mississippi River, a new dredge, the *William A. Thompson*, was built by the Dravo Corporation at a cost of $750,000. The pride of the War Department Fleet, the *Thompson* moved a half million cubic yards of sediment a month at a cost of $1,000 per day. The 210-foot-long diesel-electric craft was used to maintain the nine-foot channel in the Upper Mississippi River. Here, it is ready for duty at the Fountain City Boatyard in May 1937.

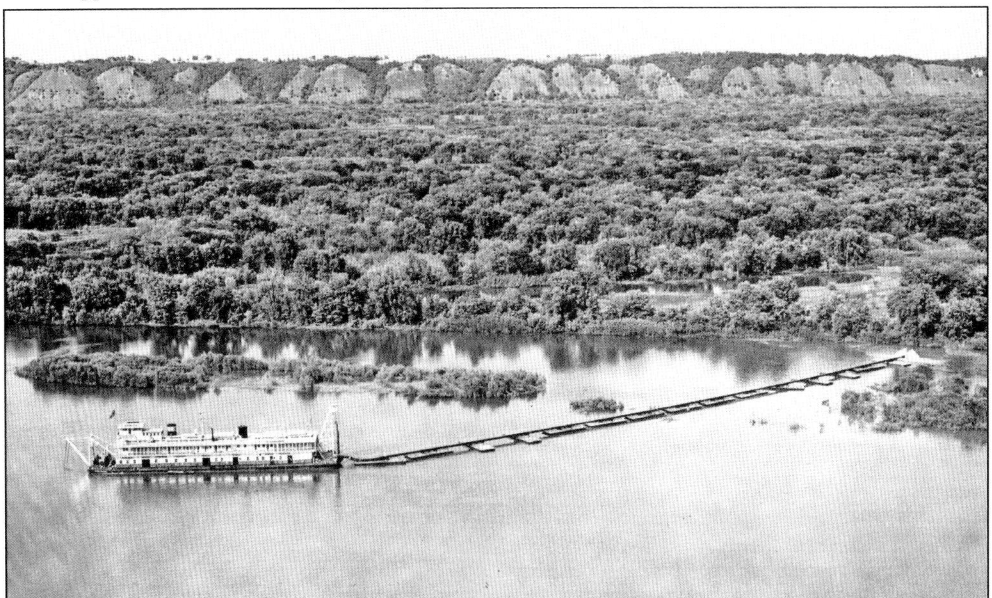

Dredge *William A. Thompson* is pictured at work soon after its arrival on the Mississippi River south of Winona near Lansing, Iowa. The dredge's pumps move sediment from the river bottom through the pipes to a different area of the river. The *Thompson* kept some 850 miles of waterway open for navigation for 76 years before it was retired in 2005. In 2012, it was sold to Community Development Alternatives of Prairie du Chien, Wisconsin, for $19.37, and in June 2012, it was moved to its new home in Prairie du Chien.

On August 25, 1983, the Army Corps of Engineers and a private contractor prepared to remove the auxiliary lock gates at the Trempealeau Dam No. 6 for reconditioning. This was the first time they were removed since the dam was built some 50 years ago.

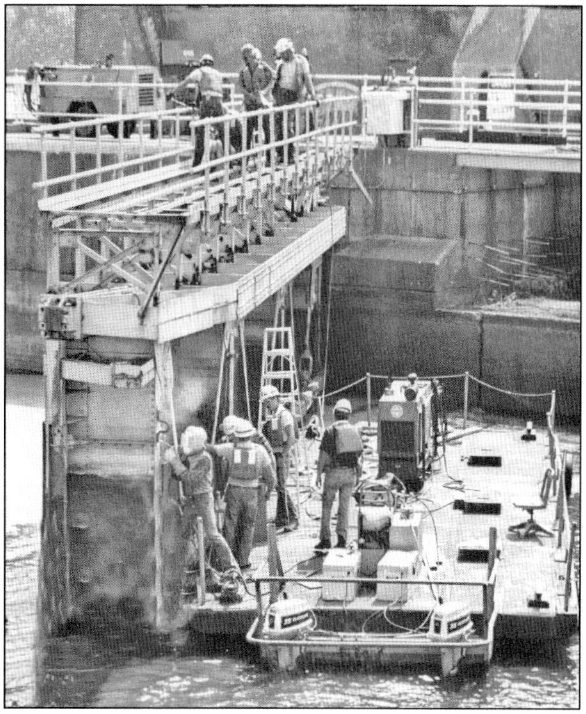

The 80-ton auxiliary gate is hanging from the hooks of *Hercules*, a high-capacity steam-powered crane owned by the corps. It is being moved to a barge for transport to Guttenberg, Iowa.

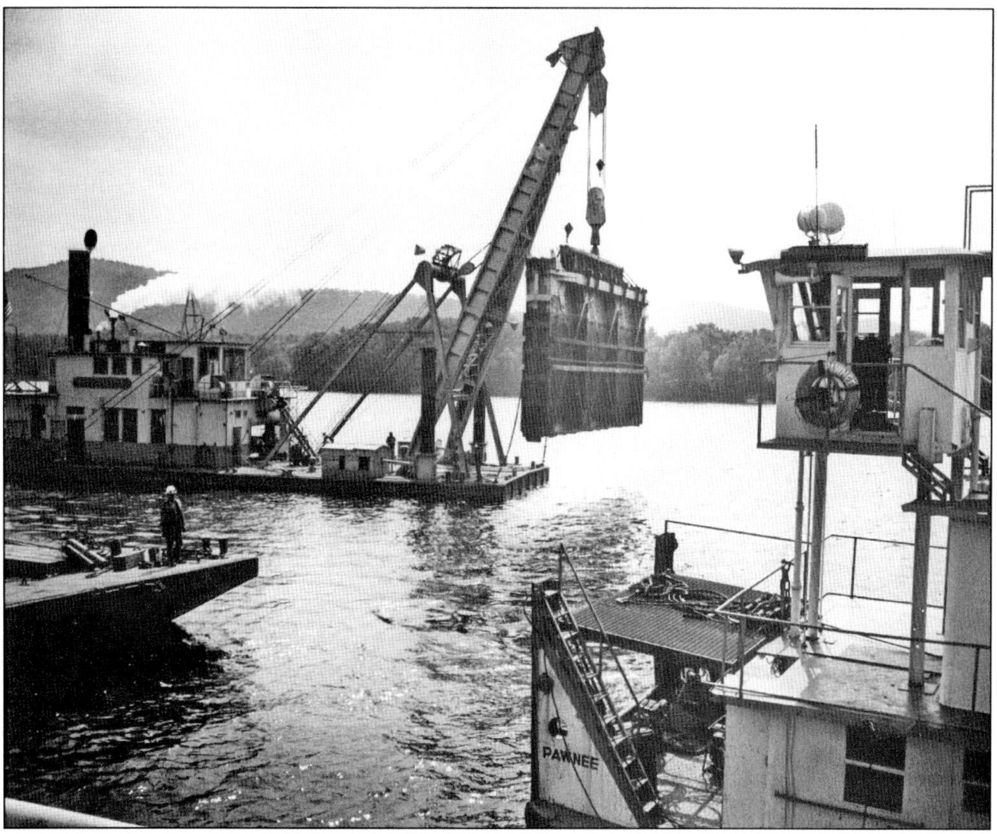

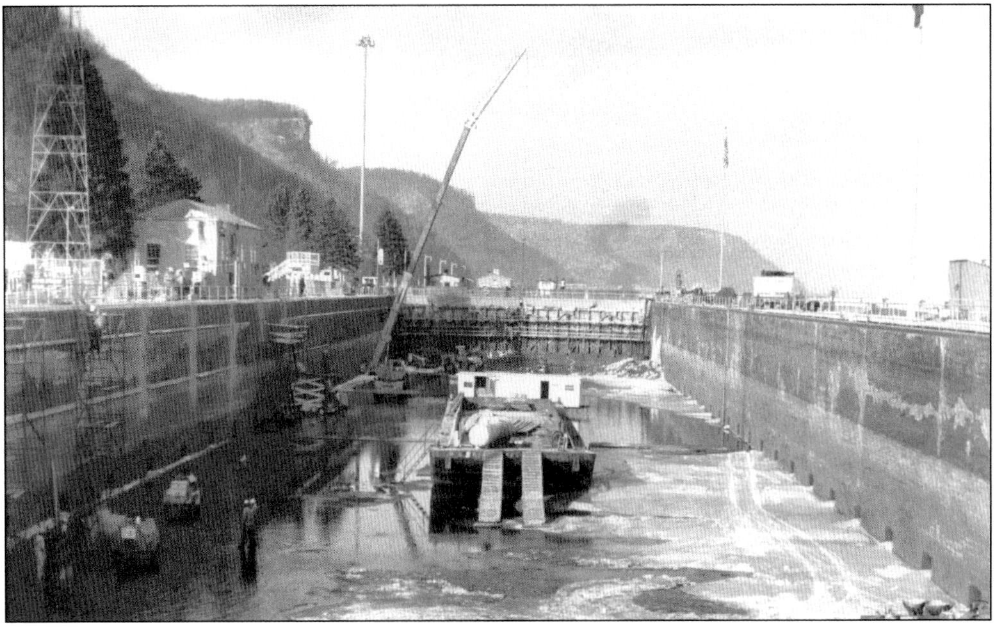

The lock at the Whitman Dam near Weaver, Minnesota, has been drained and is undergoing needed refurbishing during January 1990 by general contractor American Plumbing of Winona and the Army Corps of Engineers. The workmen are ever mindful that millions of gallons of water lie just beyond the upriver side of the lock gate as seepage covers the lock's bottom with six to eight inches of water.

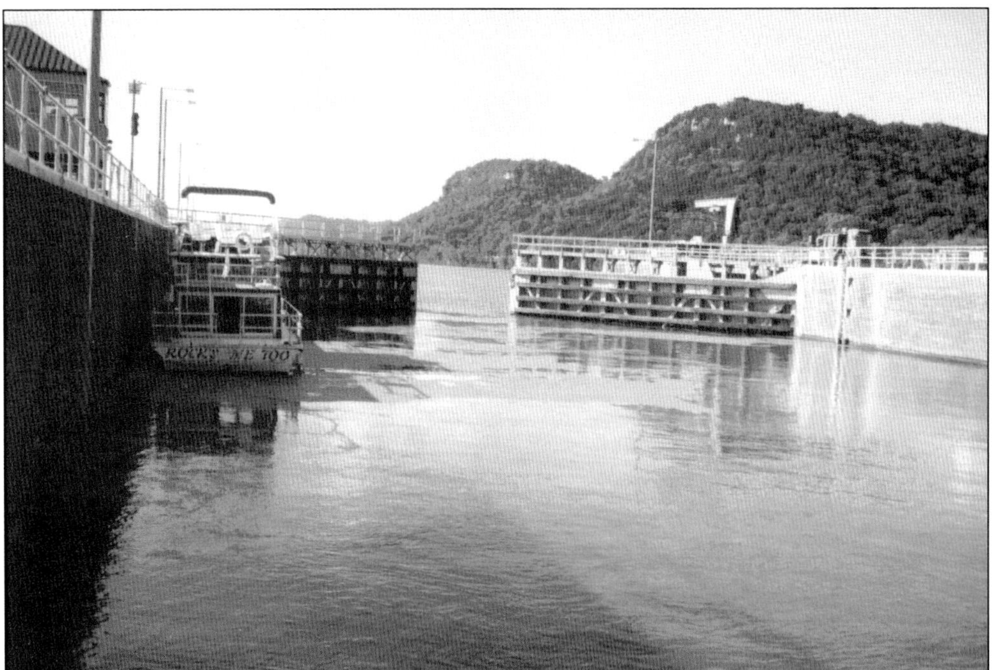

During the summer of 2007, a pleasure craft, tied up inside the lock at Dam No. 5A, is preparing to exit the lock as the gates open on the upriver side.

Four

Floating Palaces, Showboats, and Workhorses

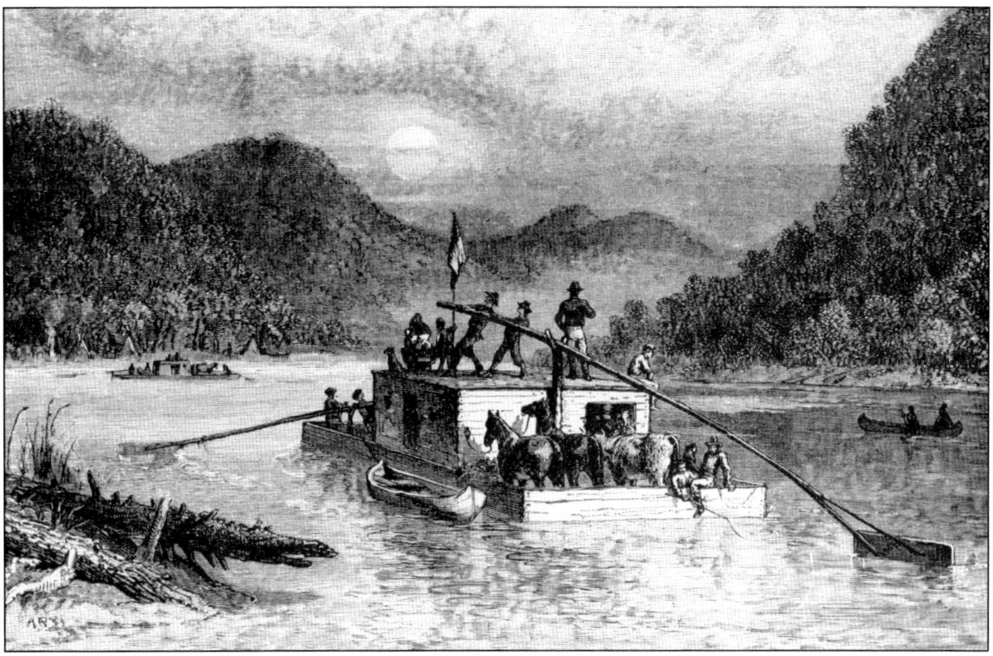

Barges made of cut lumber were an early mode of river transportation that easily carried passengers, animals, and supplies downriver with the current. These flat-bottomed boats were steered with board oars, or sweeps, that guided them around obstacles in the river. When they arrived at their destinations, they were dismantled and the lumber sold.

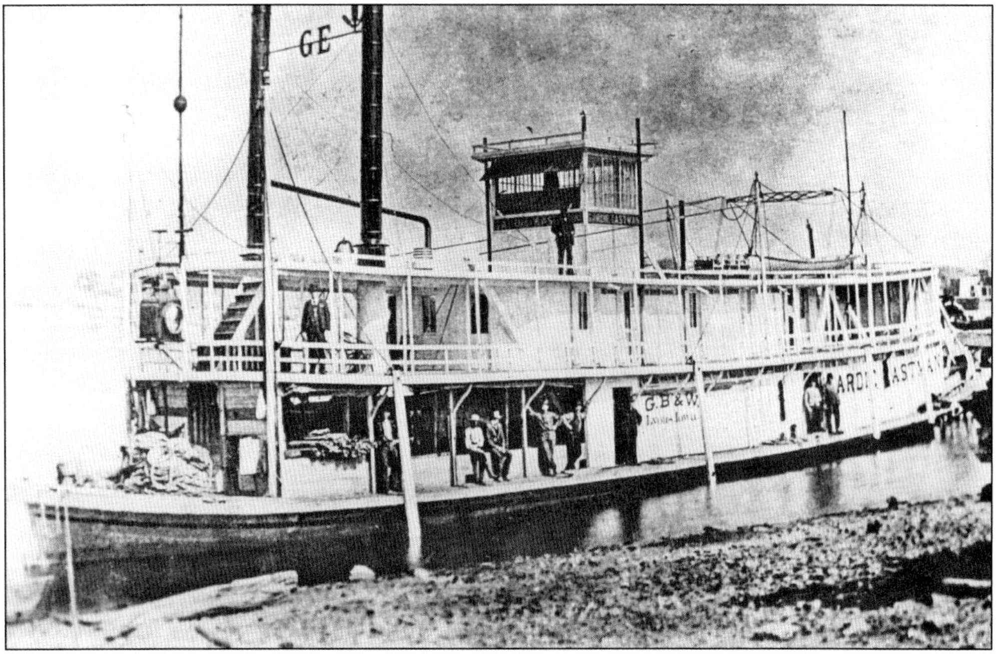

The *Gardie Eastman*, an early raft, was built at Stillwater, Minnesota, for the firm of Gardiner, Batchellor & Wells of Lyons, Iowa. It was the only boat plying the Upper Mississippi River with a woman captain, Capt. Ida Lachman. After the rafting business slowed, the boat was sold to Fetter and Crosby of La Crosse and used in river improvement work maintaining the four-and-a-half-foot channel.

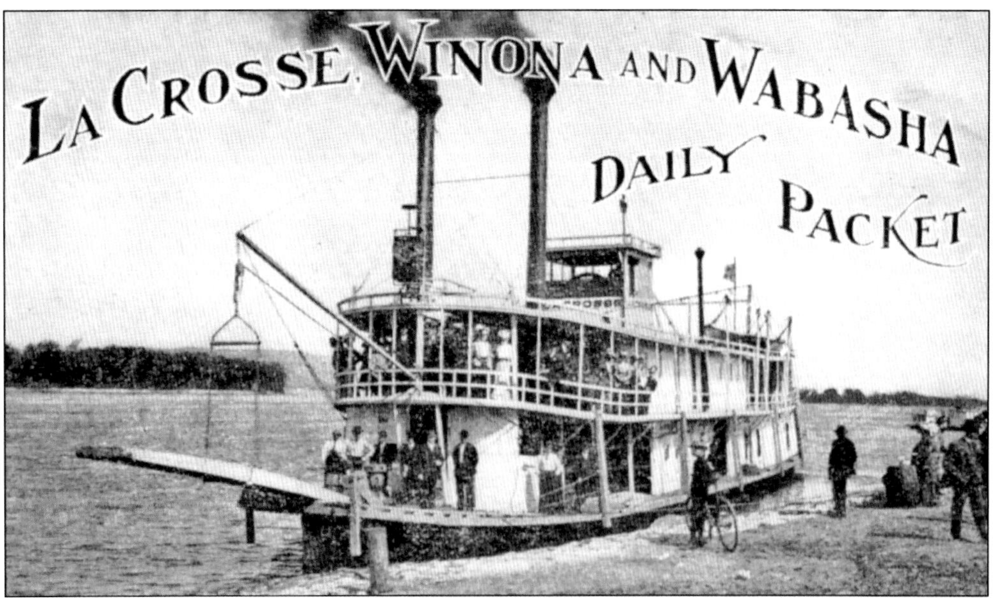

Steamer *La Crosse* of the La Crosse, Winona, and Wabasha Packet Company is pictured here. The company was one of many that offered daily trips carrying both passengers and freight between selected cities along the river.

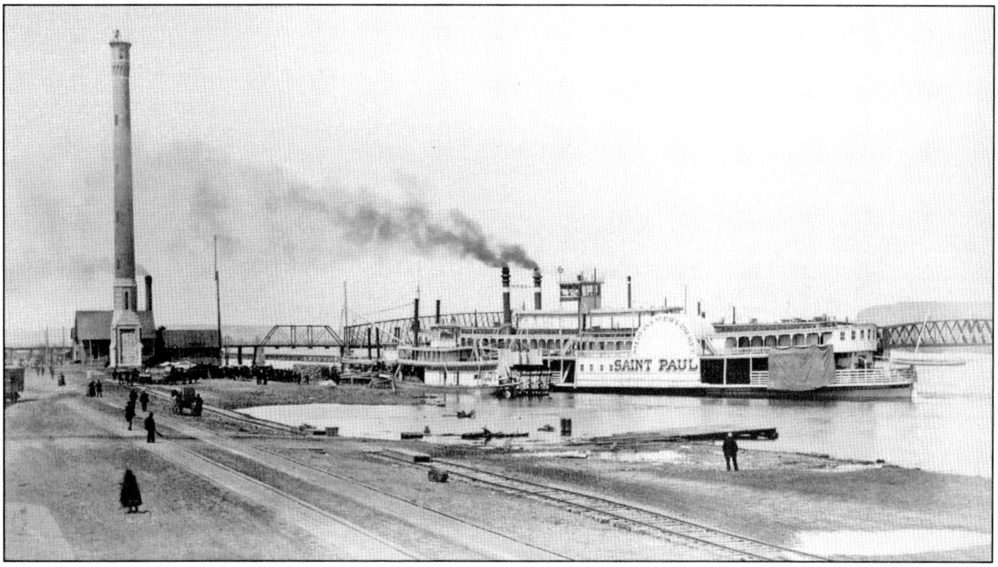

Steamer *St. Paul* is tied up in high water at the Winona Levee on its maiden voyage in July 1883. It was built in 1883 in Dubuque, Iowa, for the St. Louis and St. Paul Packet Company. The steamer is 300 feet long and has 55 elegant staterooms. In 1889, it was sold to the Diamond Jo Line and, later in 1911, to the Streckfus Line. In 1918, the *St. Paul* was converted into an excursion steamer, and its staterooms were removed and replaced with a spacious dance floor on the main passenger deck. This conversion was due to increasing competition by the railroads in hauling freight and providing year-round passenger service.

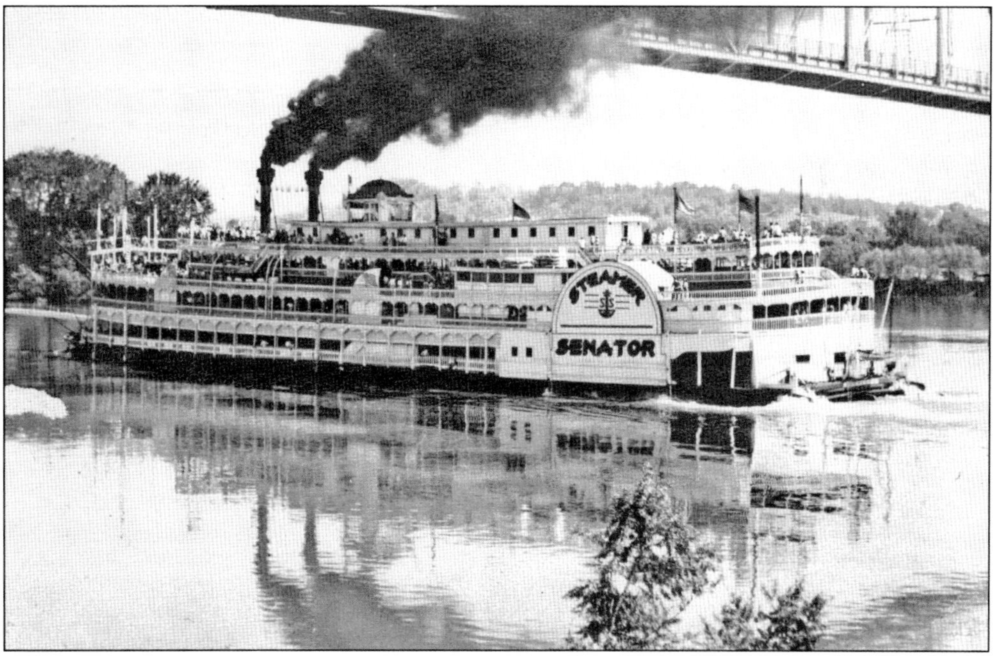

In 1939, the *St. Paul* was rebuilt and renamed the *Senator*. It toured on the Ohio River until 1942, when it was returned to St. Louis and became a training ship for Coast Guard recruits. The following year, it was used as a floating machine shop and warehouse by the Streckfus Company until it was abandoned in 1953 in the "boneyard" south of St. Louis.

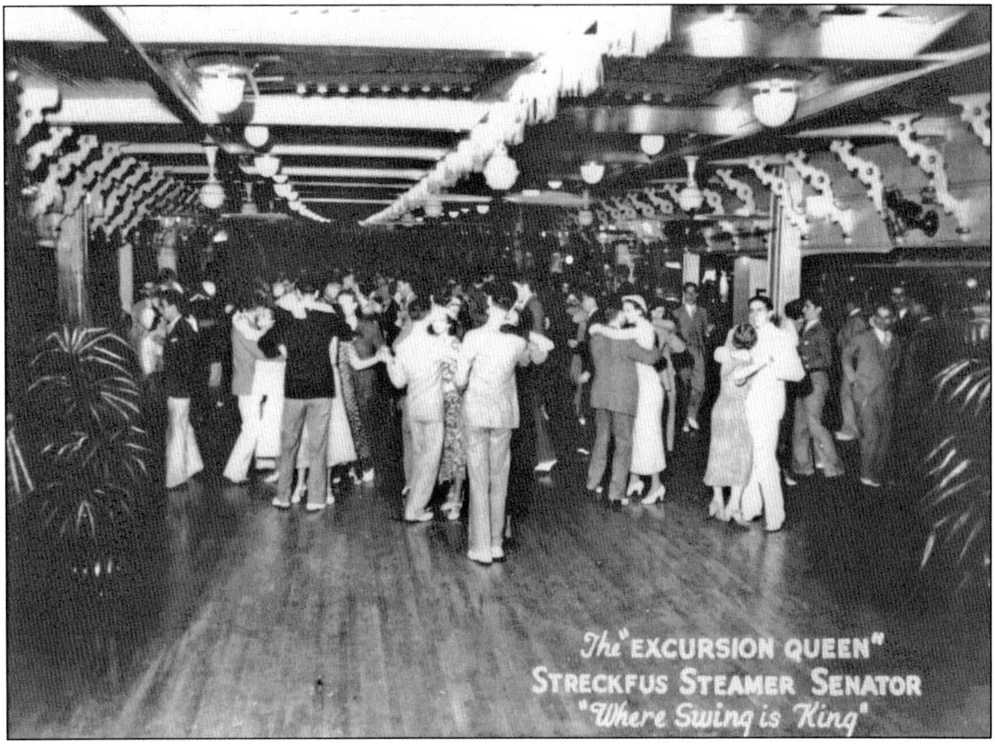

Excursion steamer *Senator* provided day and moonlight cruises on the inland waterways with every known convenience, including fans, soda fountains, table service, lunch counters, picnic tables, promenades, and the best dance music available.

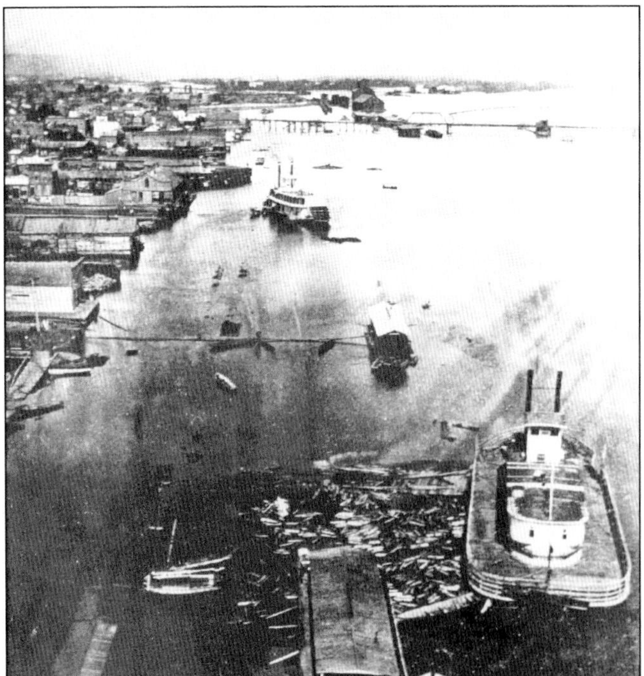

Until bridges crossed the Mississippi River, ferries were the common means for people, animals, and freight to cross the river. The *Turtle*, seen at lower right along the Winona Levee in 1872, was used in Winona until the high wagon bridge was built in 1892.

Handsome excursion steamer G.W. *Hill* is docked at Winona's Riverside Park one fine summer day around 1915, with a crowd waiting to board. The steamer was a common sight as it plied the waters near Winona. The *Hill* and its sister steamer, the original *JS*, were the first modern excursion boats to cater to the excursion trade exclusively. These boats were allowed and equipped to carry up to 3,000 persons, and many would-be passengers were turned away after the capacity was reached.

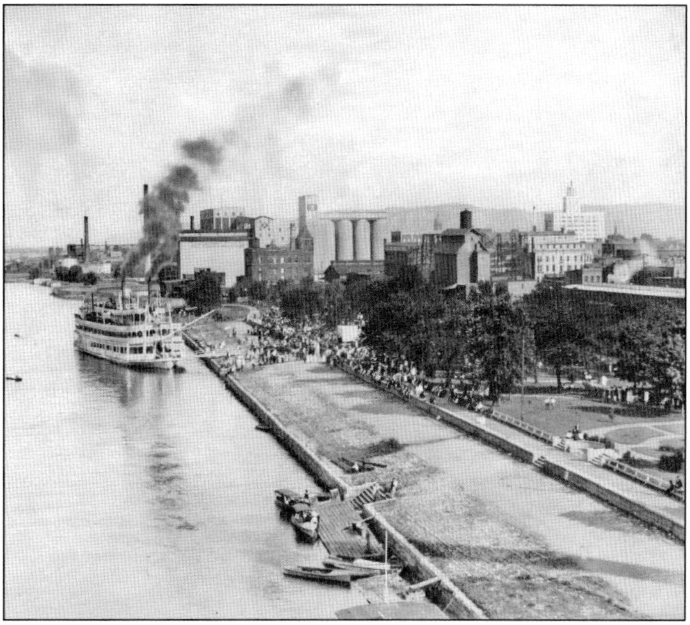

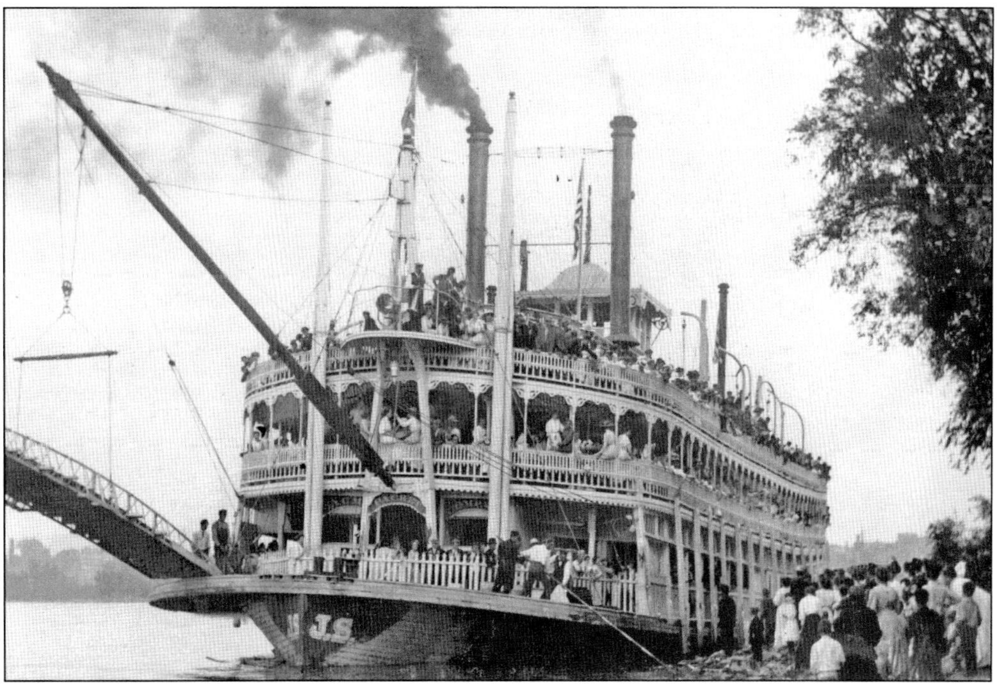

Steamer *JS*, the first steamboat built for the excursion trade, was constructed by the Streckfus Company in 1901, and the following summer, it offered excursions in the Upper Mississippi River from St. Louis to St. Paul. On Saturday, June 25, 1910, while traveling from La Crosse to Lansing, Iowa, the boat caught fire near Victory, Wisconsin, and burned to the waterline. Two lives were lost and six were seriously injured. Claims against the Streckfus Company were settled out of court in the amount of $2,500.

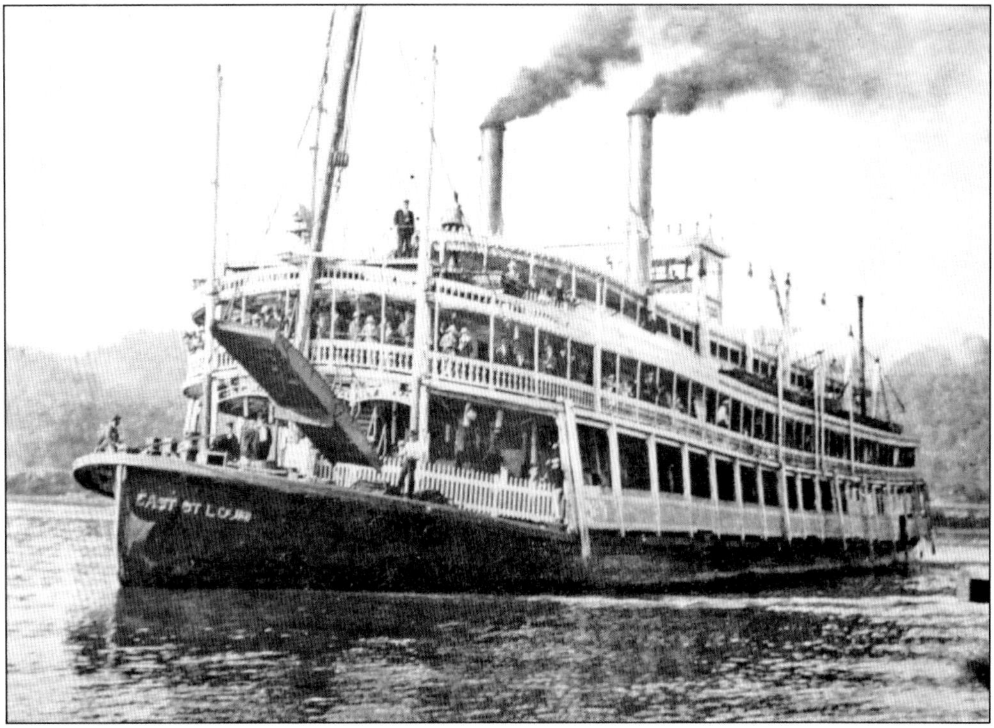

Excursion steamer *East St. Louis* was built in 1895. It was first named *Virginia*, then renamed *Steel City*, then *East St. Louis*, and finally *Island Belle* when it was sold in 1927 to the Greater New Orleans Amusement Company and rebuilt to provide excursions around the port of New Orleans as the *Ran*. After a year in the New Orleans market, it was sold to Streckfus Steamers of St. Louis and dismantled for its boilers, which were used in excursion steamer *Washington*.

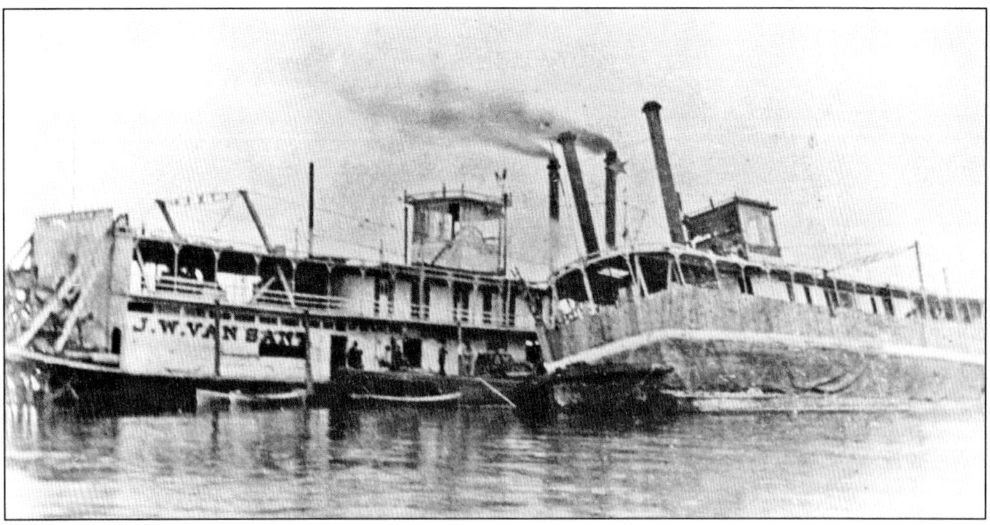

Steamer *Van Sant* is at the aid of the sinking steamer *Glenmont* in late April 1893. The *Glenmont*, a former rafter for the Laird Norton Lumber Company, was purchased by the Van Sant and Musser Transportation Company. The *Glenmont* was leaving La Crosse and sailing upstream when it struck the railroad bridge, which put a large hole in its side. The *Glenmont* was raised, repaired at the Wabasha Boatyard, and put back into service in early June.

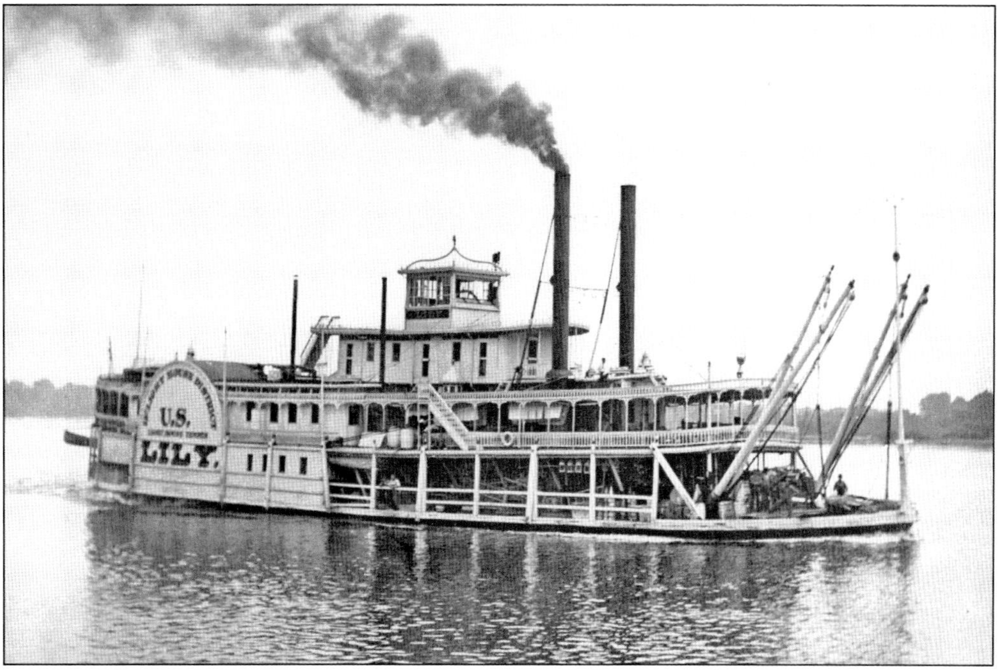

Steamer *Lily* was a lighthouse tender for the Army Corps of Engineers. The steamer, built in 1875, served the beacon lights and buoys between St. Paul, Stillwater, and St. Louis for many years. The *Lily* made three trips a year up and down the Mississippi River, providing the lightkeepers with oil and supplies for the beacons in their charge. The Lily was taken out of service in 1907 and sank near St. Albans, Missouri, in 1911.

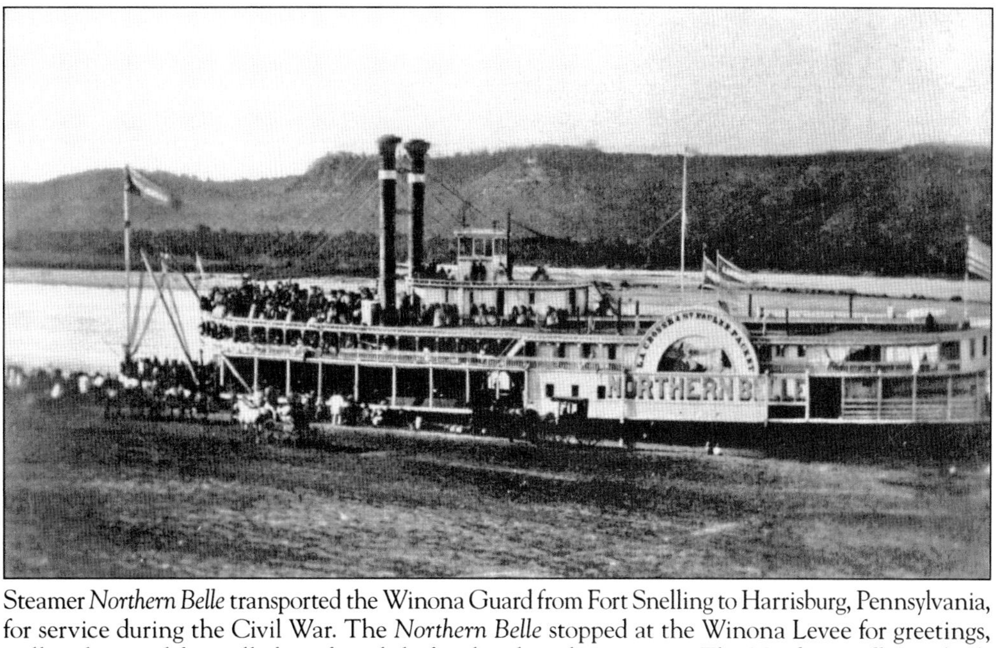

Steamer *Northern Belle* transported the Winona Guard from Fort Snelling to Harrisburg, Pennsylvania, for service during the Civil War. The *Northern Belle* stopped at the Winona Levee for greetings, well-wishes, and farewells from friends before heading downstream. The *Northern Belle* was built in Cincinnati in 1856 and sank near Wabasha in 1868. The steamer was raised and moved to La Crosse, where it was dismantled. Its cabin was used for the steamer *Belle of La Crosse*.

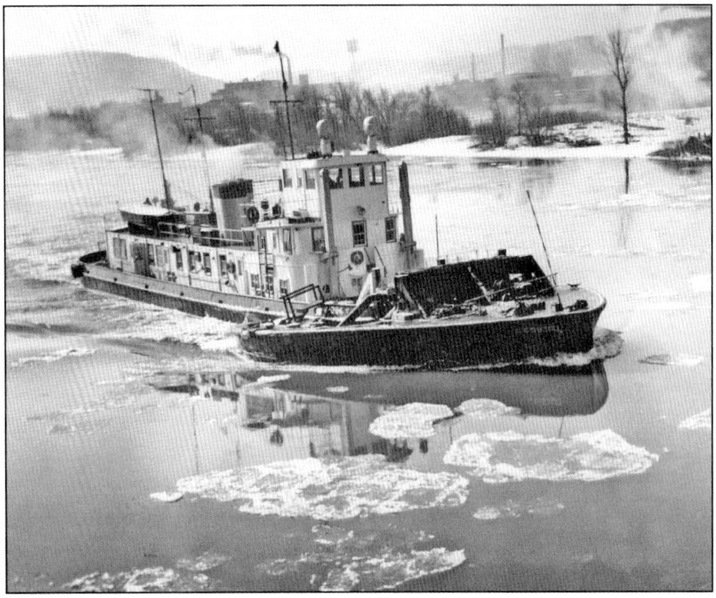

Coast Guard cutter *Fern*, with a detachable 85-ton ice plow attached to its prow, passes the Burlington Railroad swing bridge on March 18, 1955. The 114-foot cutter was commissioned in 1942 and served a variety of navigational duties for 29 years. It was decommissioned in 1971 and sold.

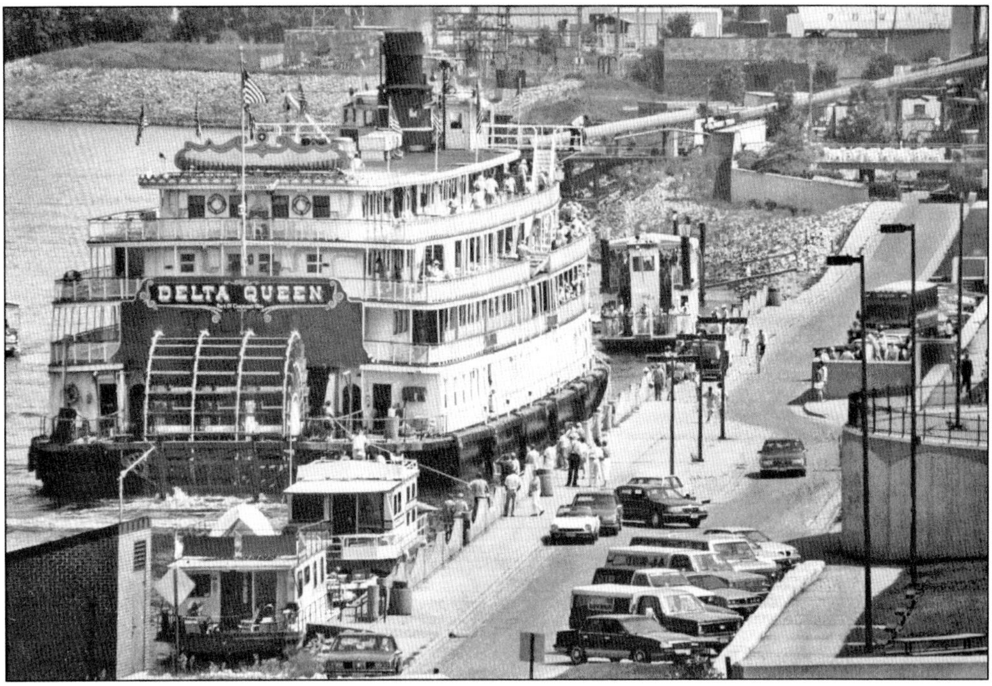

The *Delta Queen* is docked at Winona's Levee Park on August 14, 1991, to allow passengers to tour the city. The *Delta Queen* had cruised the Mississippi River and its tributaries since 1948. Built to serve the central California excursion market, it was commissioned in 1927. It 1948, the *Delta Queen* was sold to the Greene Line and sailed through the Panama Canal to New Orleans for service on the Mississippi River. In 1966, it was declared exempt from the Safety at Sea Act and was announced a National Historic Landmark in 1989. In 2008, it was taken out of service when its exemption ended, now serving as a floating hotel at Chattanooga, Tennessee. In 2013, Congress allowed an exemption for the *Delta Queen*, and it was brought to New Orleans for restoration and eventual cruising on the Mississippi River.

Five

Life on the River

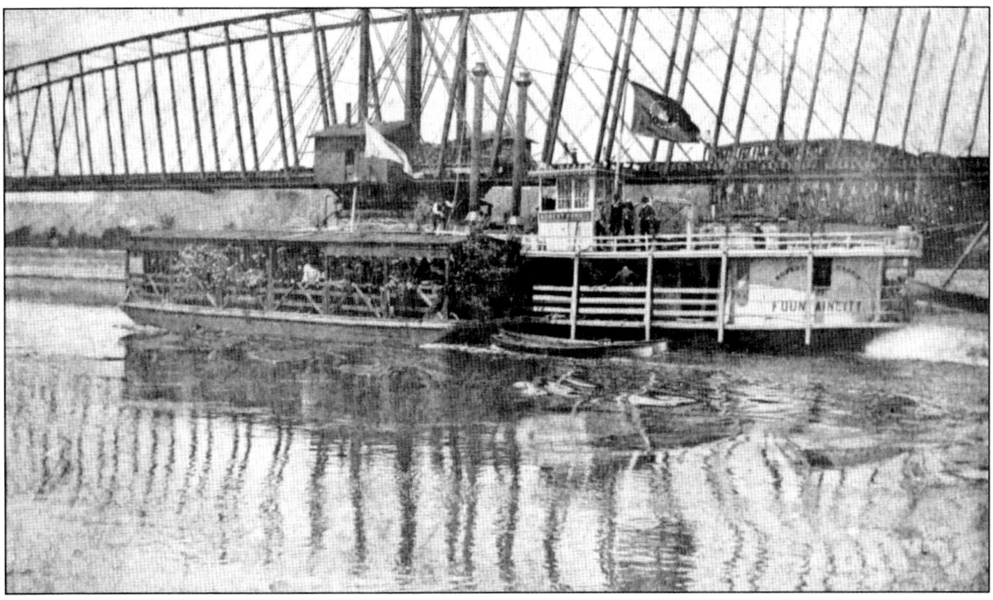

Steamer *Robert Harris* offered a Christmas Day excursion in 1888 on the ice-free Mississippi River between Winona and Fountain City. The barge, pushed by the steamer, was amply decorated with evergreens. By the end of the trip, the weather was turning cold, and the river began to freeze over the next day.

1888 **Merry Christmas!** 1888

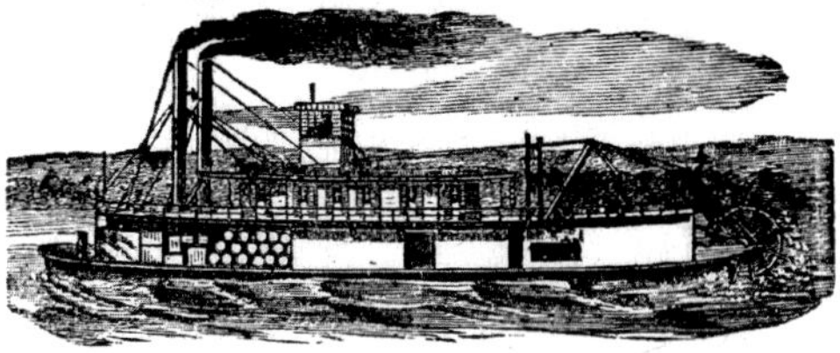

STEAMBOAT EXCURSION!

TO

Fountain City!

On Tuesday, Dec. 25th.

STEAMER ROBERT HARRIS

And two barges will leave the levee at 2 o'clock in the afternoon for Fountain City with the Gate City Band aboard. All excursionists will please uniform in linen dusters and straw hats. Refreshments will be served on board, consisting of Minnesota Strawberries and Cream, Soda Water, Pop, Lemonade and Ice Cream.

FANS DISTRIBUTED FREE OF CHARGE.

What is Home without a Mother? What is Winona without an

Excursion on Christmas Day?

Capt. Shorty will furnish Pop Corn to the boys and Boquets, Sweet Violets, Roses and Water Lillies to the Girls. O the Flowers that Bloom in the Spring, Tra La.

ROUND TRIP TICKETS ONLY 50 CENTS.

At Haesly's Cigar Store. For State Rooms apply to

W. C. PIERCE, Manager,

162 & 164 Walnut Street.

The Christmas excursion on the steamer *Robert Harris* and its barge is advertised in 1888. Another such excursion also took place the following year.

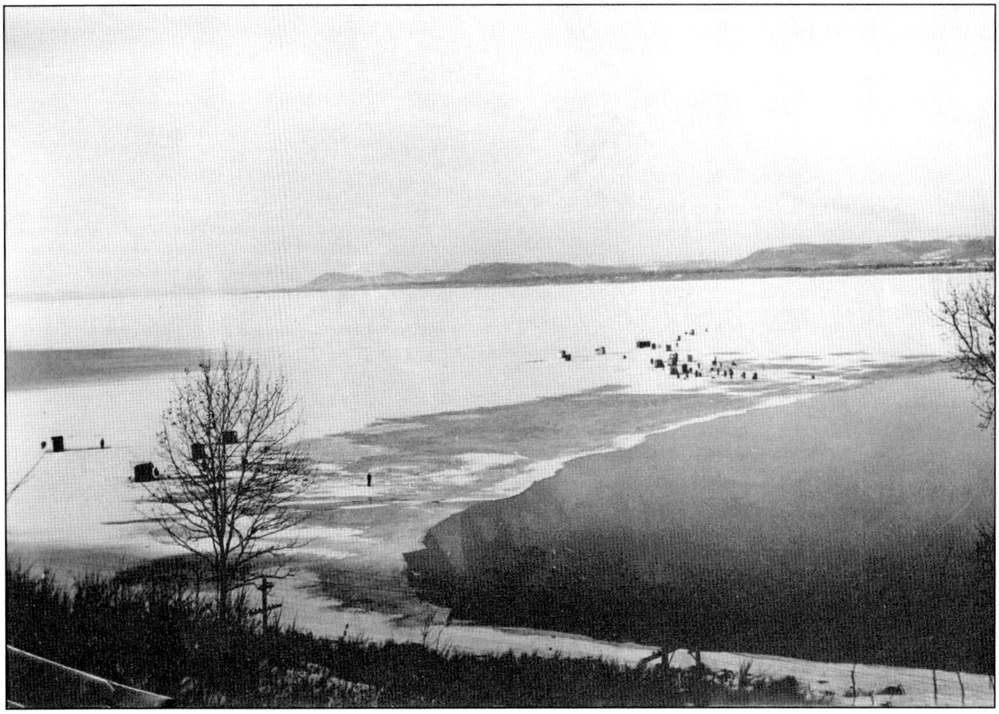

On the sunny Friday afternoon of January 10, 1955, a number of ice fishermen enjoy themselves on the Minnesota side of Lake Pepin, where ice fishing is a popular sport—both from the shelter of a fish house and in the open.

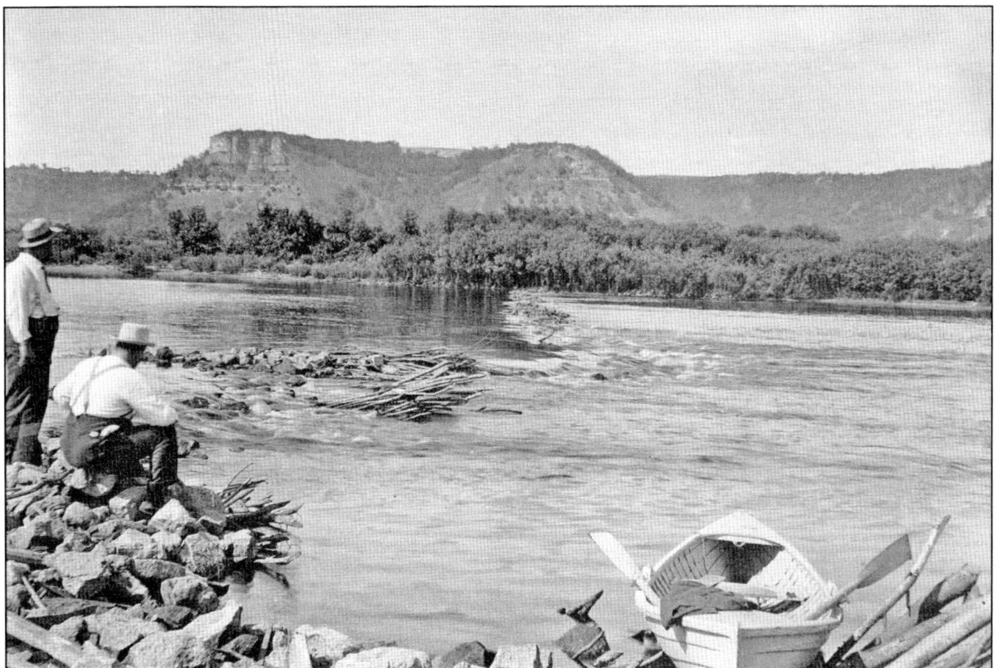

On a warm summer day during low water, these men have found a great place to catch their fill of fish below a wing dam on the Mississippi River.

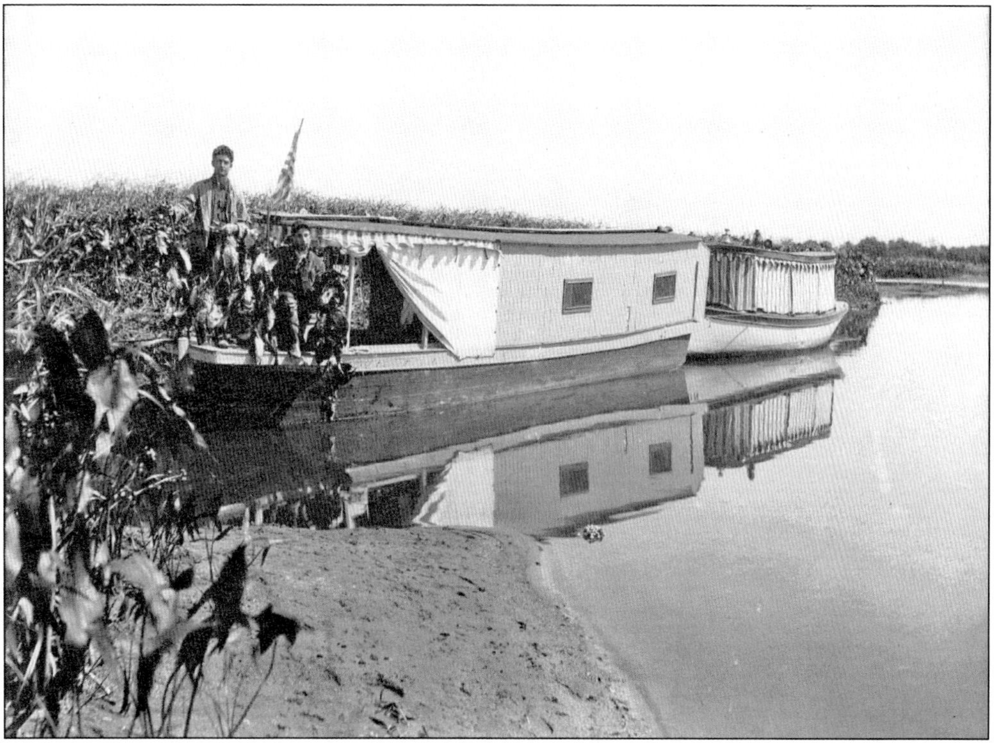

Conrad Heintz's hunting boat and barge are out in the bottomlands of the Mississippi River Valley, where he and John Burmeister are ready to get their bag limit of 10 ducks—most of them Mallards.

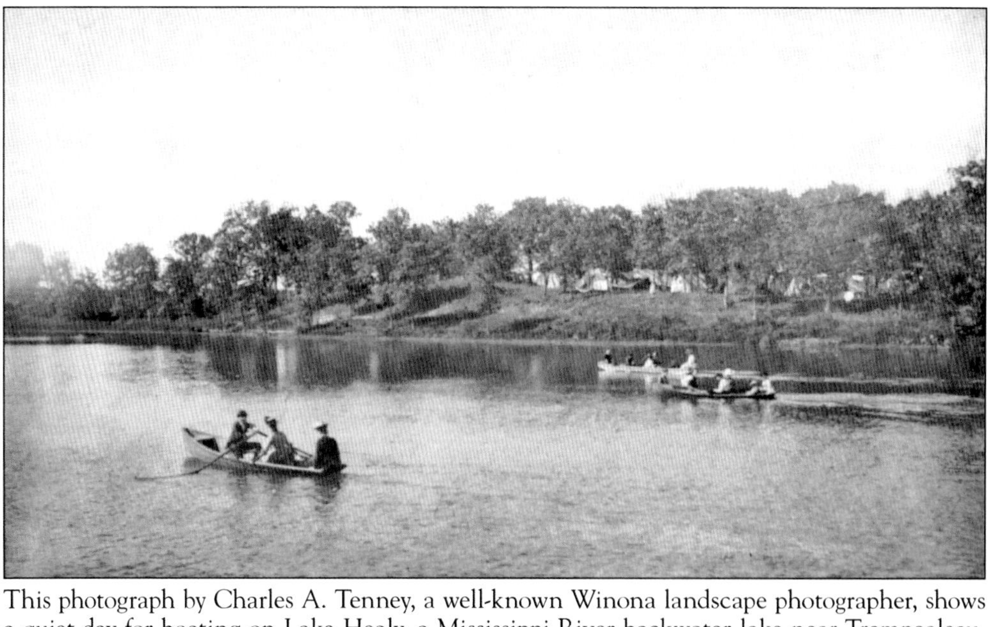

This photograph by Charles A. Tenney, a well-known Winona landscape photographer, shows a quiet day for boating on Lake Healy, a Mississippi River backwater lake near Trempealeau, Wisconsin, in August 1888. In the background is one of three camping sites occupied by people from Winona who enjoy the camping life.

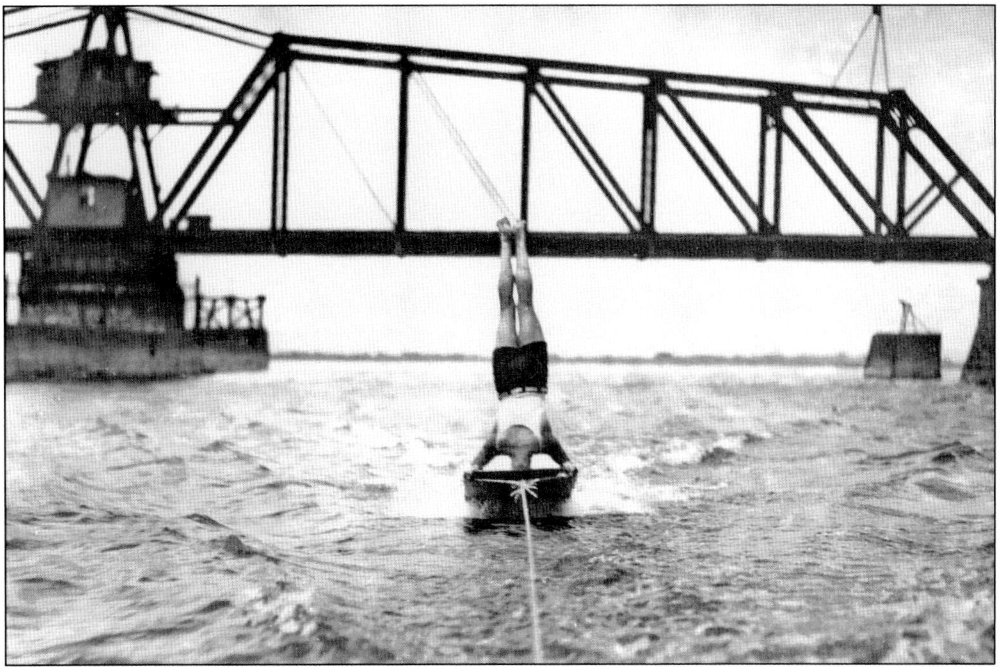

On August 11, 1924, at Winona's first annual water carnival, local Max Conrad entertains the crowd with a demonstration of his skilled surfboard stunts near the Chicago & Northwestern Railroad's swing bridge.

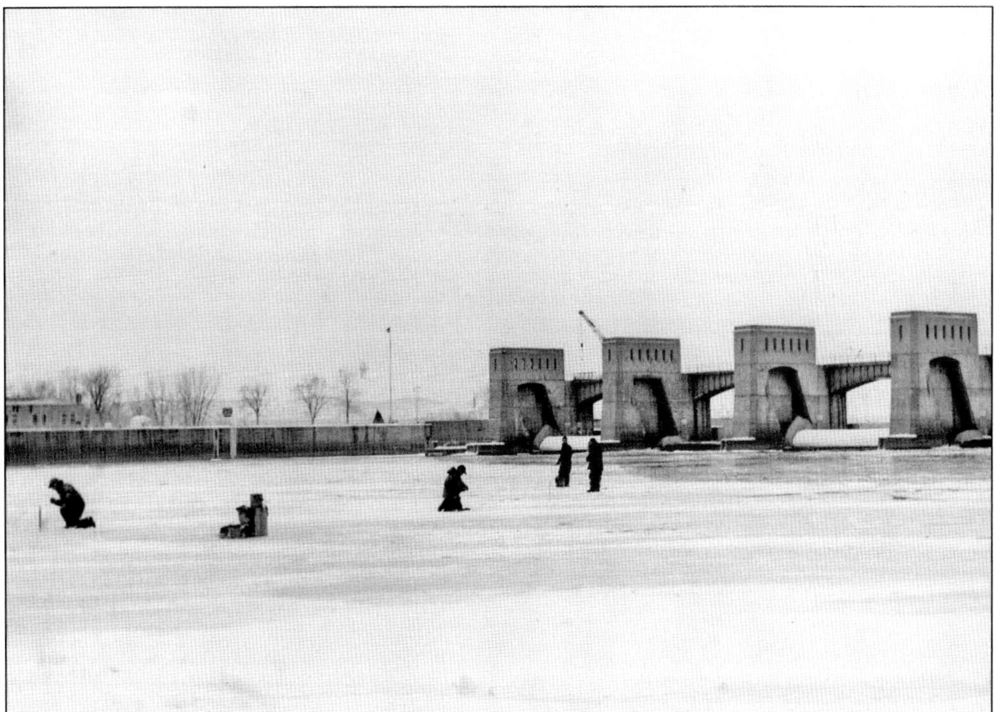

These ice fishermen are dangerously close to the open water below Dam No. 5A just upriver from Winona. These waters are a favorite habitat of large walleyes and are heavily fished.

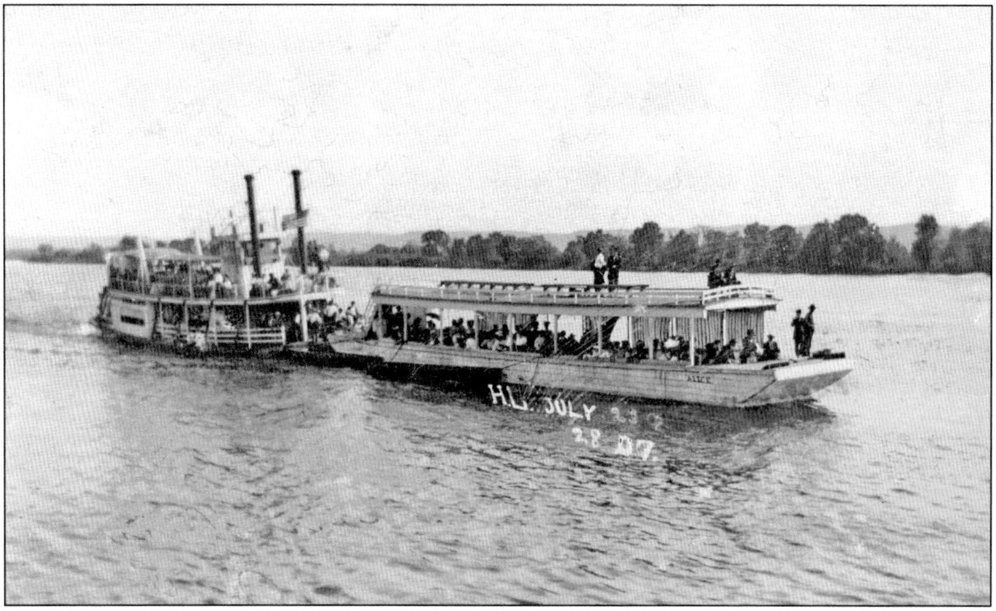

Excursion steamer *HL* and barge *Alice* embark from Winona on July 27, 1907, for a private moonlight excursion under the auspices of the Knights of Columbus. The *HL* and *Alice* were operated by Capt. Frank Fugina and Capt. William Henning and traveled primarily between Fountain City and Winona. The steamer was later renamed *Ideal*.

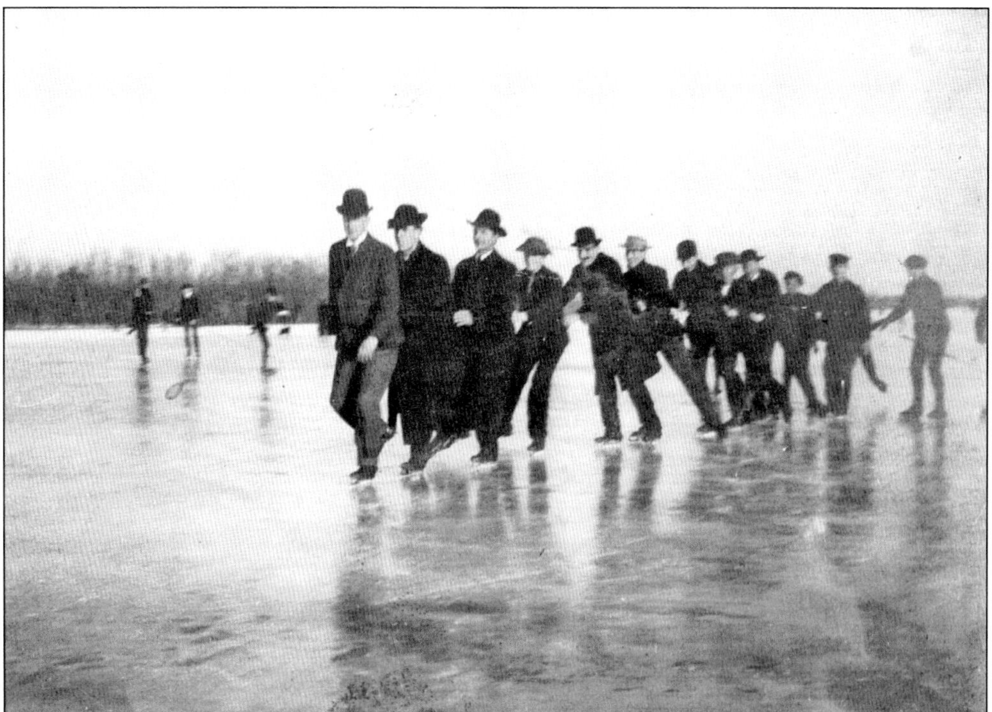

The municipal band enjoys a game of "crack the whip" during an ice skating party in the winter of 1917.

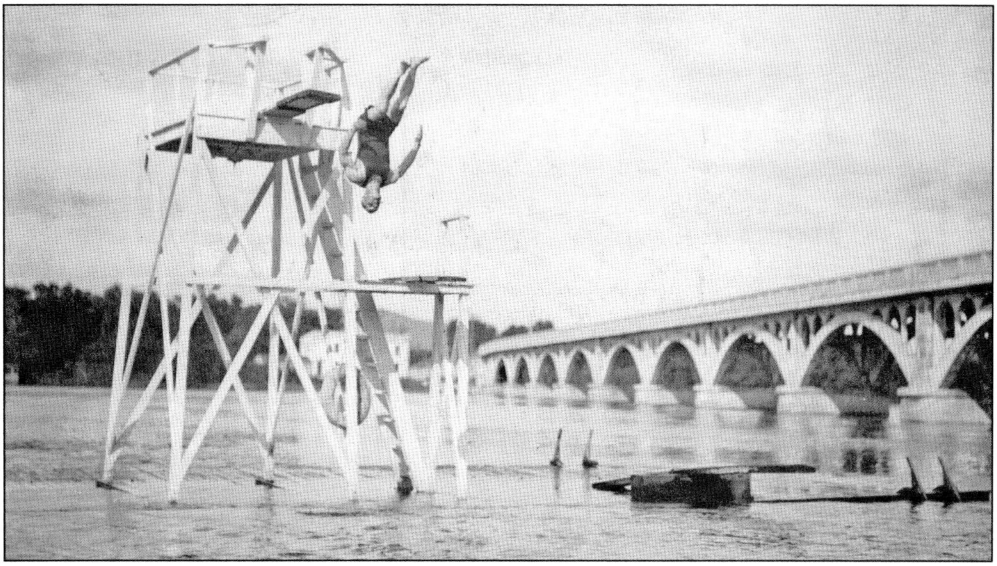

A photographer captured this back dive off the high diving board at the old Latsch Beach, which was opened in 1907 on the north side of Latsch Island. In the background is the concrete bridge that connects to the high wagon bridge, which joins Winona with Wisconsin. Behind the high dive to the right is the concrete arch bridge, which was opened in 1918 and connected to the high wagon bridge. Also behind the diving board is the Old Stone House, which served as a stagecoach stop and ferry dock for moving people and freight across the river to Winona.

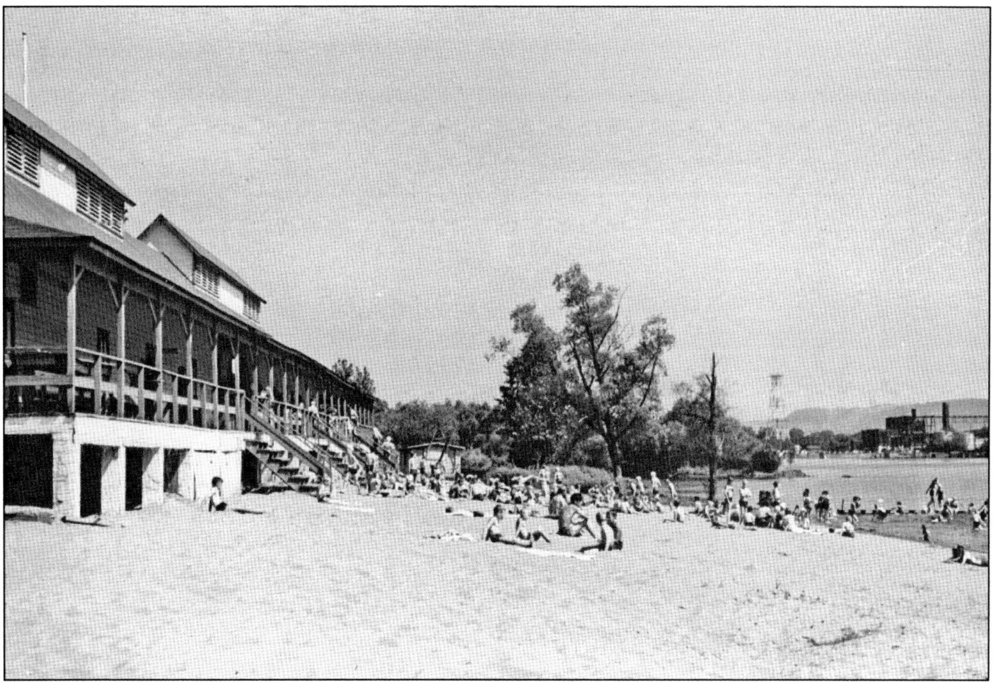

In 1924, the Latsch Island Bathhouse, built in 1907, was moved to the south side of the island because the water was stagnating due to poor flow at the site of the old beach. The beach was improved with additional sand, and the bathhouse was set on concrete piers rather than wood ones as done previously. The beach was closed in 1974, and the bathhouse was razed.

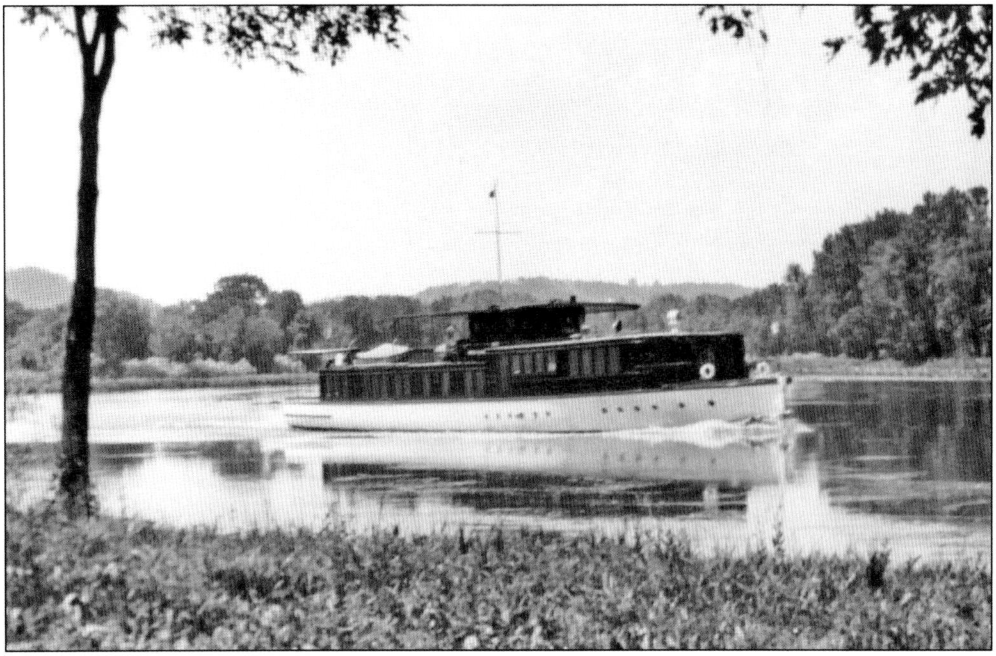

The *North Star*, Dr. William Mayo's private yacht, was 120 feet long, 22 feet wide, and powered by twin gasoline engines. It was built in 1922 by the Joseph Dingle boat yard in St. Paul and was operated on the Mississippi River from the port at Wabasha. The yacht was never operated for personal use by Dr. Mayo but for purposes connected with the Mayo Clinic and Mayo Foundation and for the benefit of the medical profession. The yacht was sold in 1938 to the Inland Waterways Corporation for inspection purposes.

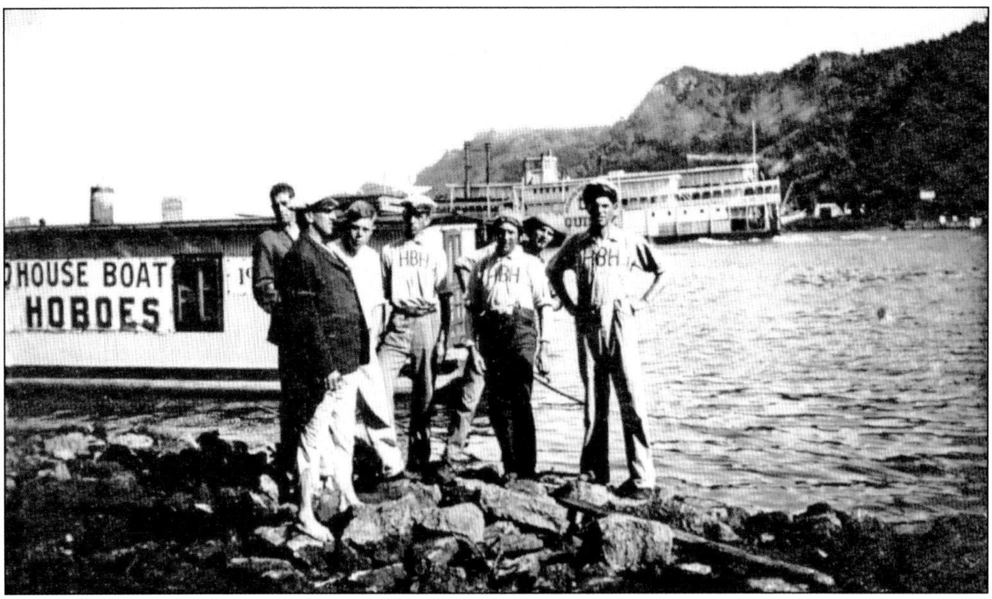

The House Boat Hobos were a group of friends from Winona who, during the early 1900s, vacationed together along the river on Carl Gerlicher's houseboat, *Milton G.* The friends, often including their wives, would camp, fish, and loaf on the sandy islands near Winona. In the background is steamer *Quincy* moving upriver.

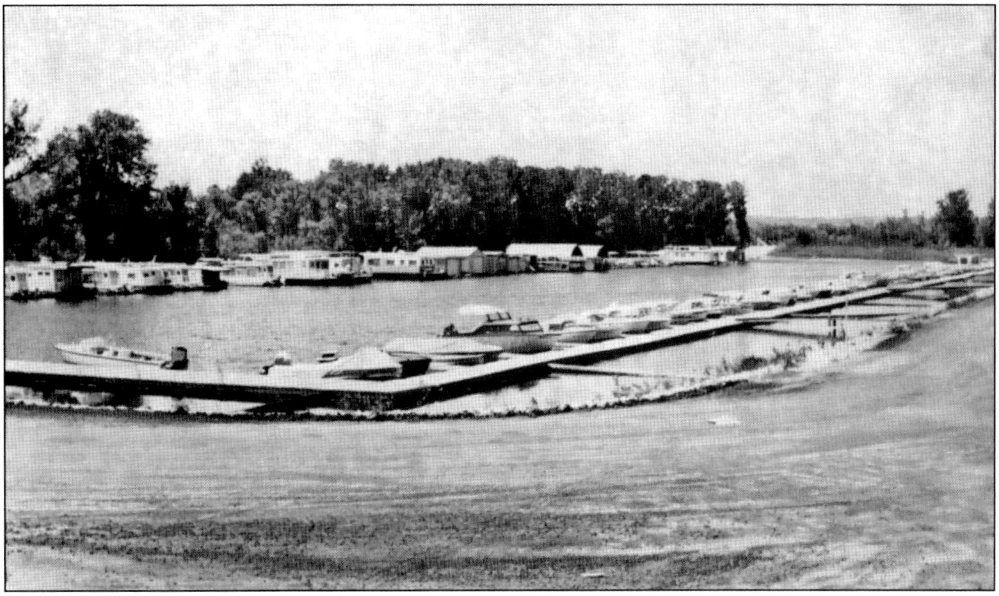

Most of the pleasure craft docked in the Winona Municipal Boat Harbor are ready for summer cruising up and down the Mississippi River. Most of these craft have been overhauled, put in the water, and given a test run. They are now ready to cruise on the Mississippi River come Memorial Day weekend of 1961. The small boat harbor was dredged by the A. Kertzman Dredging Company for the Army Corps of Engineers in 1957 and opened for business in the spring of 1958.

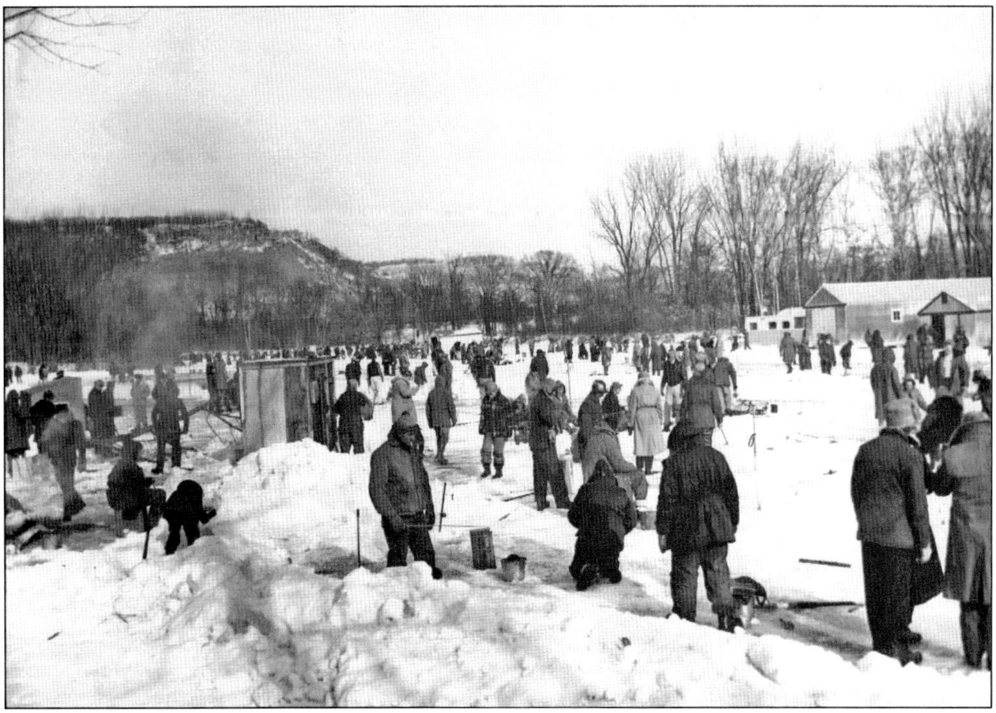

The annual ice fishing contest is seen here in January 1956 at Straight Slough during the annual Winona Winter Carnival. Of 750 contestants on the ice, only 20 fish were caught, the largest being a one-pound-seven-and-a-half-ounce northern pike.

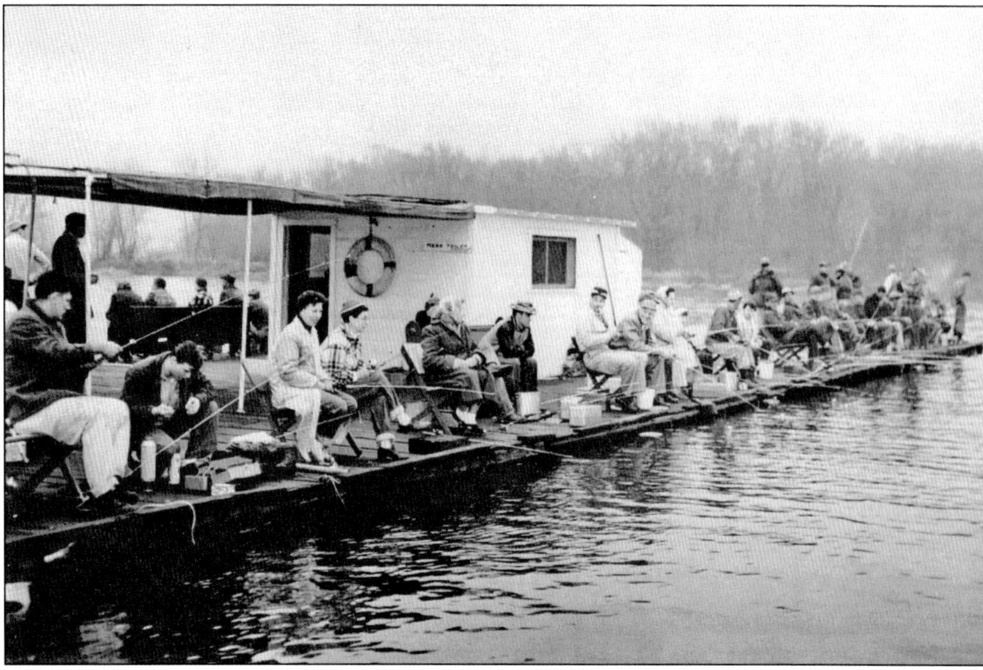

More than 150 fishermen and women were on the large *Banta* float below the Alma Dam at 6:30 a.m. when the fog lifted on May 3, 1958. The first arrival came at 3:30 a.m. Fishing was much slower than opening day a year ago at the same float.

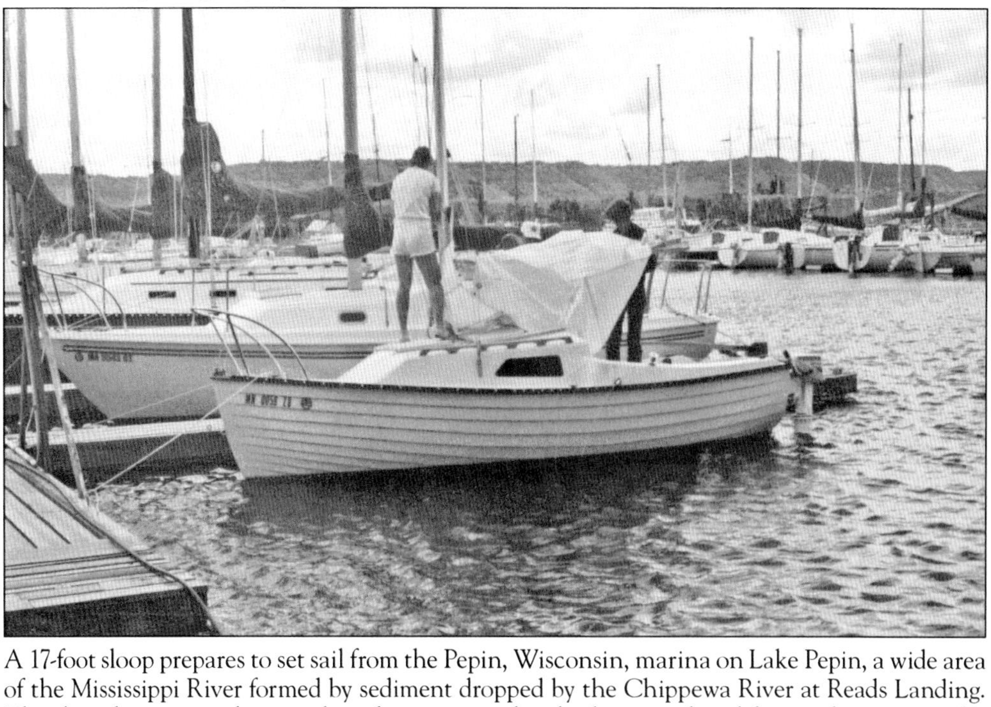

A 17-foot sloop prepares to set sail from the Pepin, Wisconsin, marina on Lake Pepin, a wide area of the Mississippi River formed by sediment dropped by the Chippewa River at Reads Landing. The sloop has an auxiliary outboard motor to aid in harbor travel and for rough going on the lake. The Pepin small boat harbor was dredged by the Army Corps of Engineers in 1965 and opened for business in June 1967.

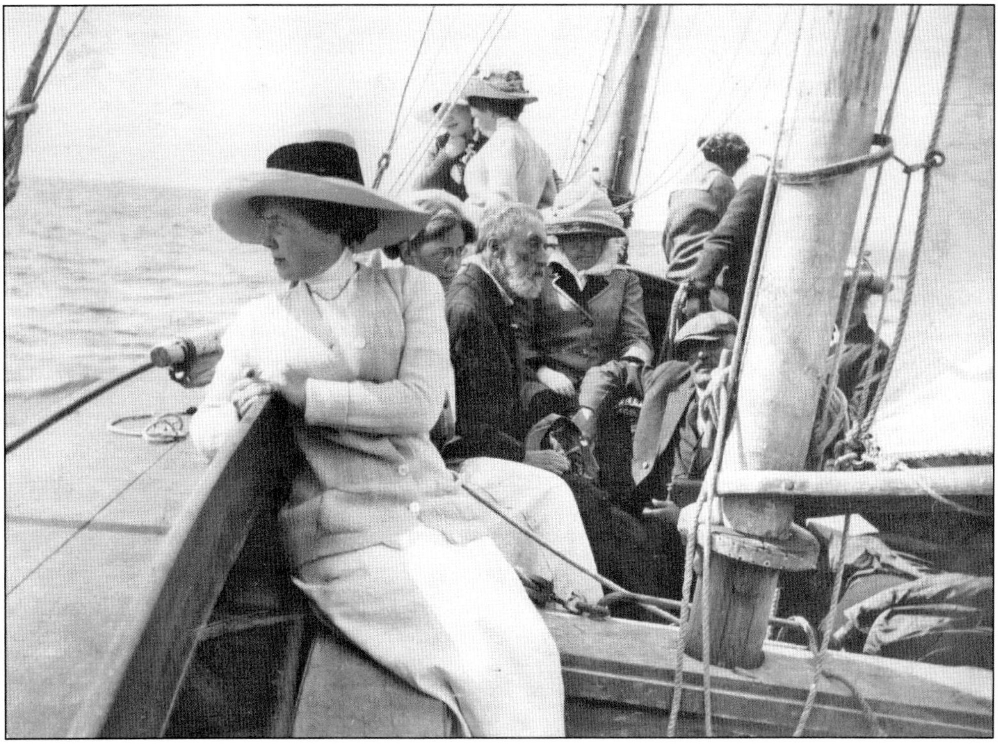

Sailing on Lake Pepin at an earlier time was rather an unsafe adventure with the lack of flotation gear and the heavy clothing worn by the individuals on the trip.

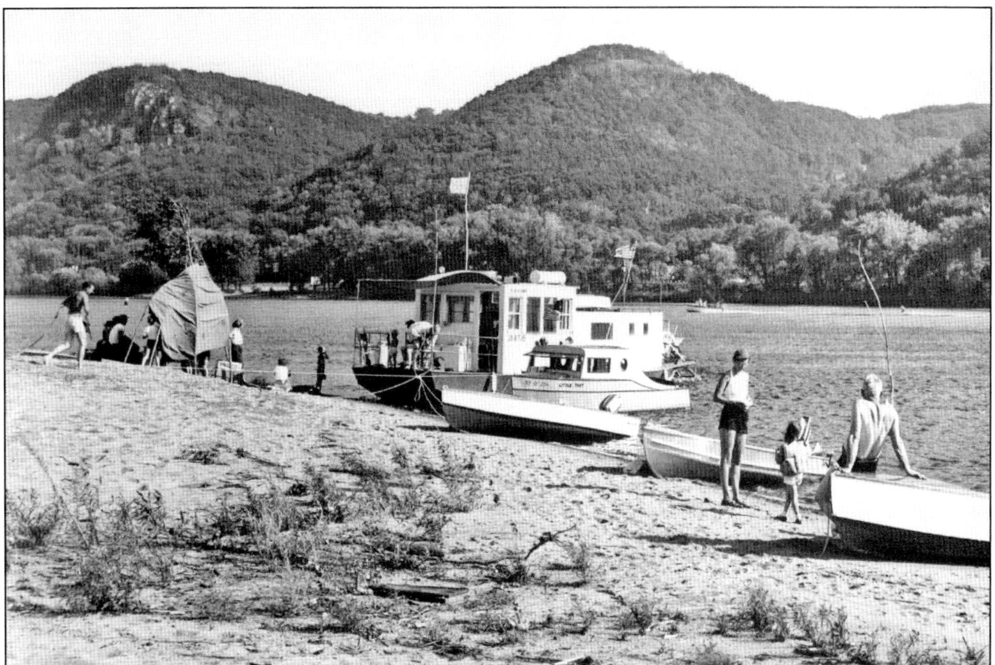

The many sandy islands on the Mississippi River are ideal places to beach a boat and spend a day—or several days—camping, swimming, or just loafing.

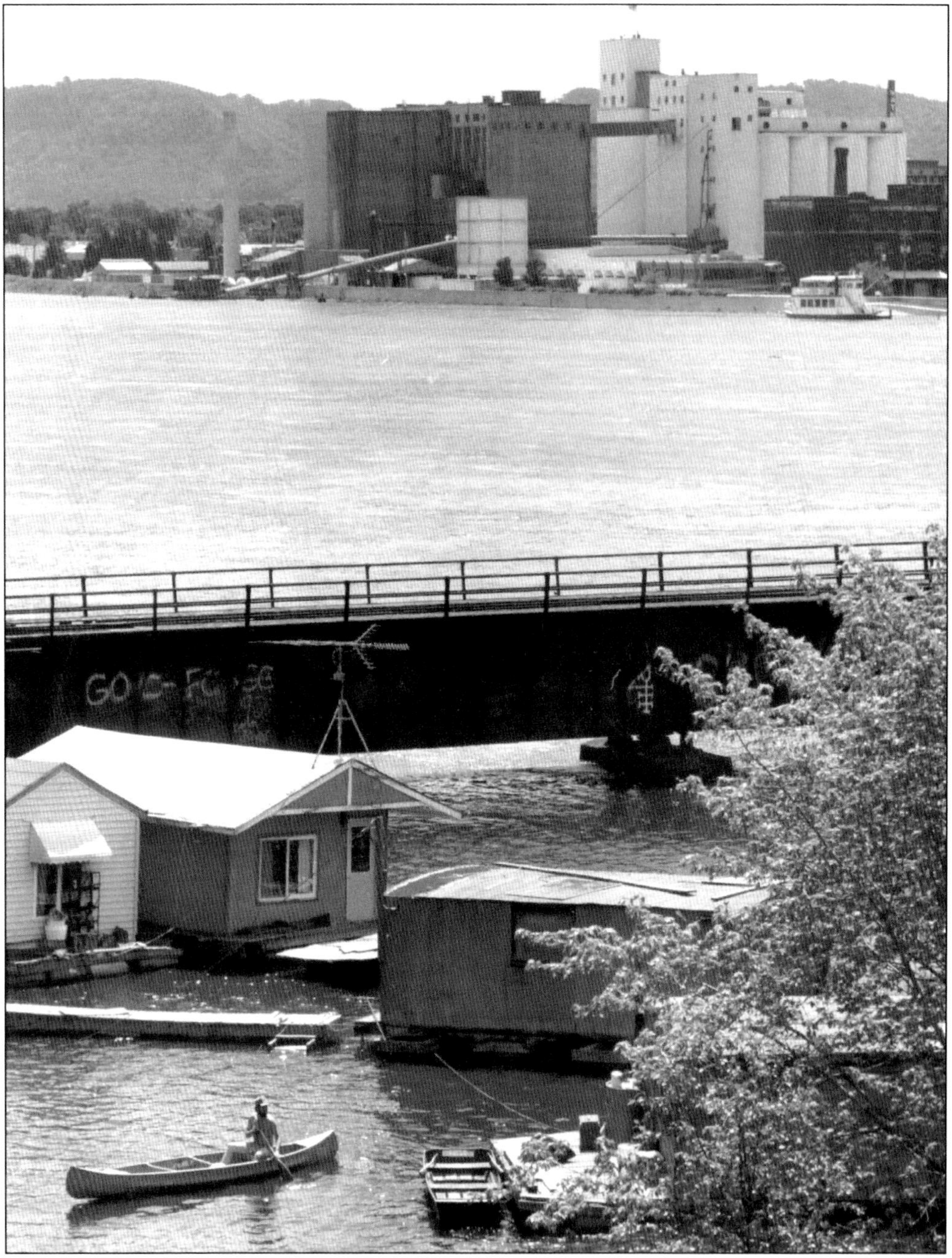

Boathouses are common along the Upper Mississippi River. A cluster of boathouses found around Winona are poled and tethering along Latsch Island, just across the interstate bridge from downtown Winona. These boathouses contain people, not boats. Since the 1960s, if not earlier, this floating village has attracted people to the water's edge for temporary and even permanent living. The community is partially tethered to the south side of Latsch Island and next to the abandoned railroad bridge. In the background are the elevators of the Bay State Milling Company and the *Jollie Ollie* excursion boat. The *Jollie Ollie* operated from the Winona Levee between 1988 and 1993.

Six

Working on the River

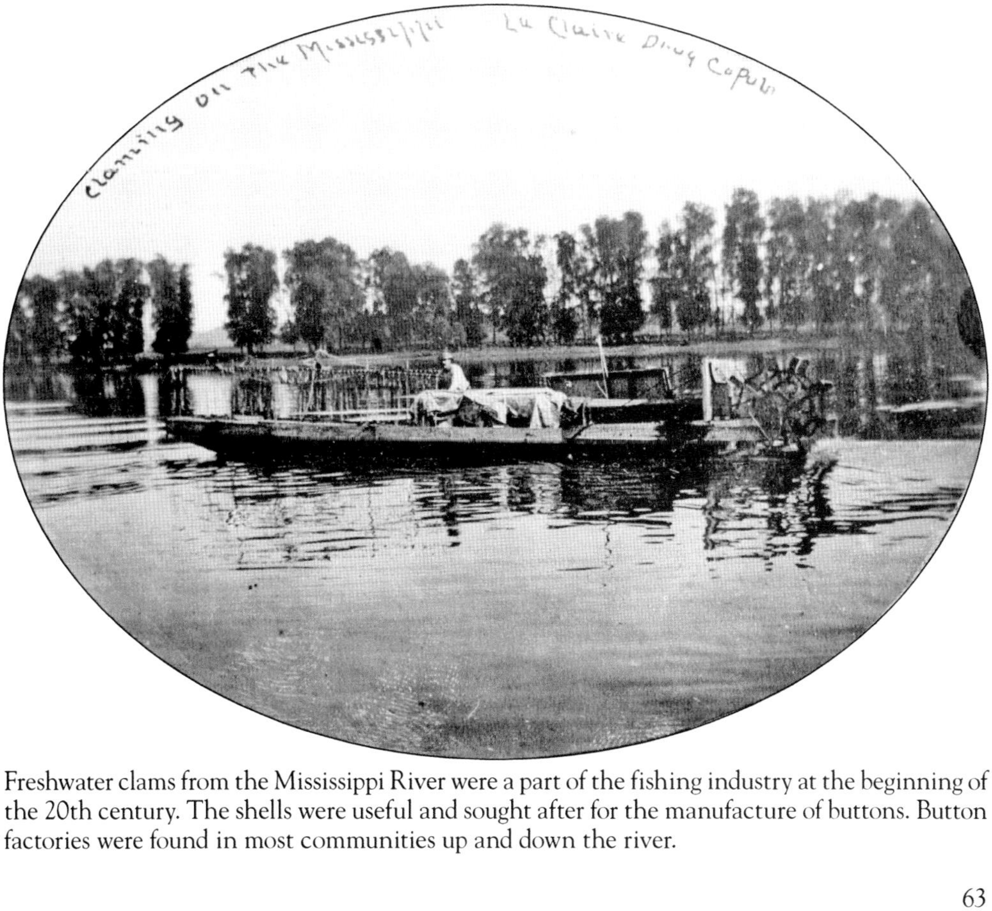

Freshwater clams from the Mississippi River were a part of the fishing industry at the beginning of the 20th century. The shells were useful and sought after for the manufacture of buttons. Button factories were found in most communities up and down the river.

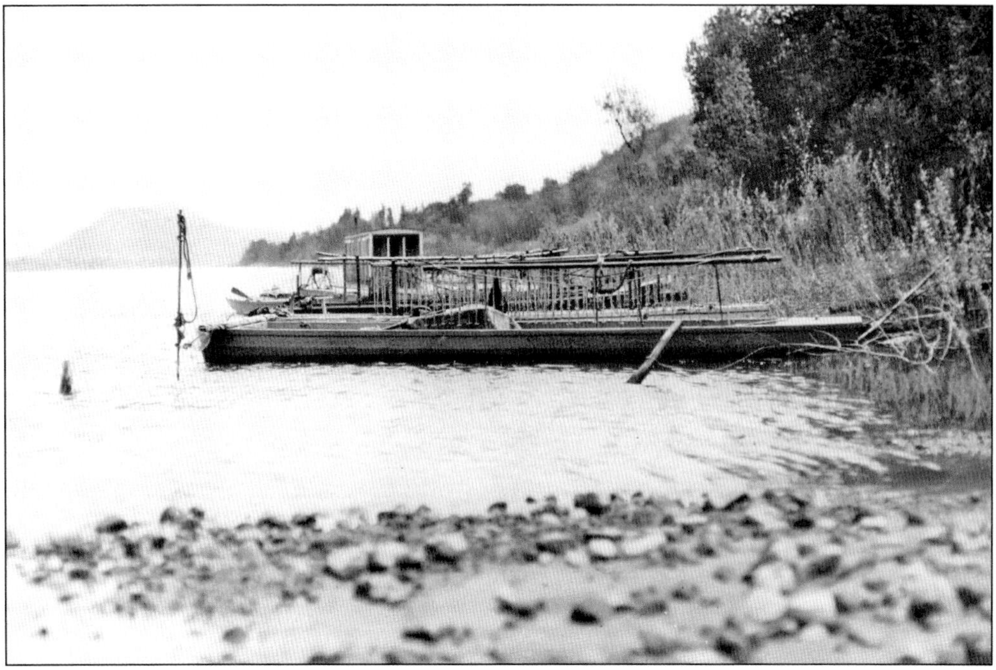

The last clammer's scow on Lake Pepin and probably on the upper river is pictured as a relic of a bygone era. Clammer's scows were a common sight on the Upper Mississippi River until about 40 years ago. Before then, the clamshell was used for the manufacture of buttons. Circular pieces were cut from the shells and sent to eastern markets to be made into pearl buttons, especially for fancy gowns.

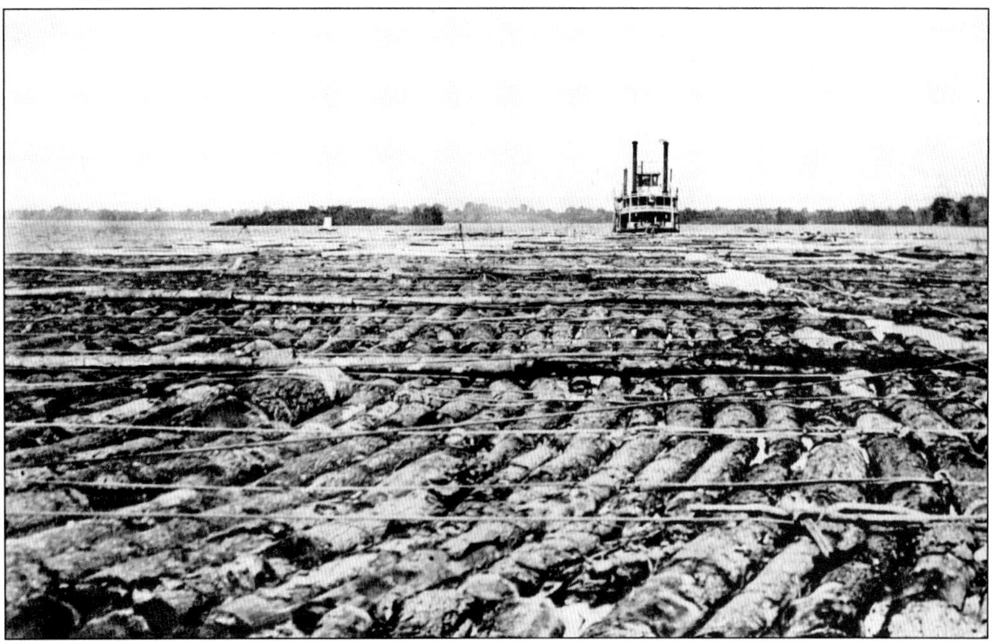

Log rafts were common on the Upper Mississippi River until the pine forests were decimated in the early part of the 20th century. These rafts were made of logs, cut the previous winter, and chained together to be towed by steamboats to the sawmills.

The cut timber was floated down the Chippewa River and other such tributaries of the Mississippi River to boom areas, such as at Beef Slough at the mouth of the Chippewa River or West Newton Slough near Wabasha, Minnesota, where it would be assembled into large rafts and towed to waiting sawmills.

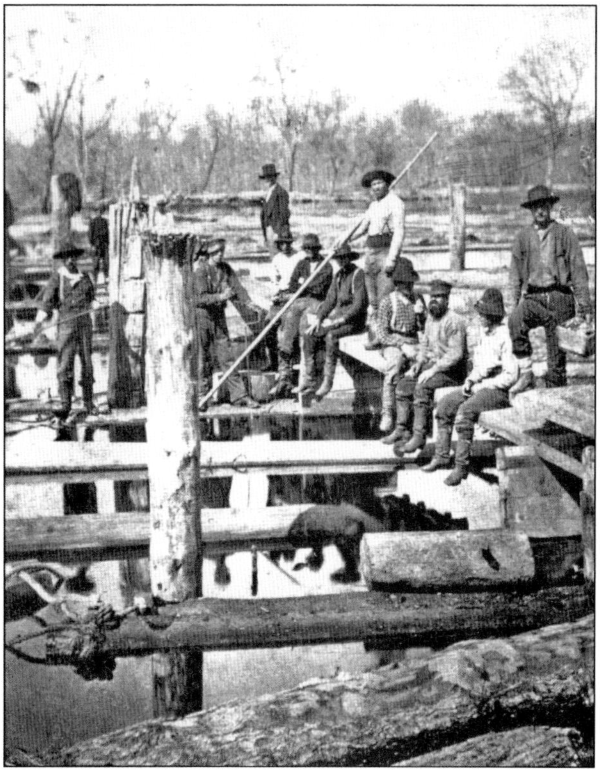

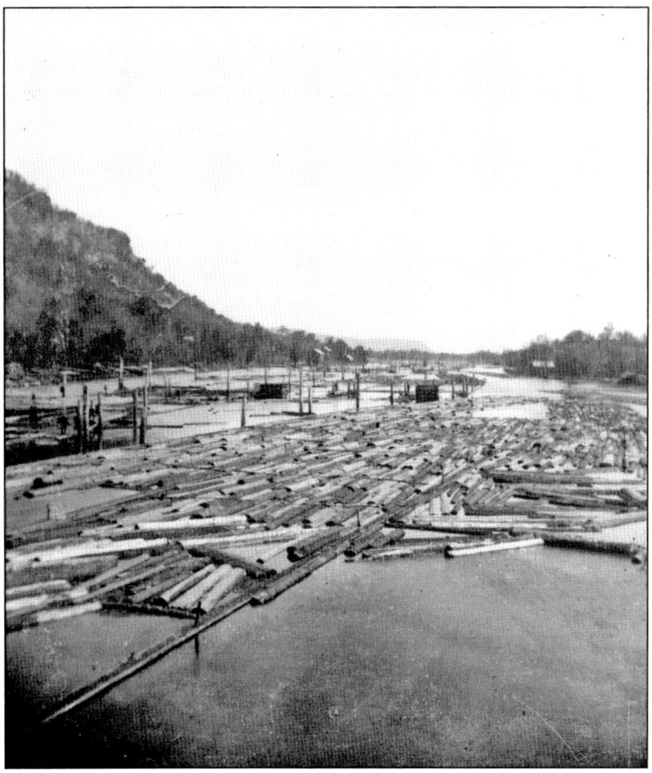

Pictured is the log assembly area, or boom, at Beef Slough. Here, the loose logs that floated down the Chippewa River were chained together in groups and assembled into the large rafts commonly seen being towed by steamers to the sawmills.

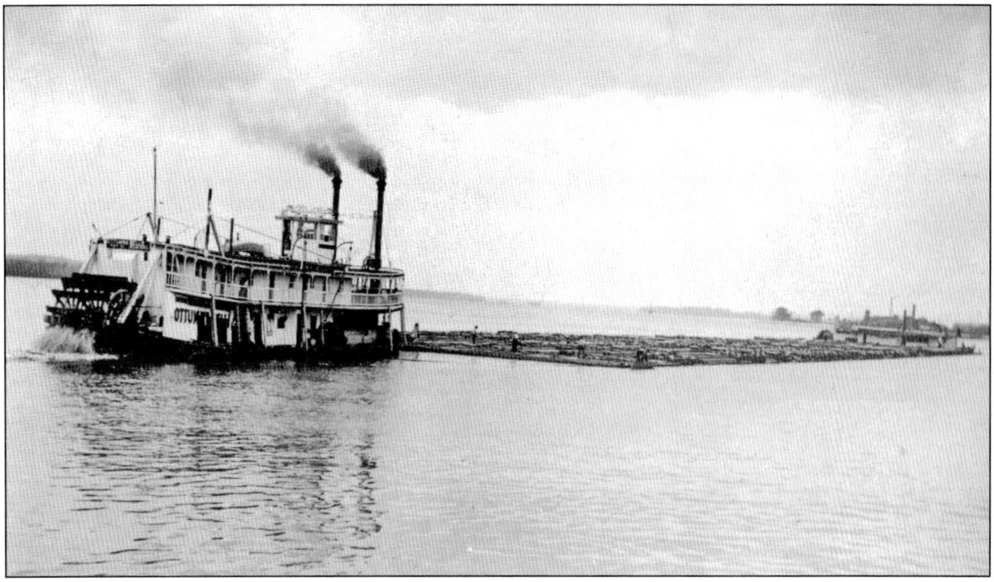

On August 7, 1915, steamer *Ottumwa Belle* and bow-boat *Pathfinder* guide the last lumber raft to go past Winona on its way to Fort Madison, Iowa. The steamer, under the command of Capt. Walter Hunter, was towing some five million feet of sawed lumber, the scraps of the logging industry of the Upper Mississippi Valley. This lumber had been accumulated in Stillwater, Minnesota, and Hudson, Wisconsin, as the last of the scattered stands of pines were cut down, thus bringing the logging industry to a close.

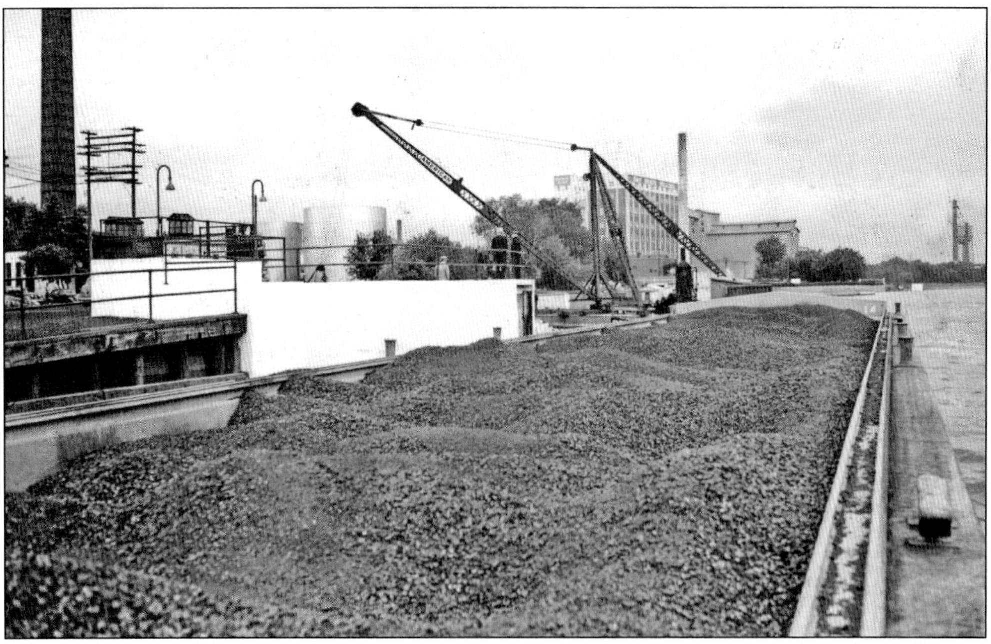

On June 16, 1939, a new transportation era opened in Winona with the arrival of a coal barge at the Mississippi Valley Public Service Company electric generating plant at the foot of Liberty Street. Towboat *William T. Warner* delivered the barge to the power company's waterfront dock to determine if the company should build its own terminal facilities. Since the unloading was successful, a terminal was constructed and operational by late summer.

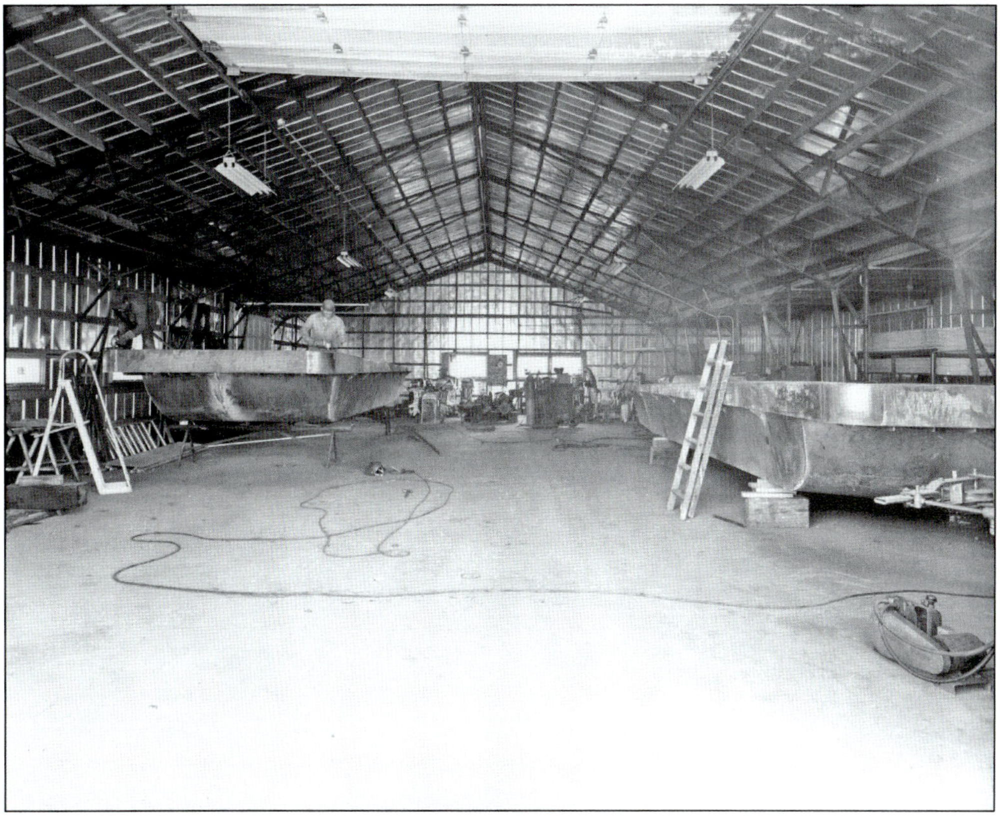

In 1954, Richard Whittaker was approached by seven influential Winona men to help construct a houseboat for use on the Mississippi River. From this humble beginning, Whittaker established Whittaker Marina at the foot of Laird Street. Within the main construction facility, a workman is working on the hull of one of two houseboats.

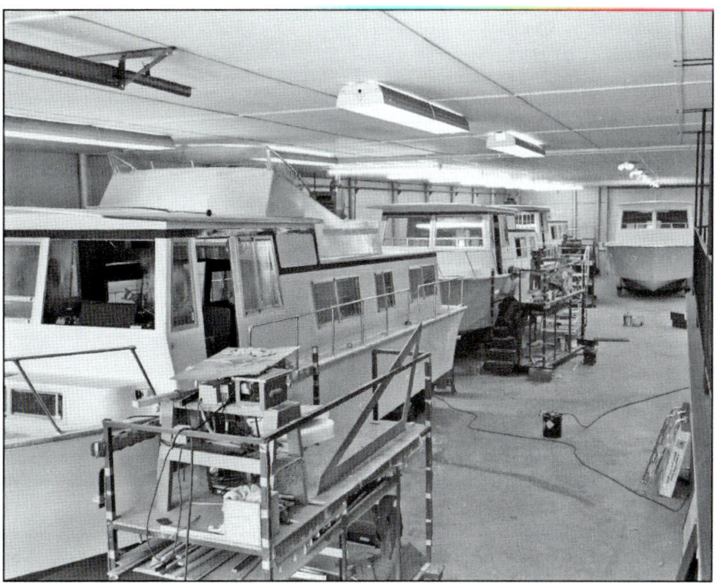

In another part of the plant, finishing touches are being installed and the electric circuitry is being tested on two nearly completed houseboats.

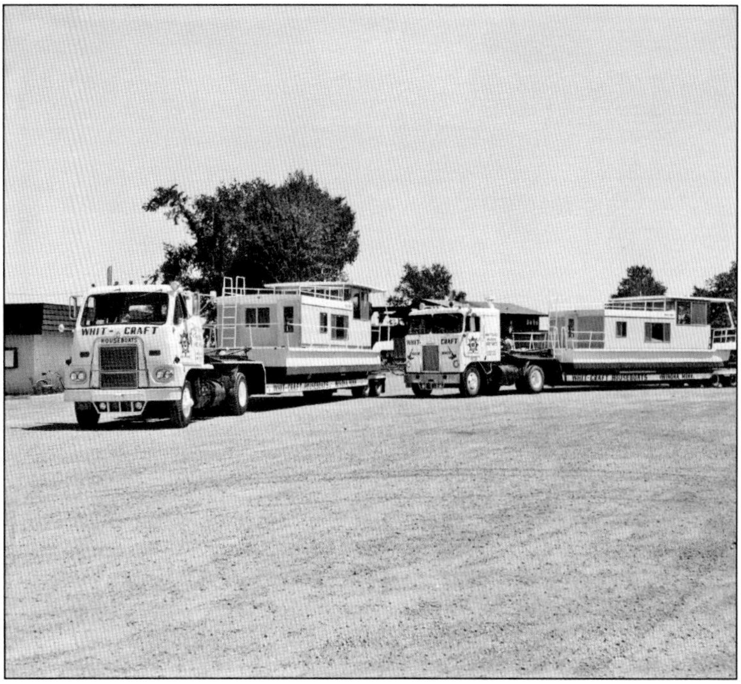

Two houseboats have been loaded onto specially built trailers to be hauled overland to their new owners. In 1969, Whittaker sold his company to North American Rockwell Corporation, and the new owners closed the houseboat manufacturing plant in mid-1972, with a loss of 104 jobs.

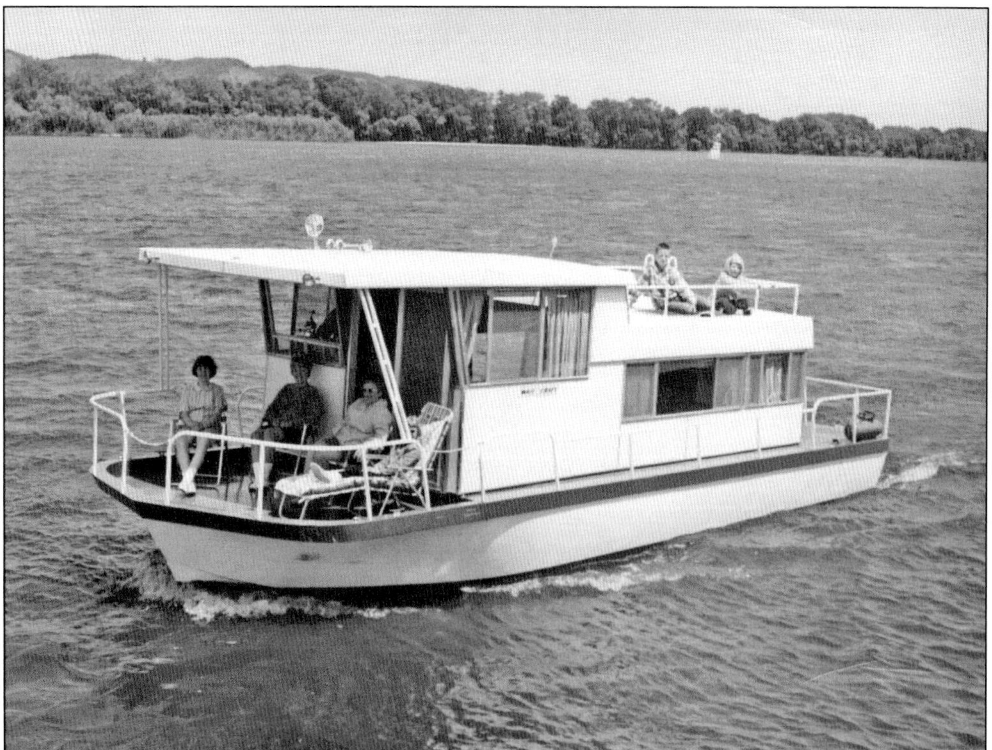

The Whitcraft Catamaran 36-foot houseboat was manufactured in Winona in the mid-1960s and included sleeping space for two and a full galley. It was constructed of heavy gauge steel and equipped with twin 210-hp Interceptor V-8 engines.

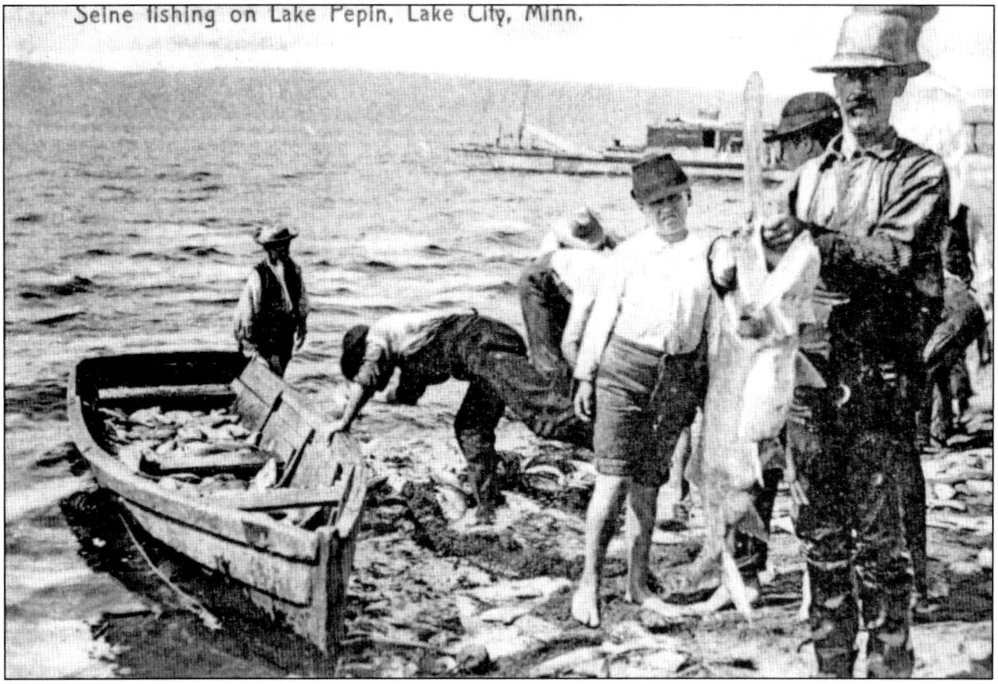

Seining, or net fishing, was a popular method of obtaining large masses of fish for the eastern market. This method was limited to rough fish only, such as carp, which had been introduced into the Mississippi River. The seining of rough fish was permitted on the Mississippi only with a license.

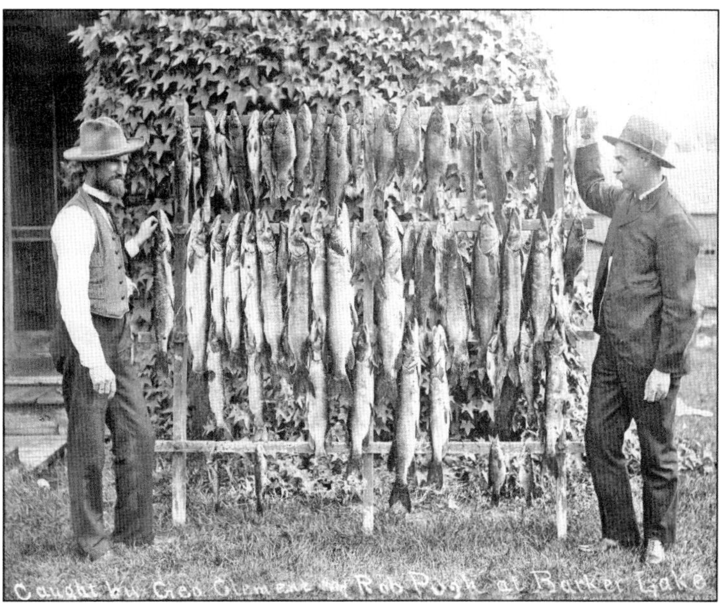

Game fish were also caught in the Mississippi River, often in large numbers, for the commercial market. George Clement, on the left, and Robert Pugh caught these near Wabasha, Minnesota.

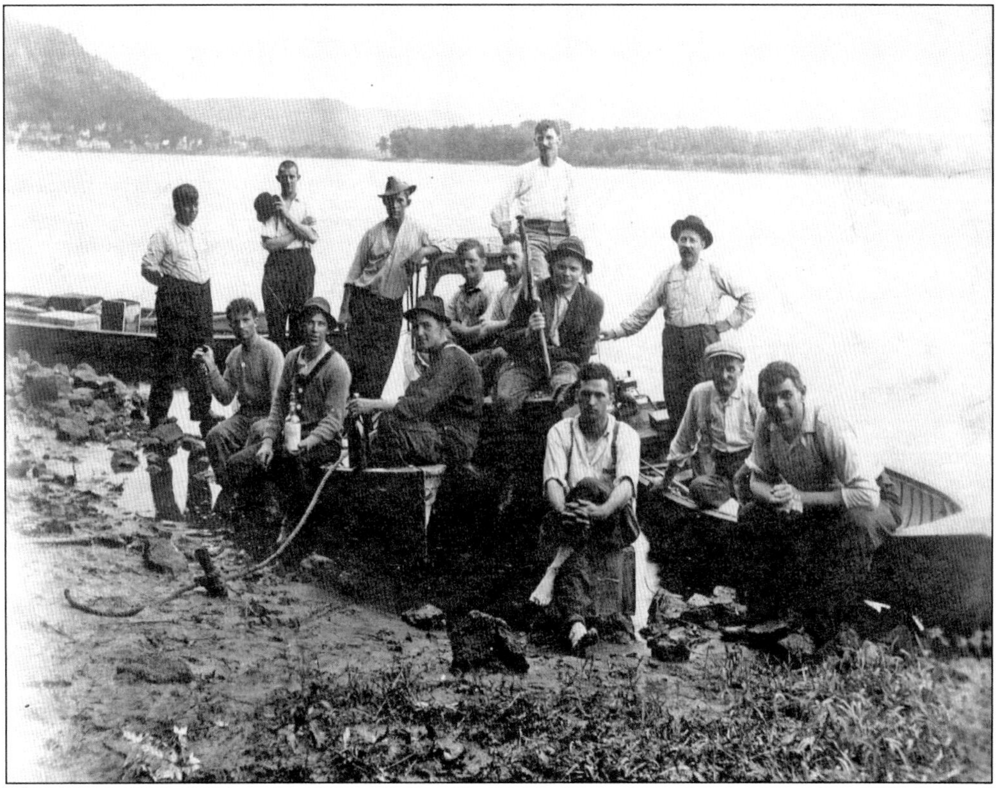

A group of fishermen prepare to go out onto the river for a day's work. Commercial fishing was a good occupation, and in the early part of the 20th century, millions of pounds of fish were caught and processed for food.

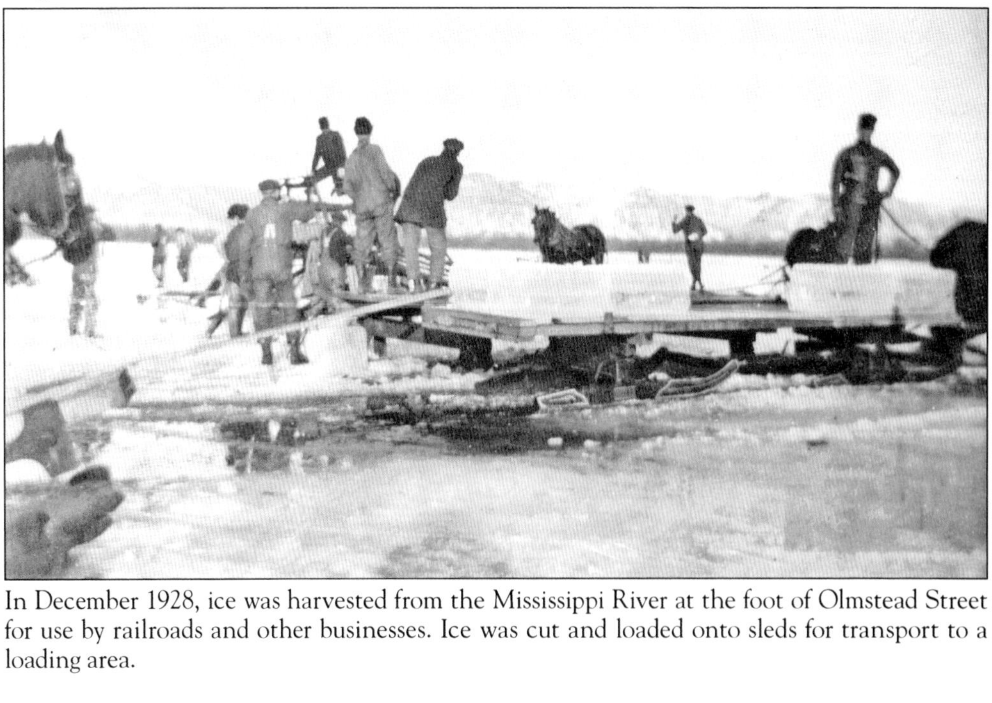

In December 1928, ice was harvested from the Mississippi River at the foot of Olmstead Street for use by railroads and other businesses. Ice was cut and loaded onto sleds for transport to a loading area.

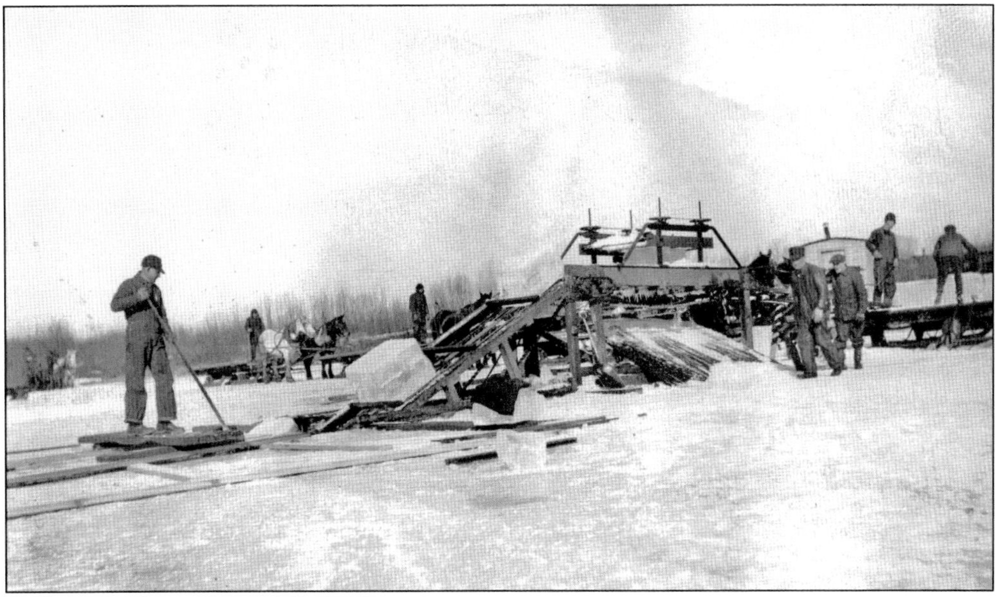

The harvested ice was slid onto a conveyer belt and carried up to sleds for transport to icehouses for storage.

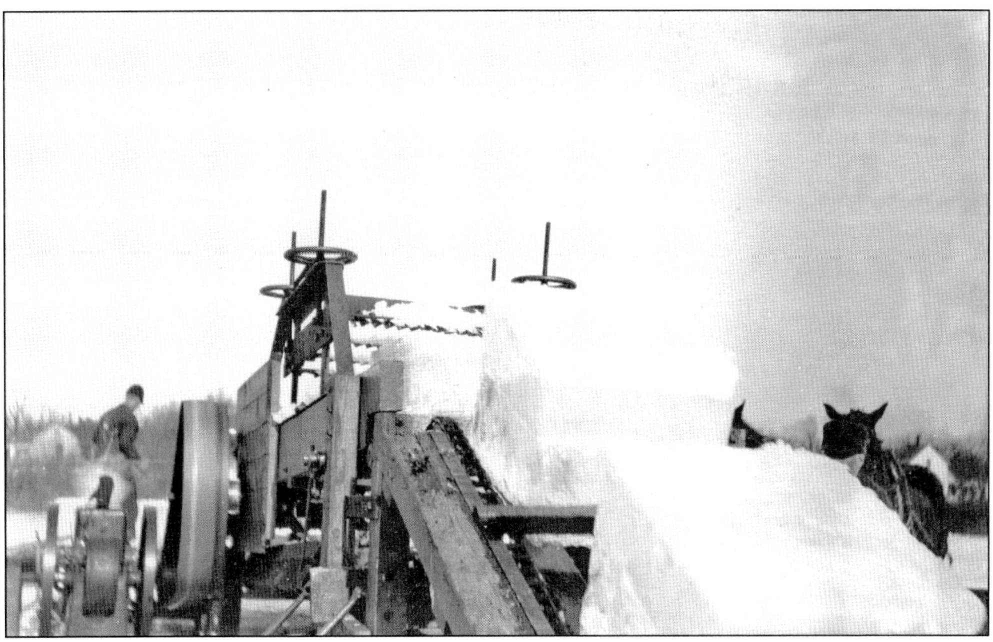

This photograph shows the ice being transported via conveyer belt to the sleds.

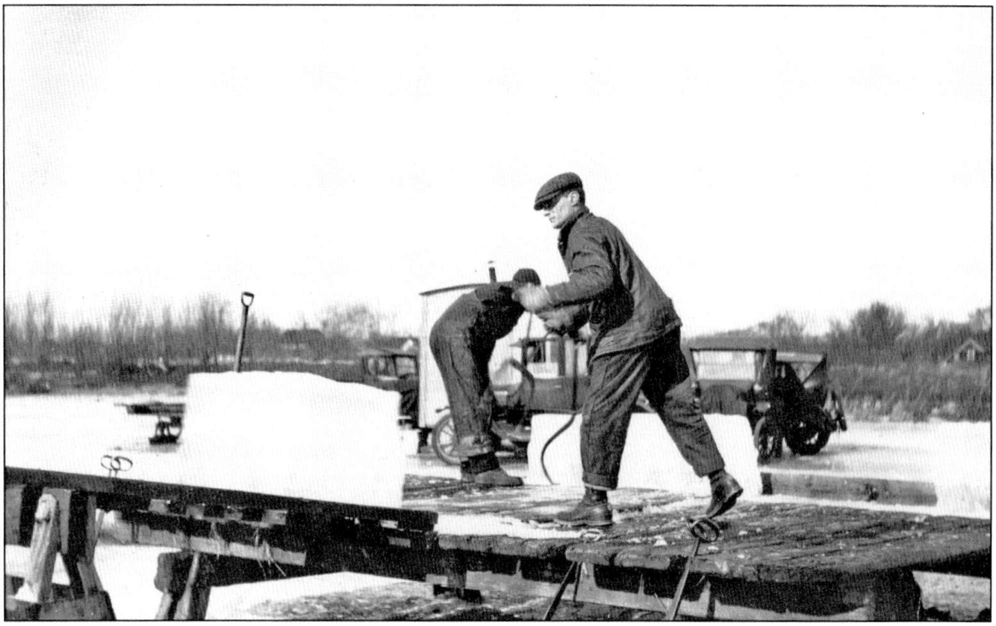

The large blocks of harvested ice were moved off the conveyer belt with ice tongs and onto the sled for transport to the icehouses or other facilities.

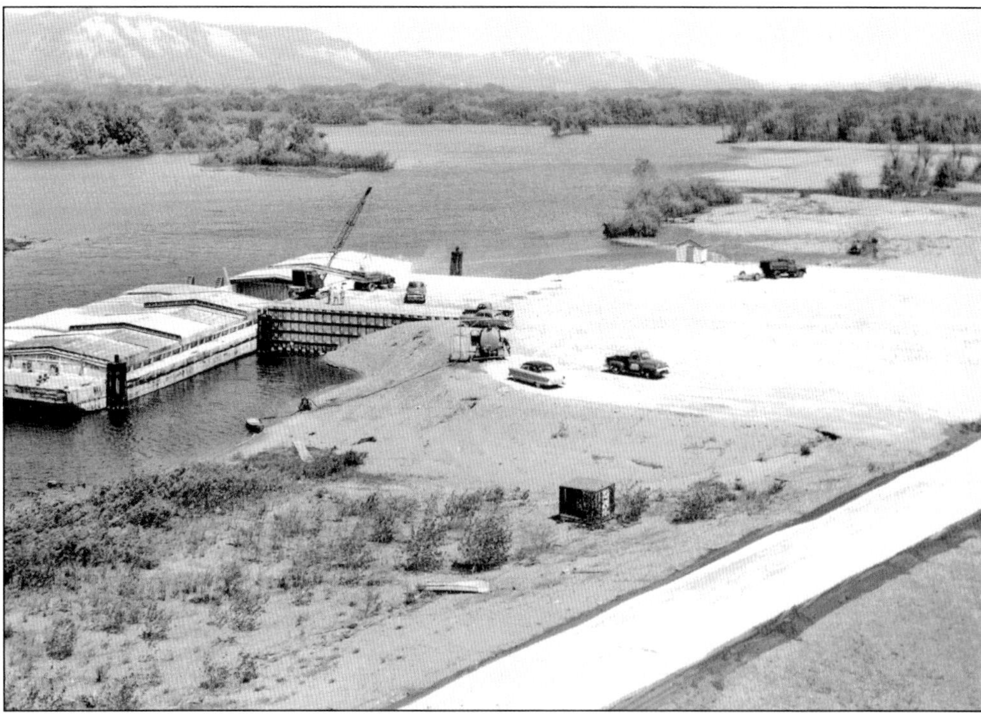

Winona's commercial harbor was dredged by the Kertzman Dredging Company in Crooked Slough in 1956. The large 100-foot-wide dock was installed in 1957, and the harbor was put into operation in the spring of 1958. The first use of the harbor was in May 1958, when a barge loaded with 1,200 tons of triple superphosphate was unloaded for the Northwest Cooperative Mills. Previously, the barges were unloaded along the levee between Walnut and Johnson Streets.

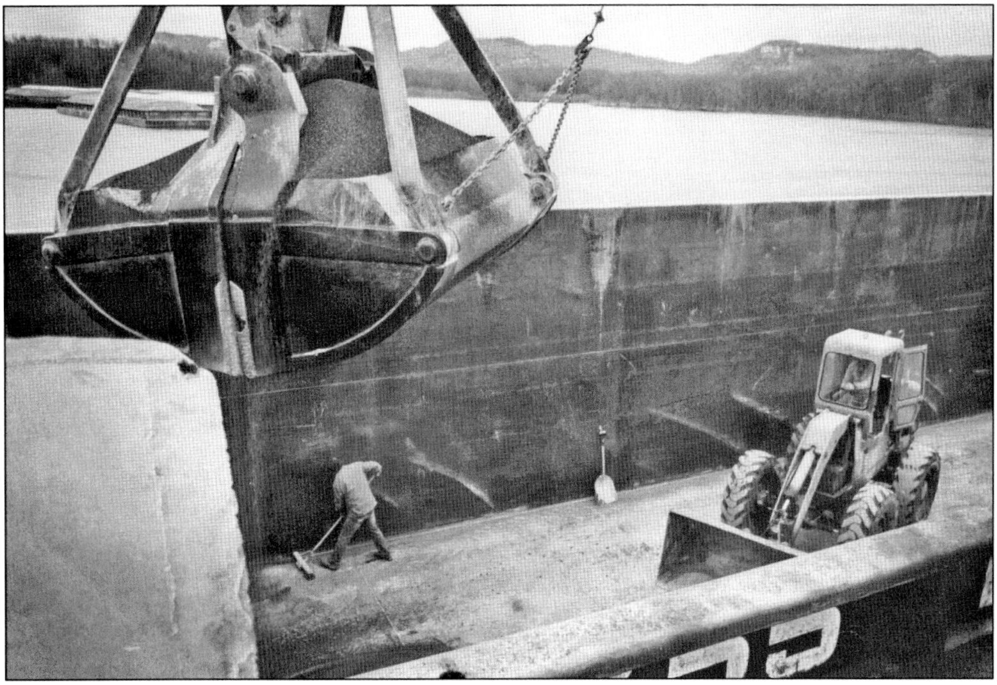

In late fall of 1983, this barge is swept clean as fertilizer is unloaded at the Kujak Transportation loading dock at the commercial harbor. The barge was unloaded with the aid of the front-end loader. After cleaning, the barge will be filled with corn and sent downriver.

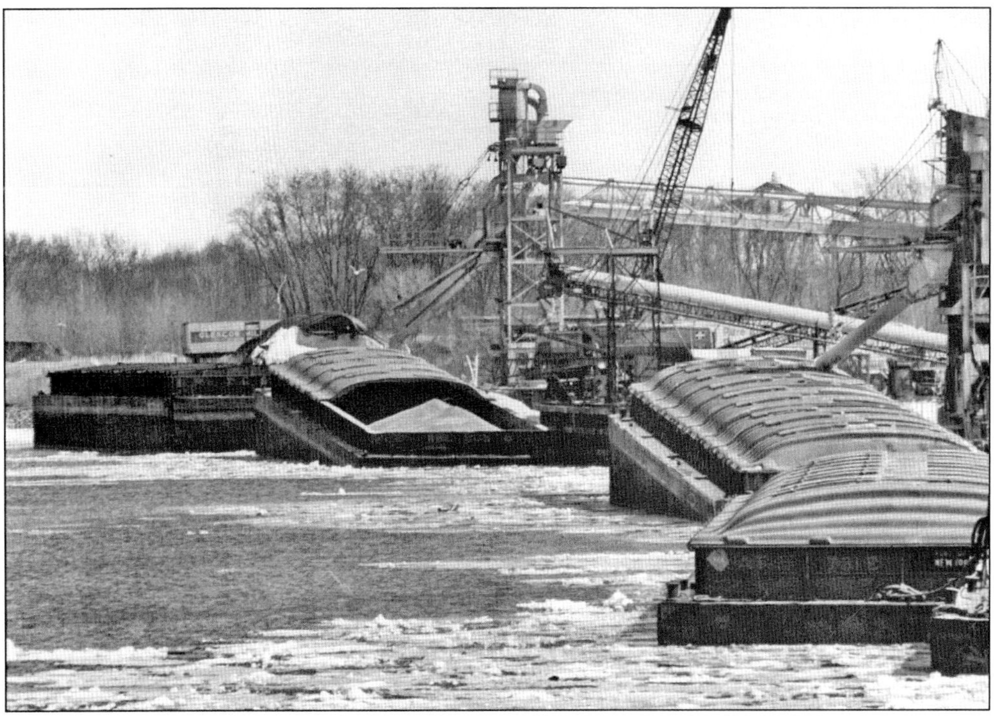

Early in April 1993, grain elevators fill the barges after a tugboat broke up the ice in Winona's commercial harbor previously in the week.

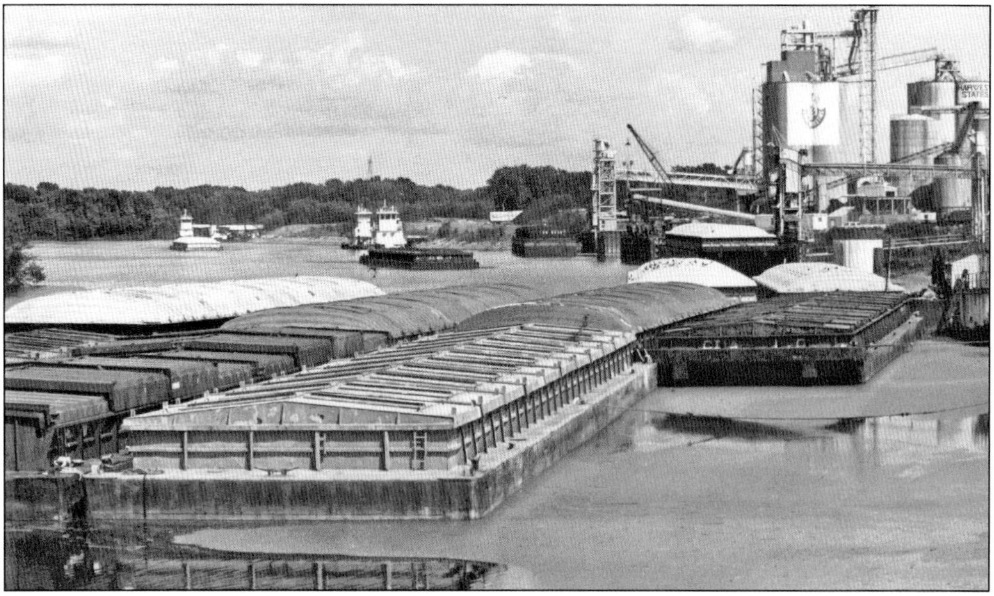

The Port of Winona, the third busiest in Minnesota, is full of barges waiting to head south. The river, which was at flood stage most of the summer of 1993, is slowly receding, thus allowing barge traffic to pick up. In the background is the Harvest States Cooperative grain elevator, which is loading a barge with grain.

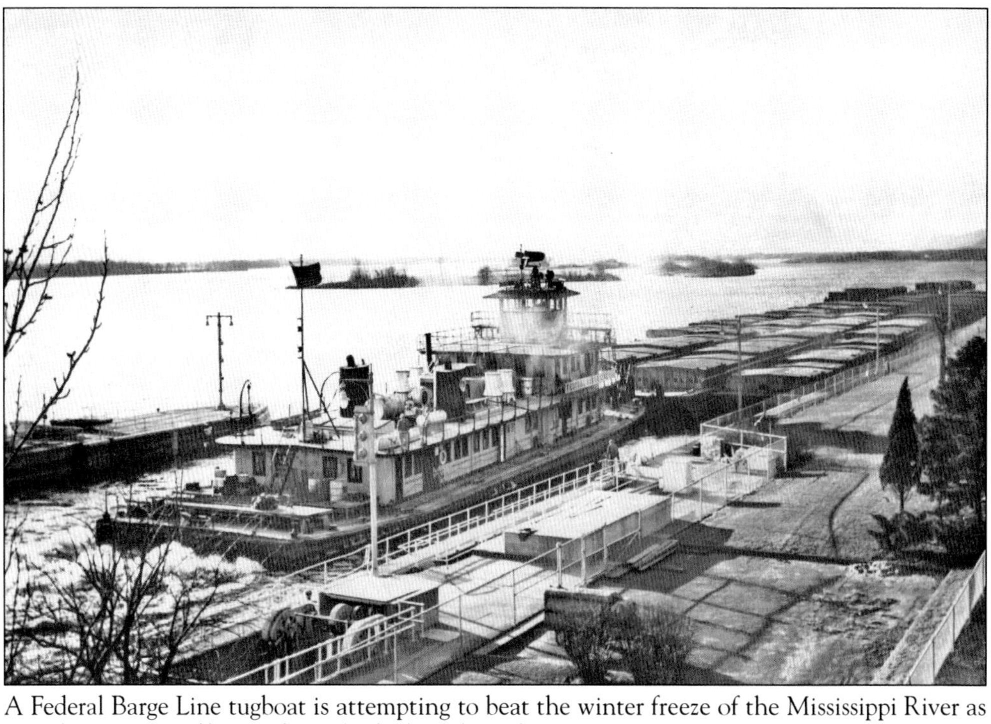

A Federal Barge Line tugboat is attempting to beat the winter freeze of the Mississippi River as it pushes a string of barges from the lock at the Whitman Dam in the late fall of 1985.

Seven

PRESERVING AND ENJOYING THE RIVER

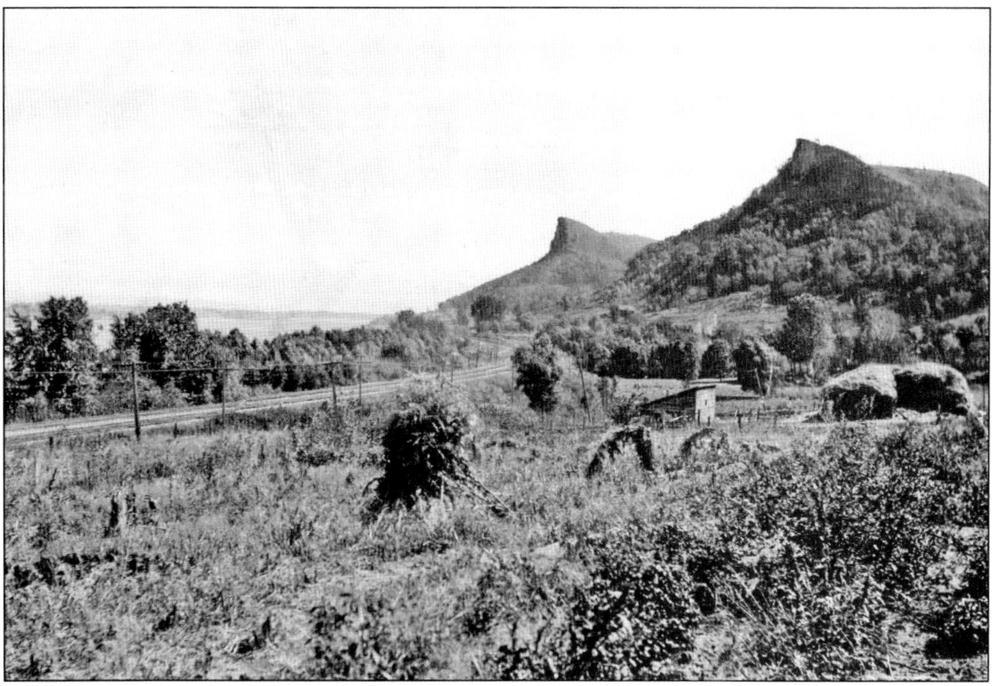

King's Bluff, closer of the two, and Queen's Bluff are erosional remnants found near La Mollie, Minnesota, noted for their goat prairies. However, many goat prairies have all but disappeared due to the invasive plants that have taken root.

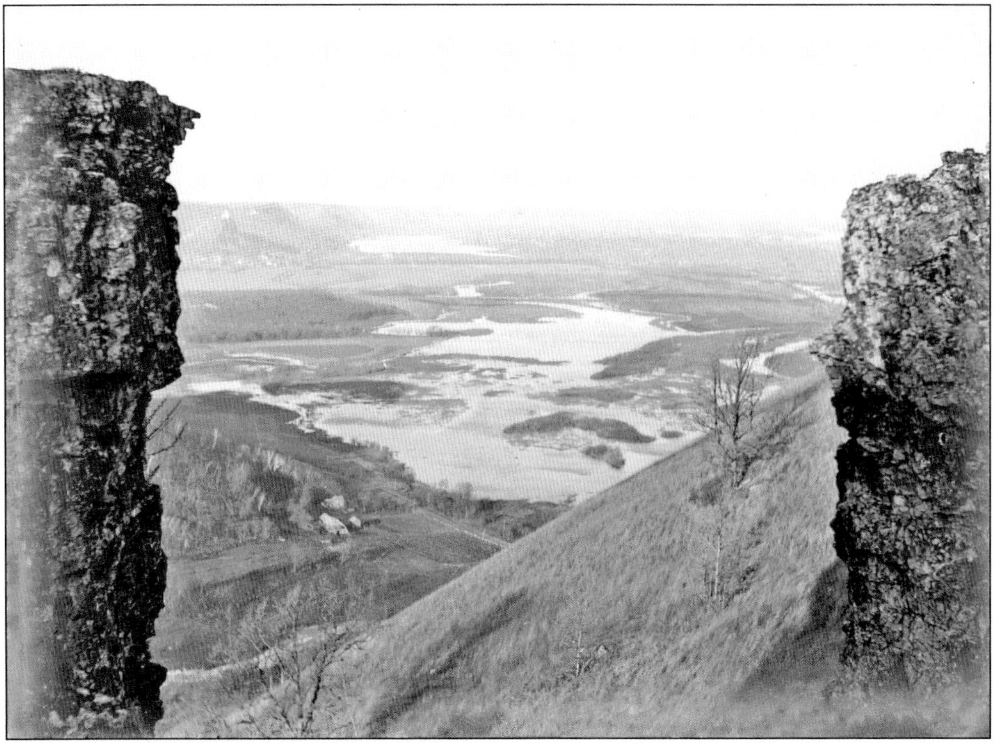

This late 1890 photograph of the Upper Mississippi River Valley near Winona was taken from a break in the Wisconsin bluffs. The valley, mostly untamed, is characterized by sloughs, marshes, and a braided underfit stream. On the south-facing slopes of the valley are the relatively barren goat prairies, which are devoid of most vegetation. Sugar Loaf, a quarry remnant and Winona icon, is just visible in the distance.

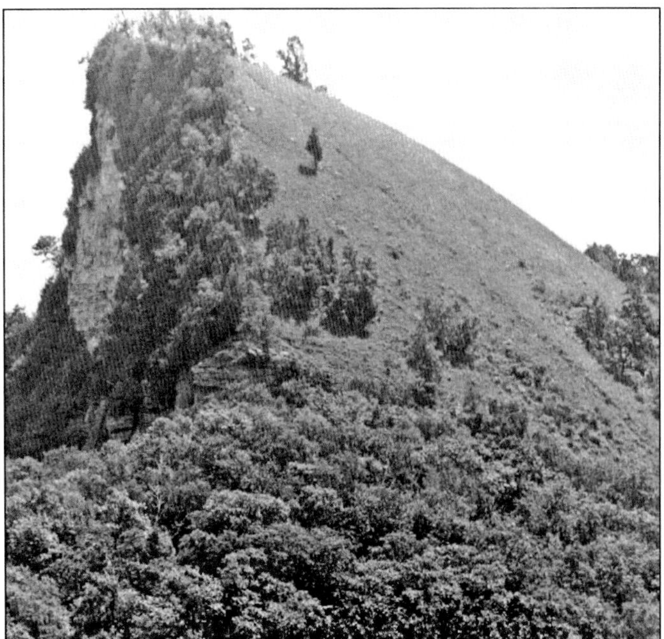

The goat prairie on Queen's Bluff is found on the south-facing slope, which receives a considerable amount of sun that dries the limited soil. The dominant growth on these features is prairie grass.

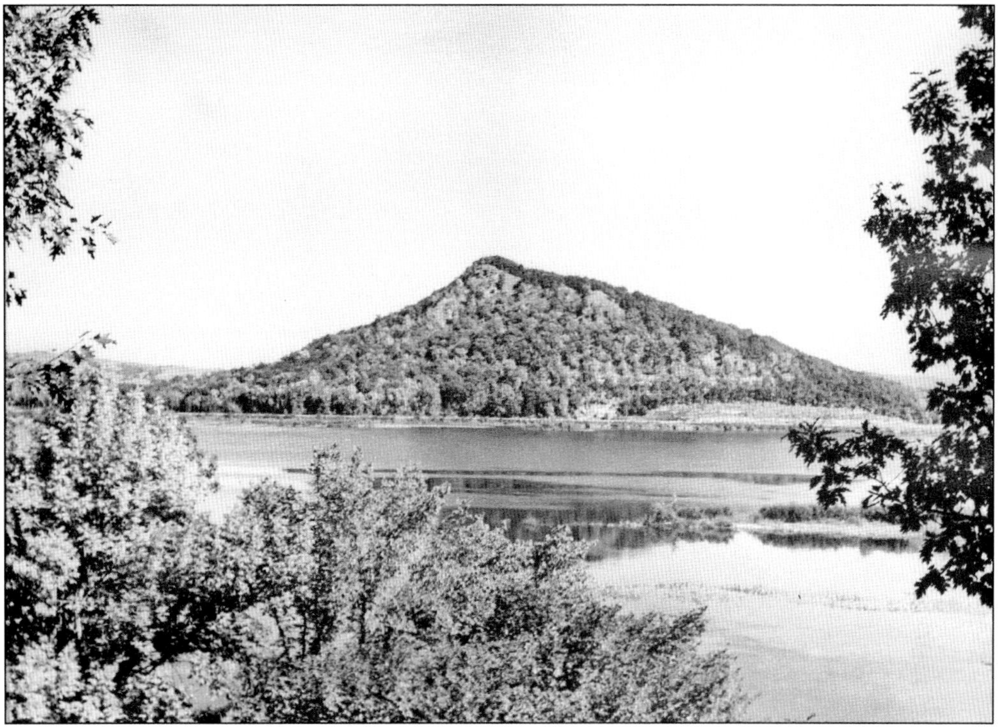

Trempealeau Mountain, as seen from La Mollie, Minnesota, has a goat prairie near its peak. It is designated a Wisconsin Department of Natural Resources State Natural Area and consists of a 425-foot conical rock mound, which is surrounded on three sides by the Mississippi and Trempealeau Rivers. It is part of Perrot State Park and was donated to the State of Wisconsin by John A. Latsch in 1918 to be used as parkland.

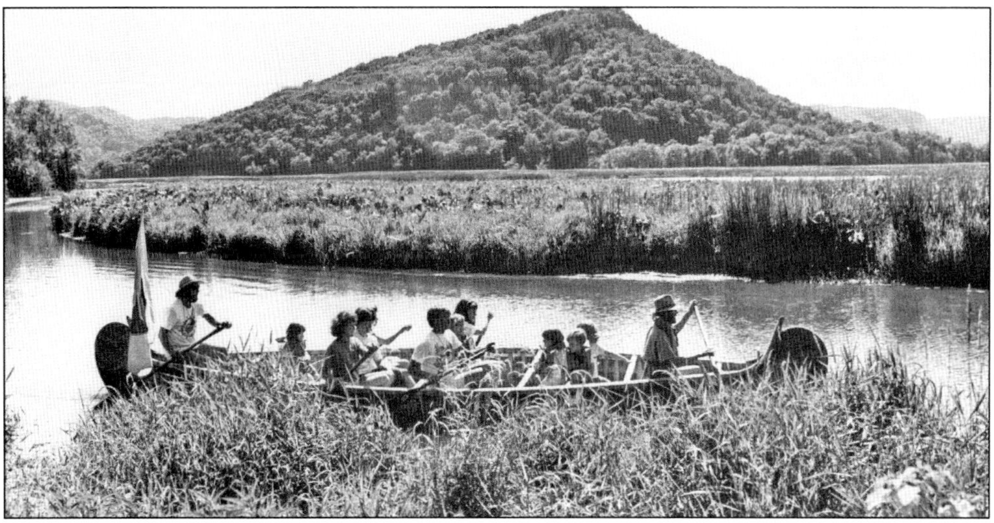

These environmental camp participants and members of the Mississippi River Revival group are exploring the backwaters of the Mississippi River near Perrot State Park in a handmade birch bark canoe. Friends of Perrot State Park are helping to educate about 50 children during a one-day environmental camp called Twigs, which was held on August 1–2, 1991. In the background is Trempealeau Mountain State Natural Area.

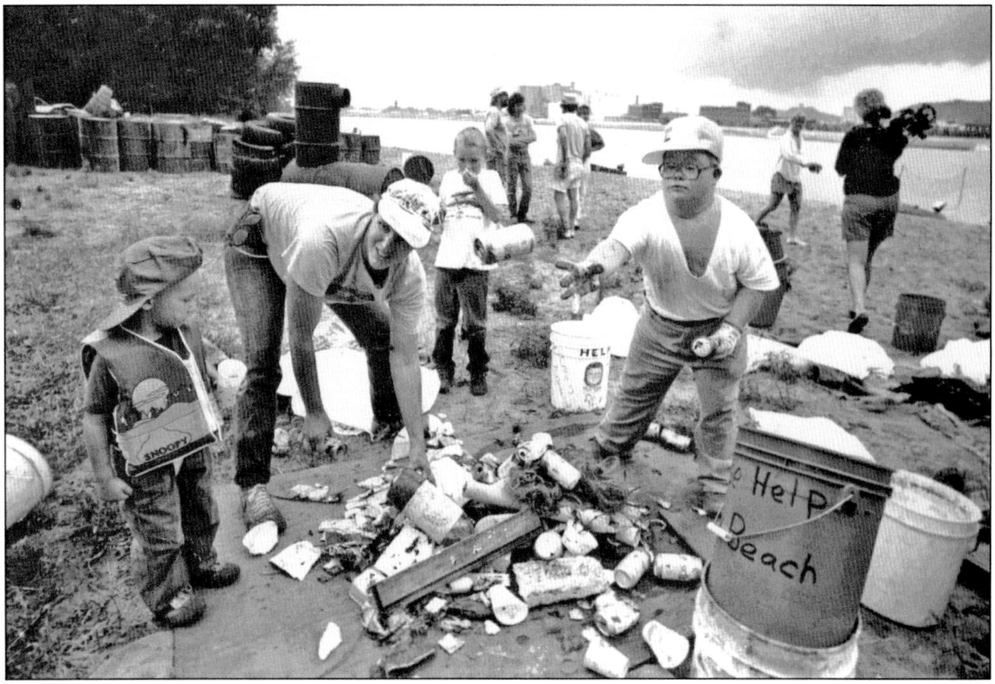

On July 28, 1990, volunteers with the Mississippi River Revival sort trash on Latsch Island. The revival was organized in 1981 in Minneapolis, Minnesota, by Larry Long as a grassroots effort to protect the Mississippi River and its watershed.

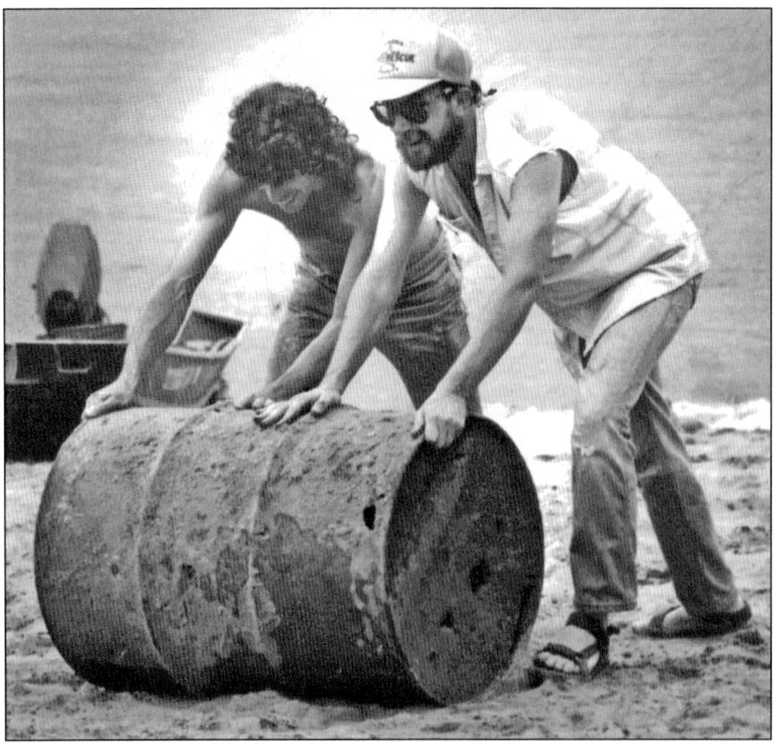

During the 1990 effort, barrels, including this one filled with sand, were pulled from the river. Each year, the volunteers collect hundreds of pounds of trash.

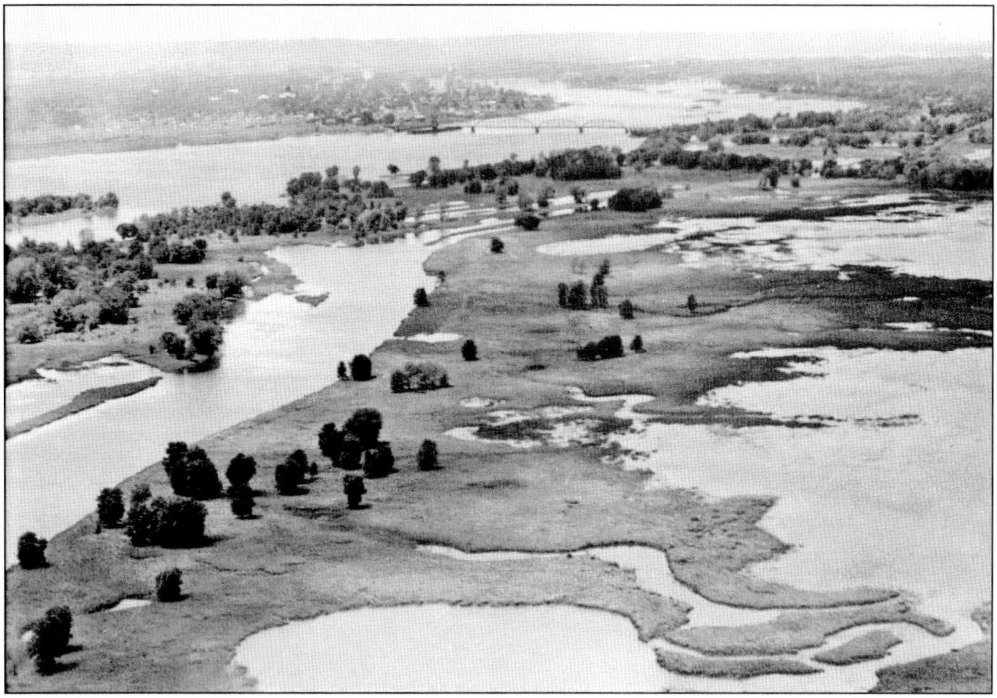

A part of the Trempealeau River Delta is pictured at the confluence of the Trempealeau River and the Mississippi River near Winona. The federal government assumed control over this bottomland after Dam No. 6 at Trempealeau, Wisconsin, was built and the area flooded. The company owning the fur farm went to court to contest the legality of the refuge, which had been established in 1924.

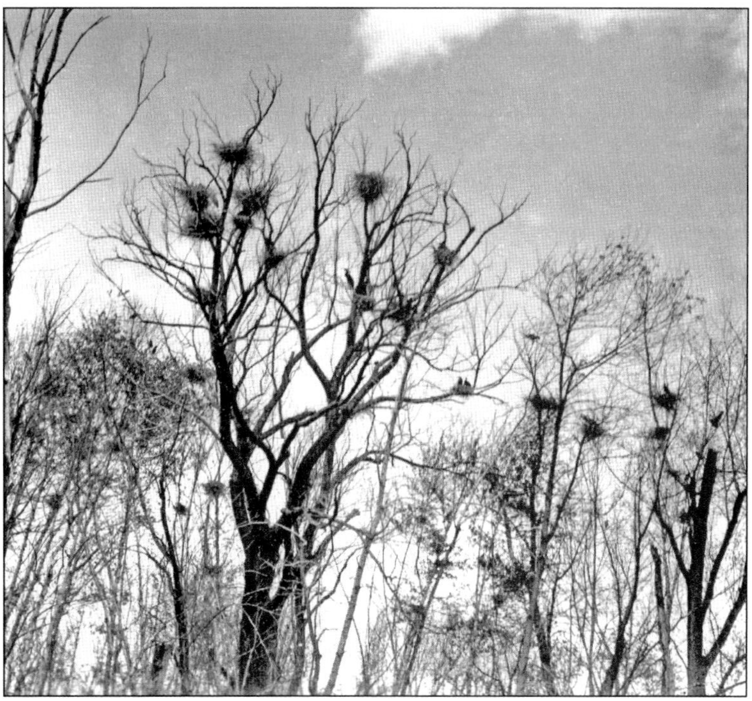

A large rookery of great blue herons, cormorants, and egrets is pictured at the old Delta Fish and Fur Farm property, which is now a part of the Upper Mississippi Fish and Wildlife Refuge. The birds nest here annually, reconstructing a nest on top of the previous year's. The nests will eventually collapse under their own weight.

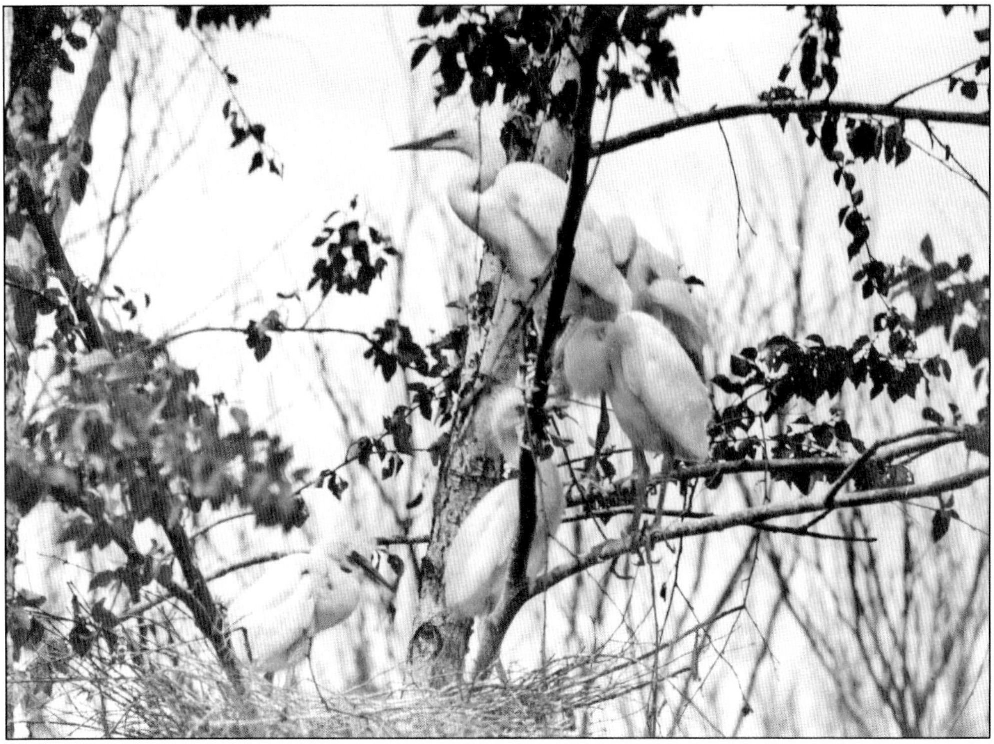

A family of egrets is pictured around a nest high in a tree.

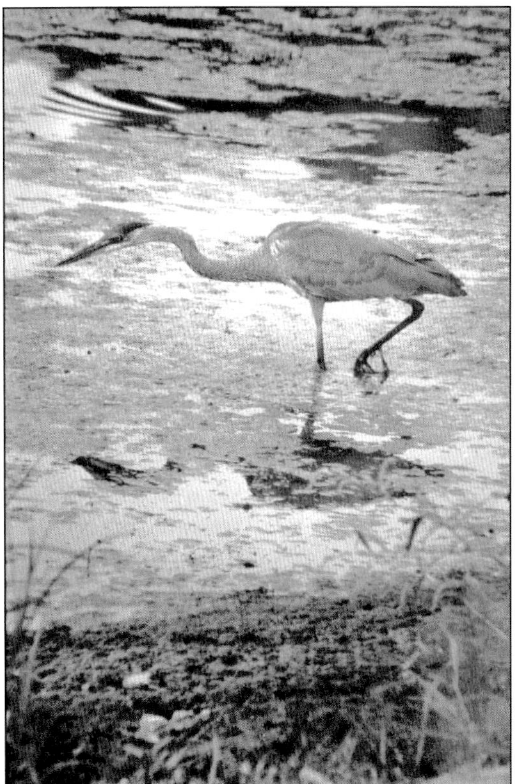

The great blue heron is a common wading bird in Mississippi River marshes. They are expert fishers, ensnaring their prey by patiently standing and waiting for fish to come in range. With a quick thrust of their bill, they grab the fish and swallow it whole.

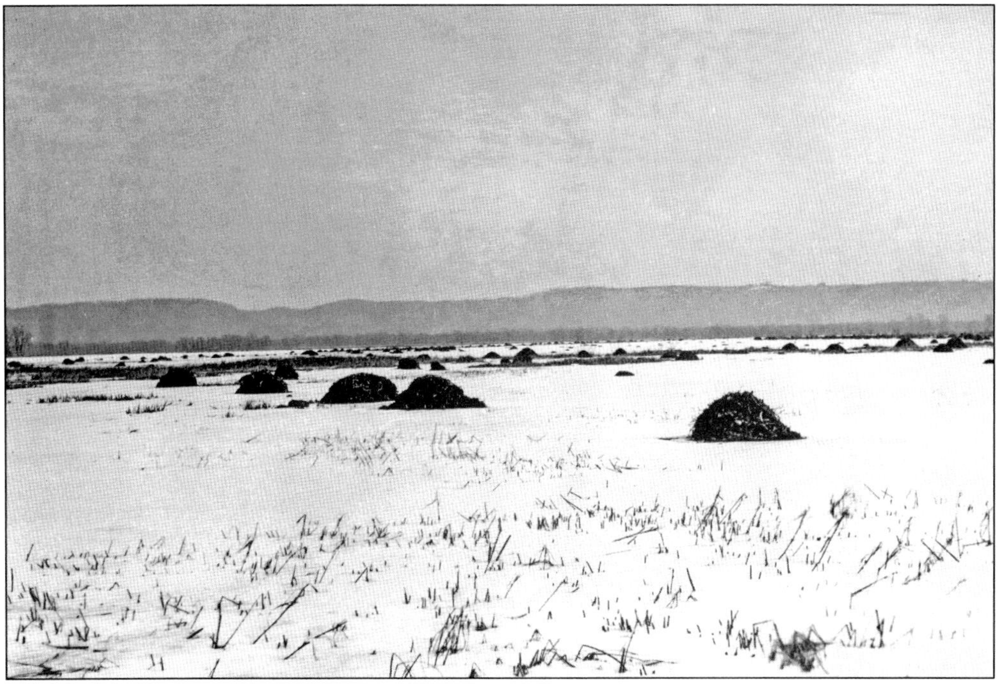

During the winter of 1937–1938, an estimated 10,000 muskrat nests populated the Weaver Bottomlands, with approximately 30,000 muskrats living within them.

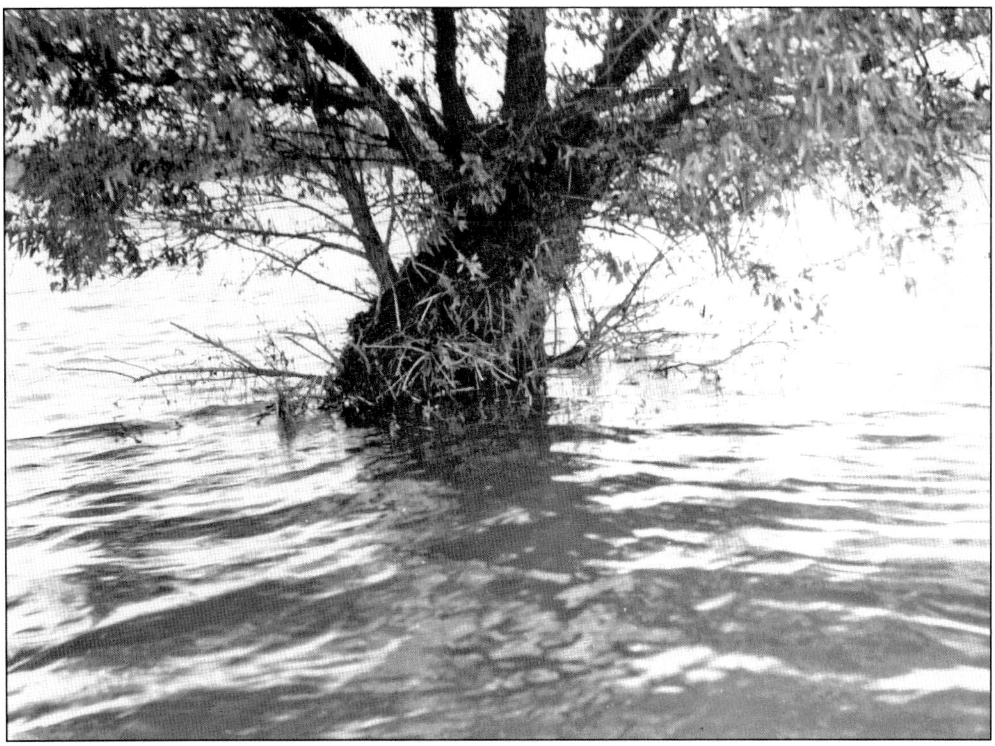

High water in the spring of 1935 forced muskrats to build an emergency nest on a willow tree branch in order for the female to have her litter.

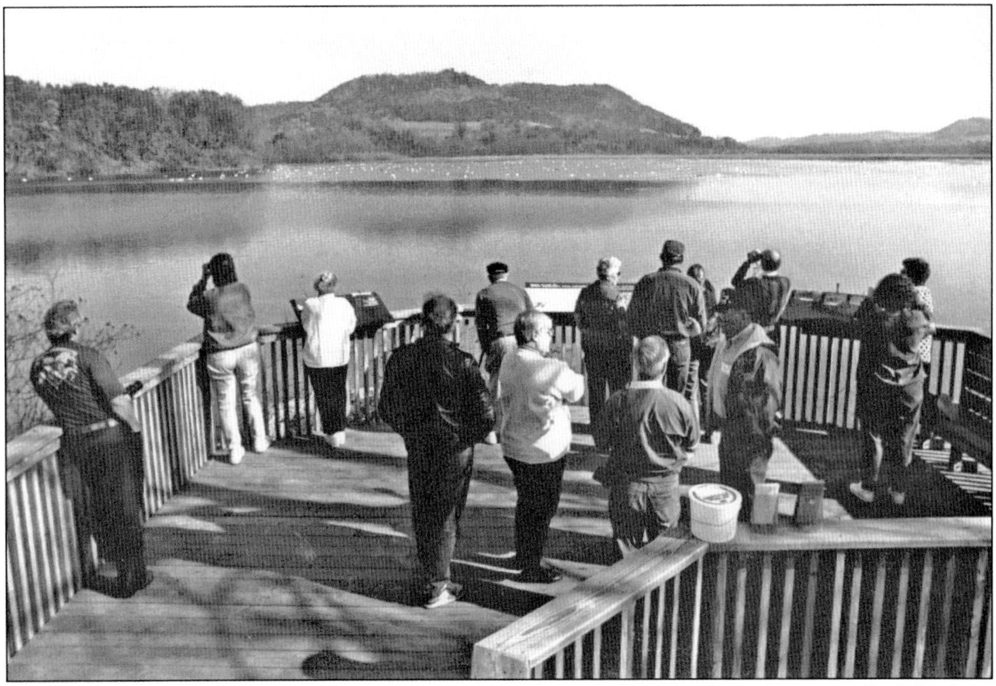

Bird watchers and other interested individuals observe tundra swans in the far end of the lake from the Rieck's Lake observation deck near Alma, Wisconsin. The deck, manned by volunteers, was built during the summer of 1992 by the Corps of Engineers, the Fish and Wildlife Service, and the City of Alma.

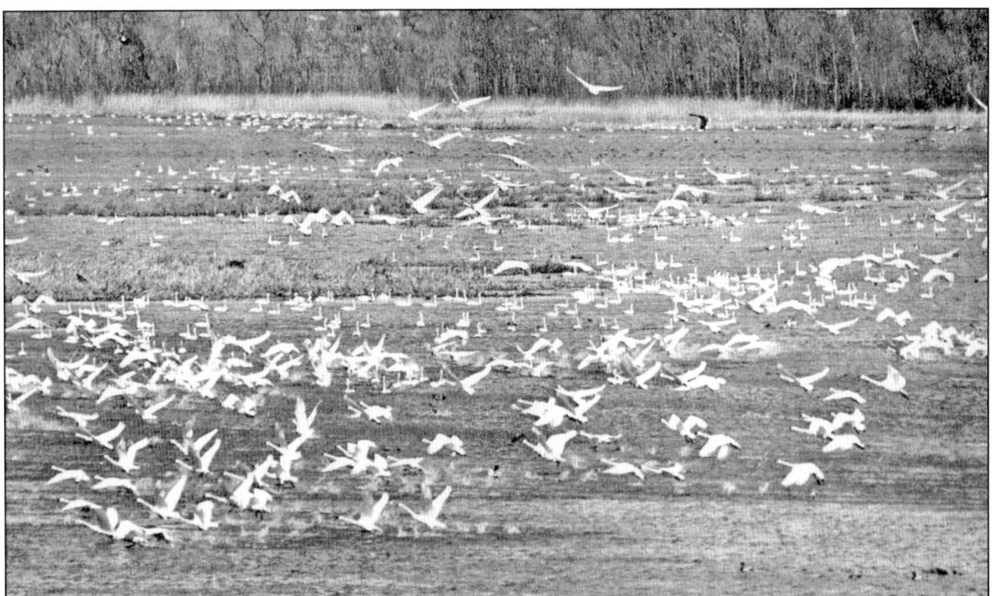

Immigrating tundra swans, pictured on their way to wintering grounds around Chesapeake Bay, rest and feed at Rieck's Lake near Alma, Wisconsin.

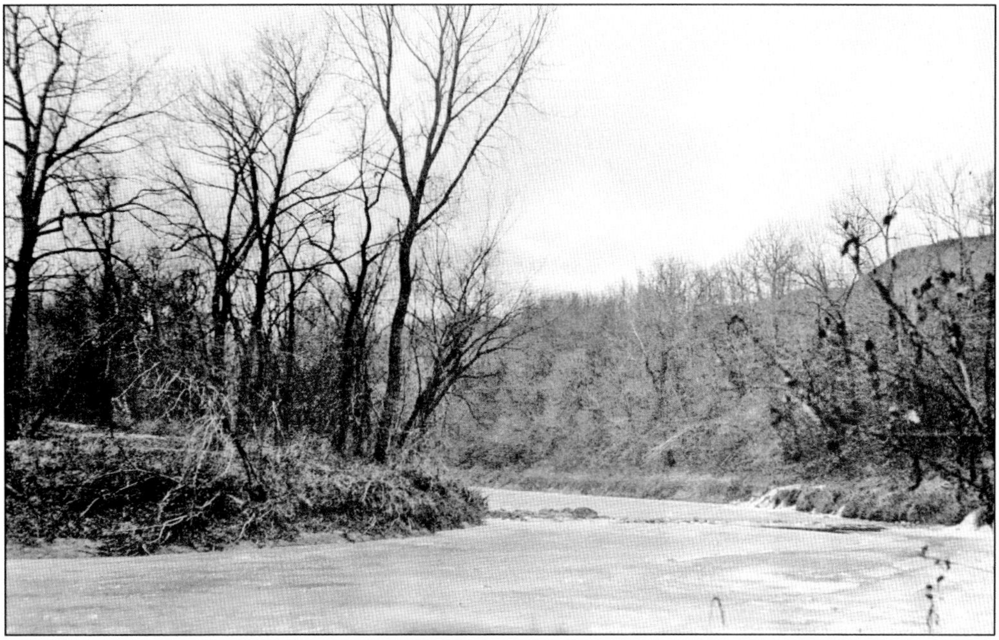
Three eagles can be seen resting in the tree above a slough in the Mississippi Valley while watching for their next meal.

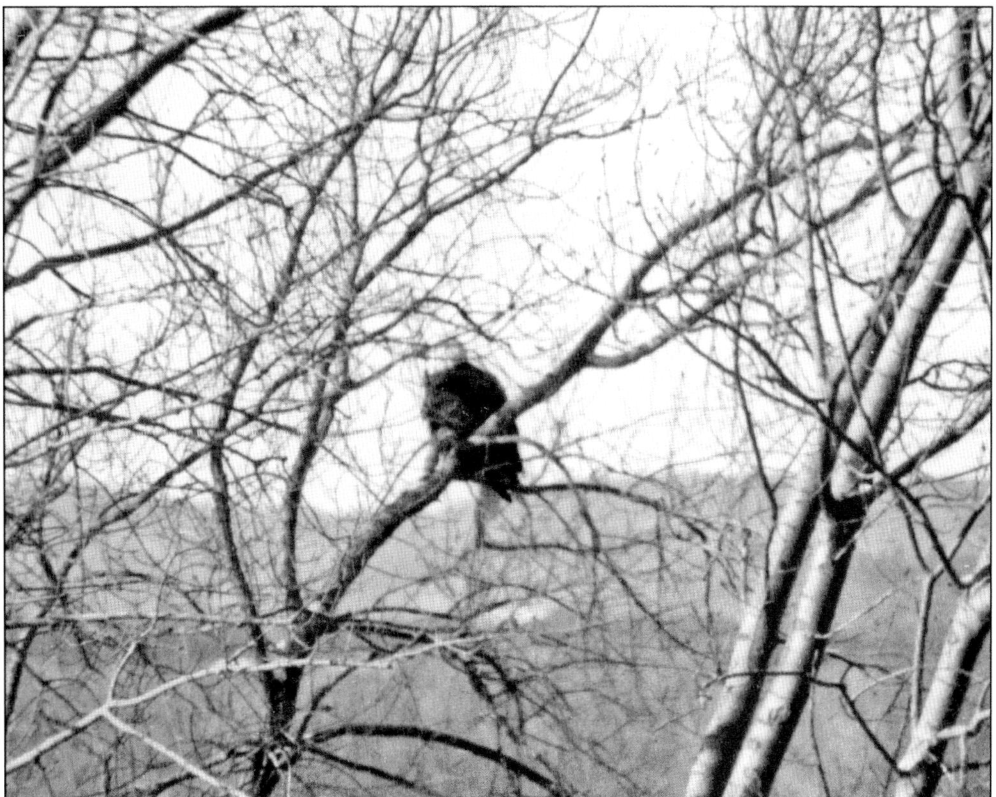
Pictured is one of many eagles that hunt for fish along the Mississippi River.

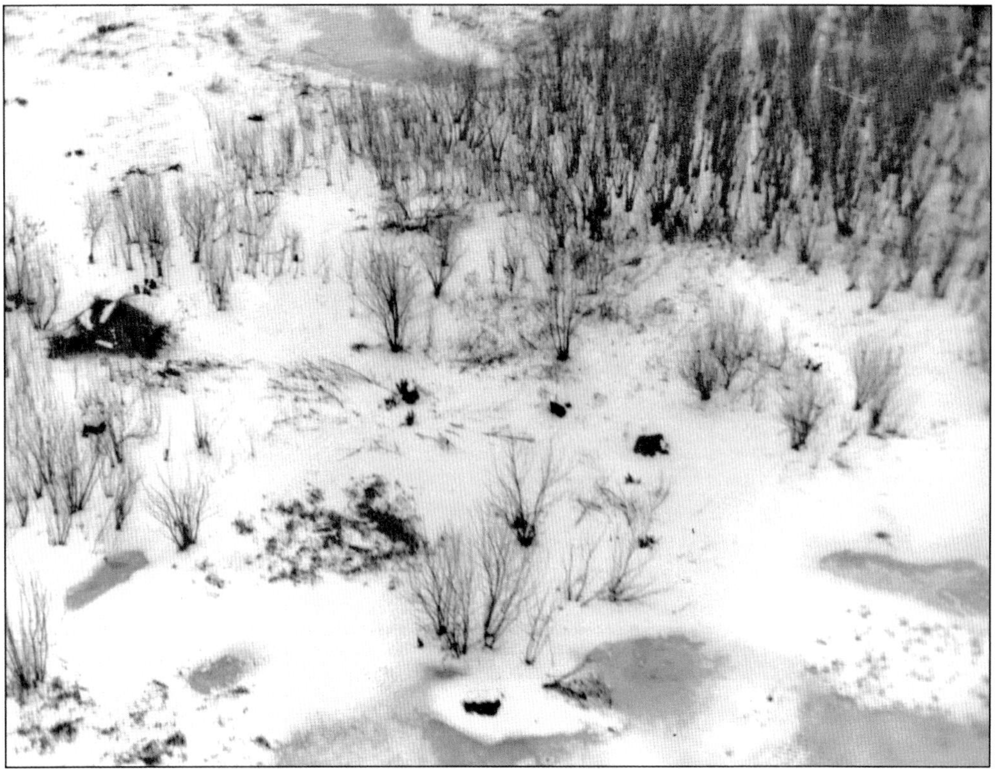

This Armistice Day 1954 aerial picture was taken by Merritt Kelley, a *Winona Daily News* photographer, of river bottomland. Here, seven hunters died 14 years earlier as the weather changed from a warm sunny day to a cold snowy afternoon when a winter storm emerged, trapping them in the valley.

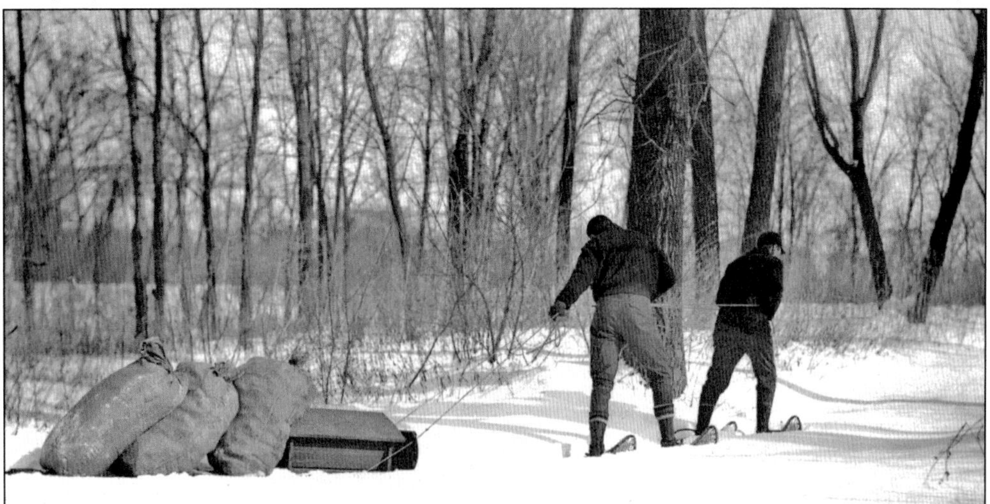

Refuge rangers Edward Knopp and John Hassinger pull a toboggan loaded with grain to restock bird feeders located in the refuge. The feeding program is routine in the refuge, and restocking the feeders is done once a week by the rangers.

Pictured is the Coast Guard cutter *Lantana*, a river buoy tender, hoisting a navigational aide out of the Upper Mississippi River.

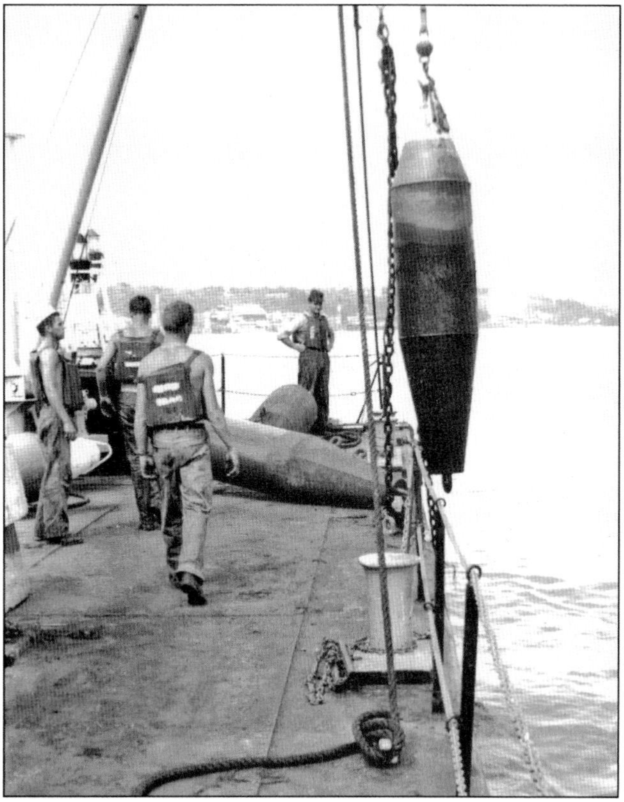

A mat of net-spinning caddis fly larvae, called retreats, was found on the navigational buoy that was lifted from the water. These retreats, composed of plant and mineral fragments, are homes for the larvae and are part of a food-gathering site.

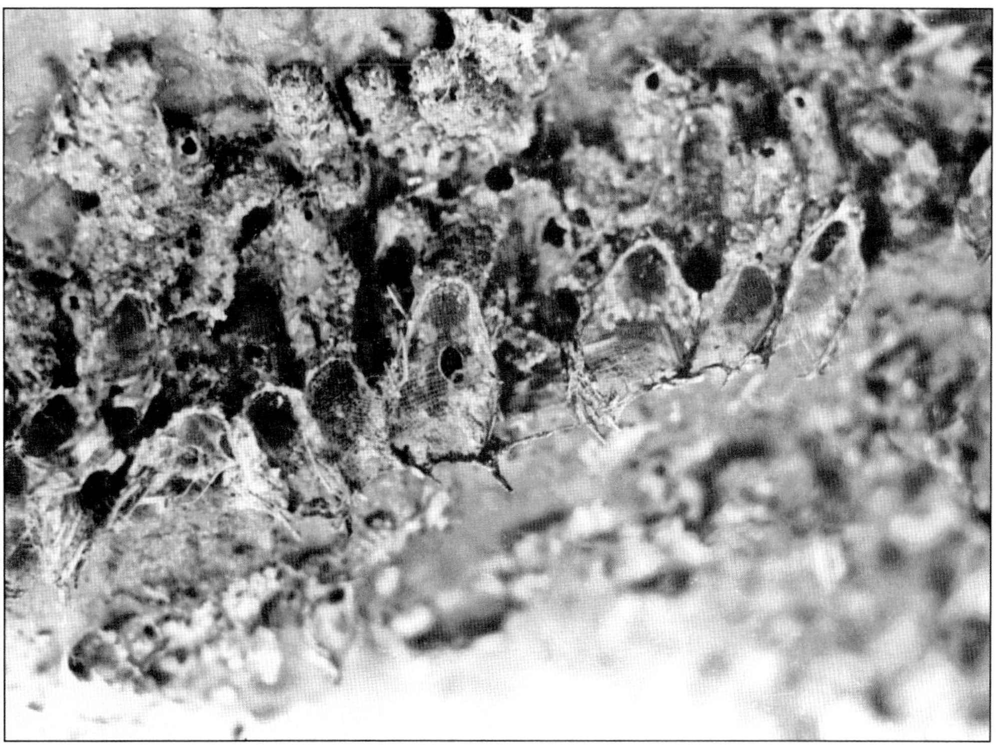

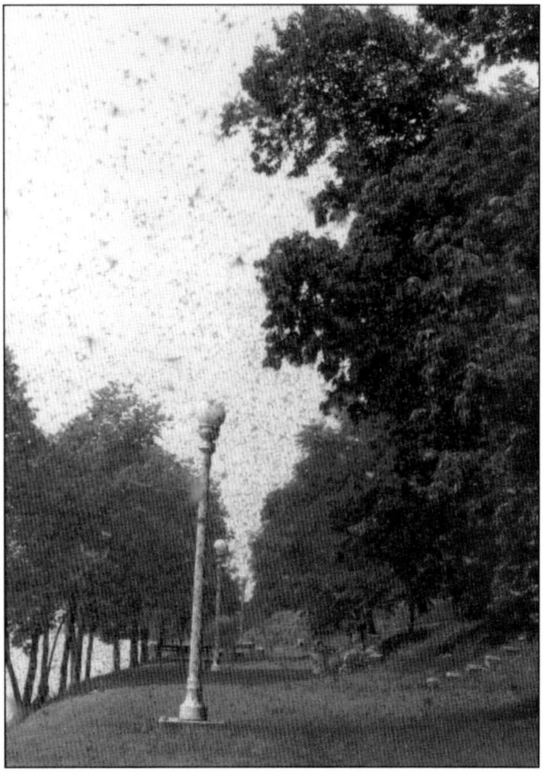

Pictured is a mayfly hatch that occurred on a July evening in 1958. The insects that are attached to the lights are females, which fly upstream for several miles before laying eggs after breeding to allow the eggs and nymphs to drift downstream.

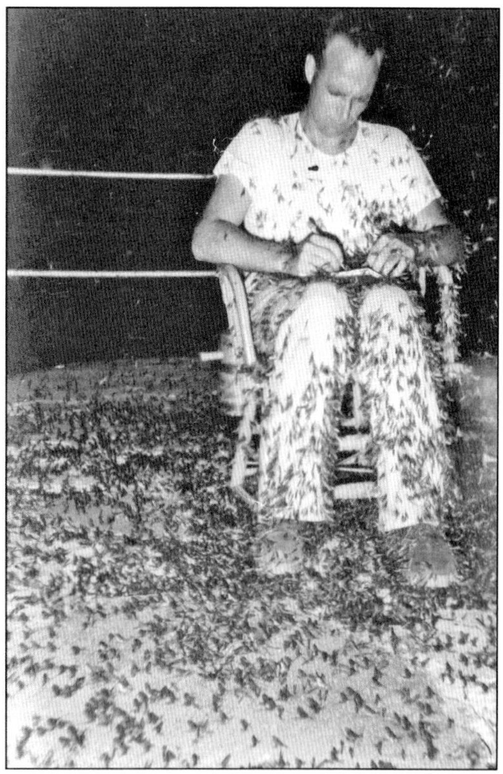

Mayflies settle on Calvin Fremling after their hatch.

Eight

The City that Saved Itself

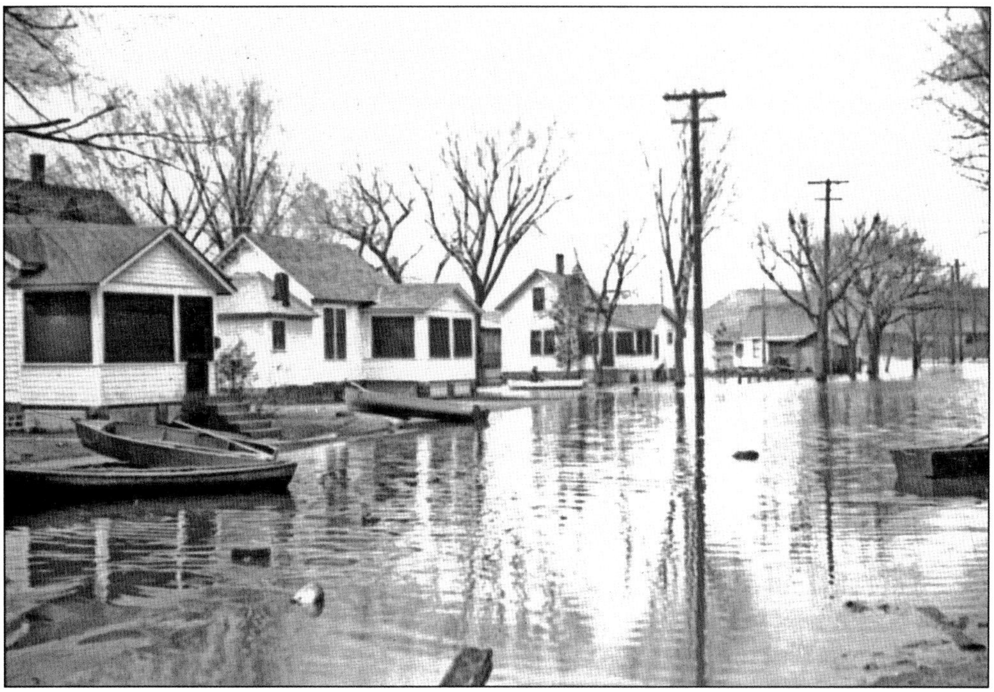

This photograph was taken in mid-April 1951 in Winona along West Fourth Street near McBride Street after a break in the temporary dike on West Third Street near Sioux Street caused the water to inundate the neighborhood to a height of 17.5 feet above flood stage. This was the worst flood ever recorded in Winona's history.

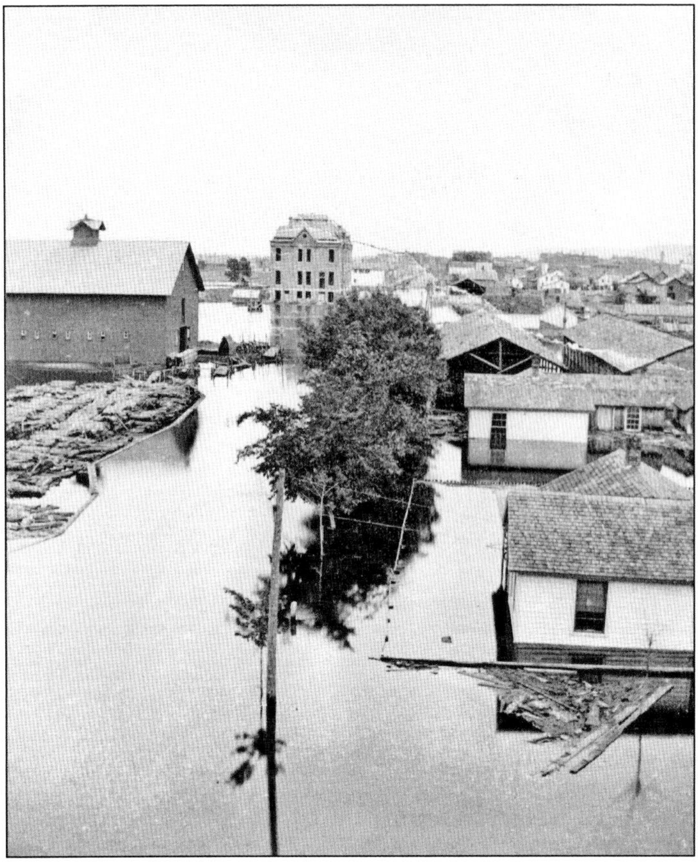

The first flood ever recorded on the Mississippi River was in 1726, when Fort Beauharnais was abandoned because of high water. About 150 years later, on June 10, 1880, a storm of epic proportions sent floodwaters—estimated to be the greatest volume of water ever to descend upon the city—into the river valley and raised the level of the river to 16.87 feet above the low water mark. However, since the river channel was much wider than it is now, there was less inundation in the city.

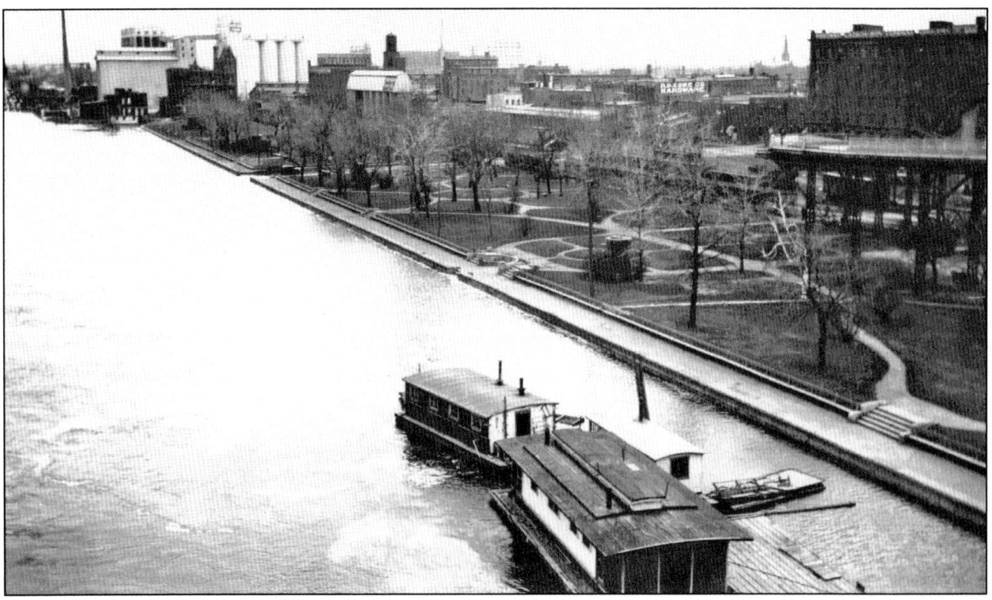

In mid-April 1916, floodwaters registered 14.4 feet above the low water mark, covering the Wisconsin approach to the high wagon bridge, flooding cellars of many residences, and washing out over 200 feet of nearby railroad bed.

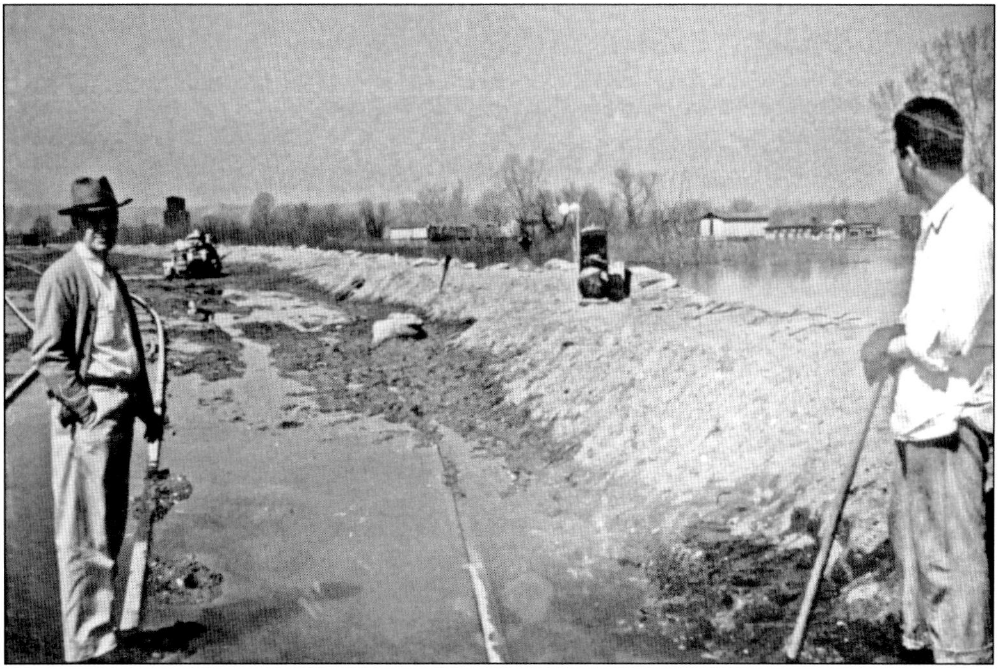

A temporary dike was situated on top of the railroad tracks westward to the Prairie Island causeway. Sandbags were placed on the water side of the dike to prevent erosion. Despite this, water was ponded by the tracks due to seepage.

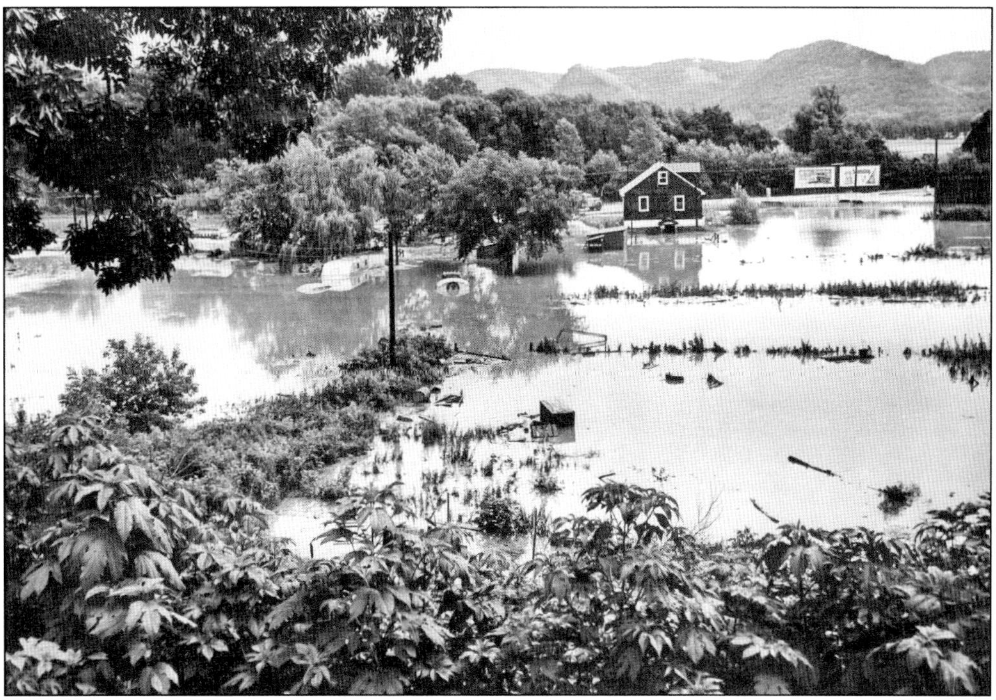

Three months later, a major storm sent six feet of water rushing down West Burns Valley Creek and into an area of Winona east of the Mankato Avenue Dike. This area had been previously flooded in April. The two signboards are to the south along Highway 61.

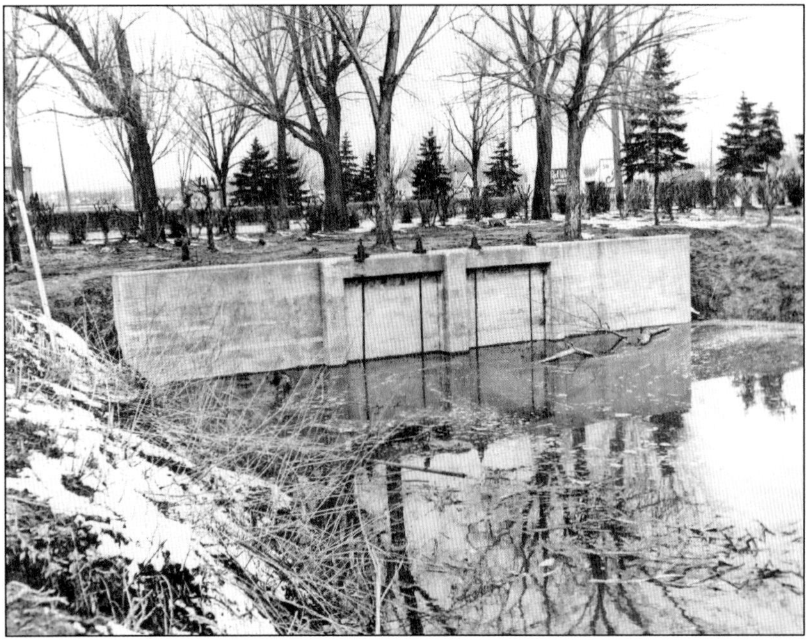

A year later, on April 3, 1952, the floodgates at the east end of Lake Winona were again closed after the water reached a level of 9.51 feet above flood stage at the levee early in the morning.

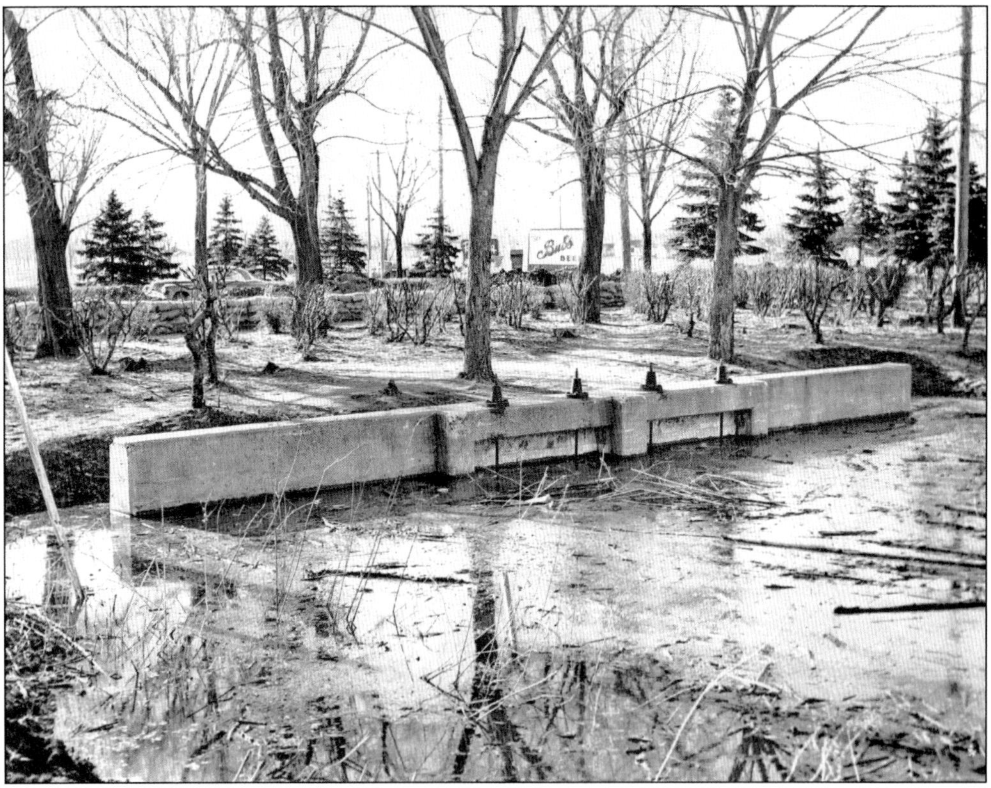

The floodgates at the east end of Lake Winona are pictured on the morning of April 16, 1952, with a water level of 17.20 feet above flood stage at the levee early in the morning. The gates are holding back about seven feet of water, which if released would flood Lake Winona and the surrounding neighborhoods.

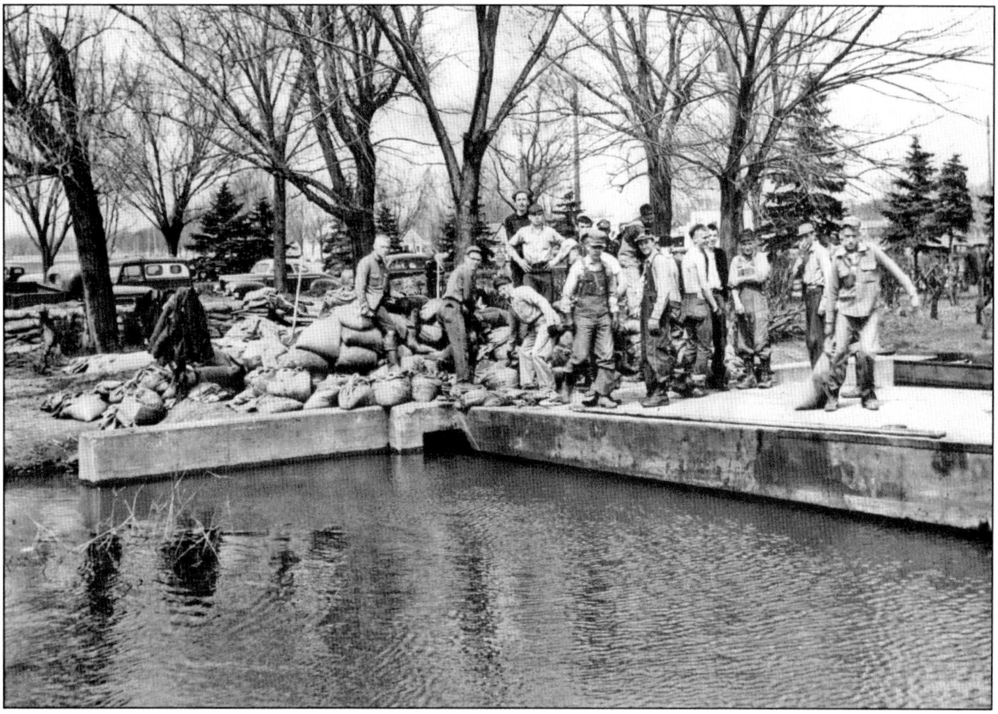

A 12-by-30-foot barge was lowered into the drainage ditch at the east end of Lake Winona and is being filled with sandbags, which were moved to the Burns Valley Ditch. From there, they were moved by wheelbarrow to seepage points along the outlet ditch.

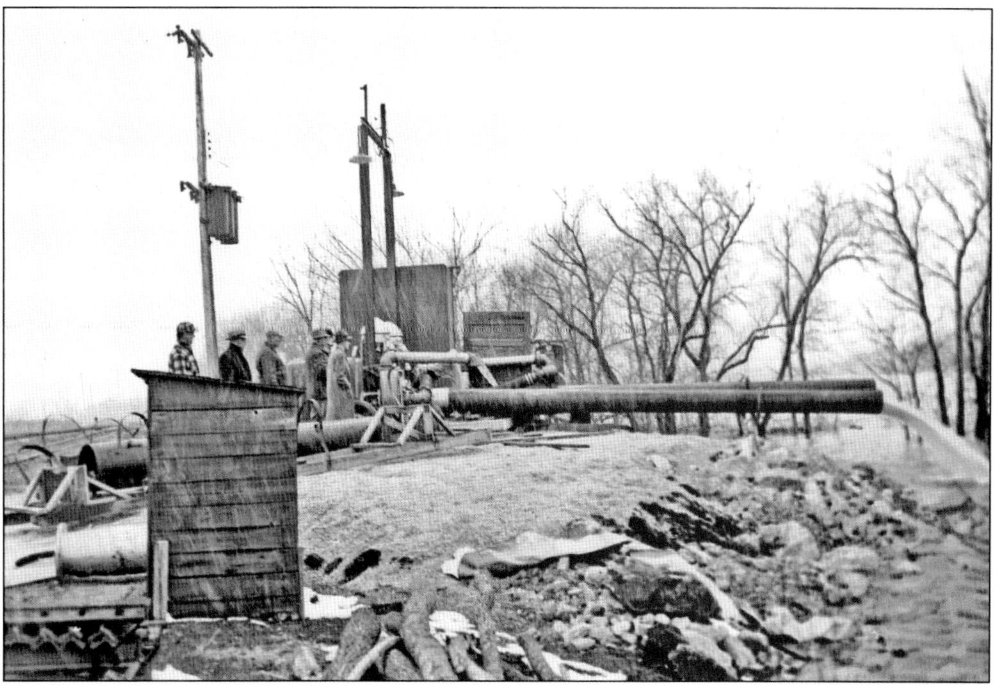

Two pumps spurt foot-wide streams of water into the flooded Mississippi River on April 12, 1952, at the foot of Olmstead Street. Each pump is capable of 3,000 gallons per minute.

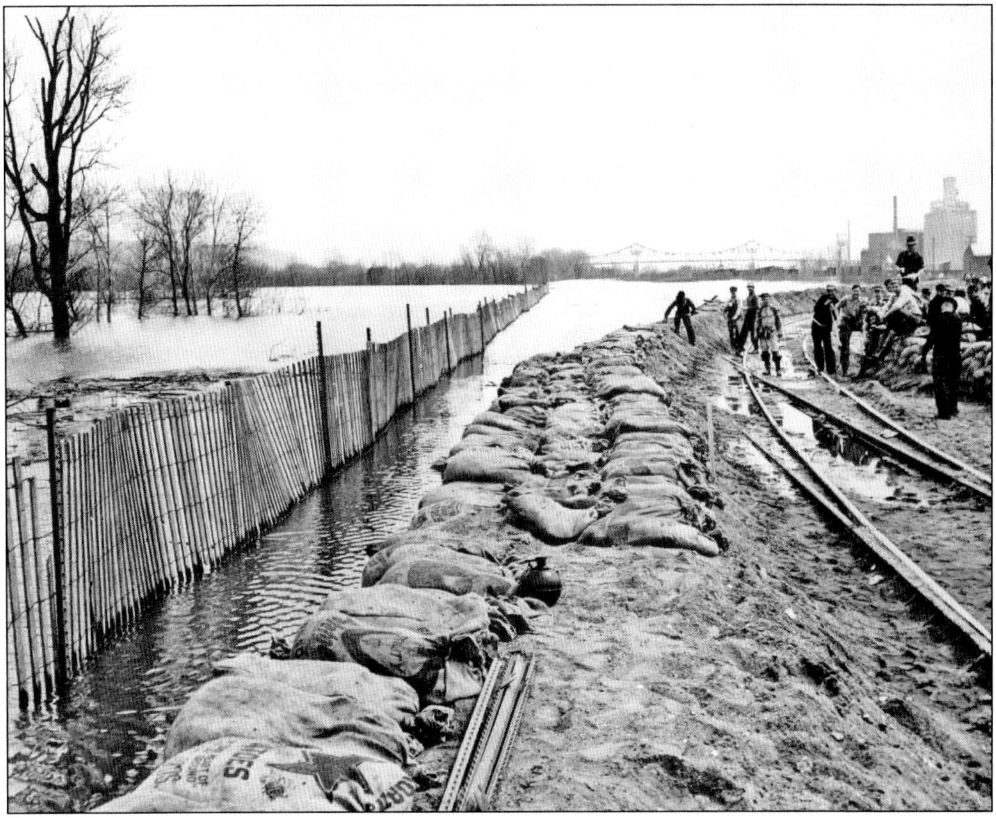

A snow fence is used along the Chicago & Northwestern Railroad dike on Winona's north side to cut down on wave action against the vulnerable face of the dike. The dike is holding back about 18 inches of main channel water from West Third Street industrial and residential areas.

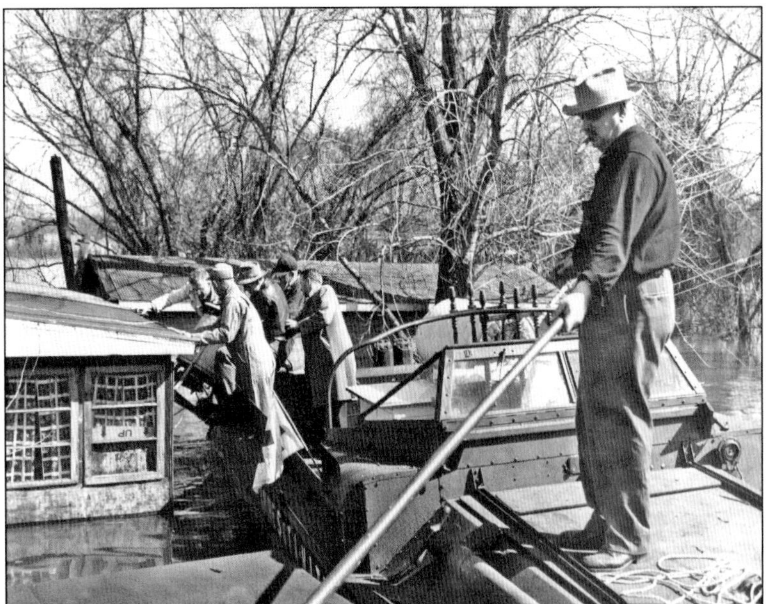

On April 17, a water rescue crewman steadies an amphibious vehicle, while others inside the house hand out furnishings to workers on the craft. The house, which stands about 400 feet from the river, was one of the first to be flooded when the river rose above flood stage.

A Red Cross disaster canteen from Hennepin County, Minnesota, was on duty on the evening of April 16 to provide coffee, sandwiches, and donuts to dike workers. Looking on from the left side of the photograph is Joseph C. Page, chairman of the Winona Chapter of the American Red Cross. The unit toured all Winona dike areas during the night.

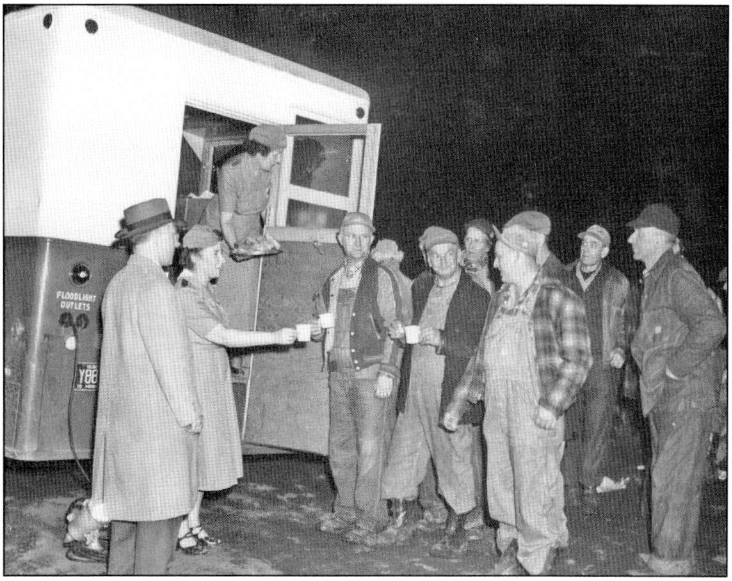

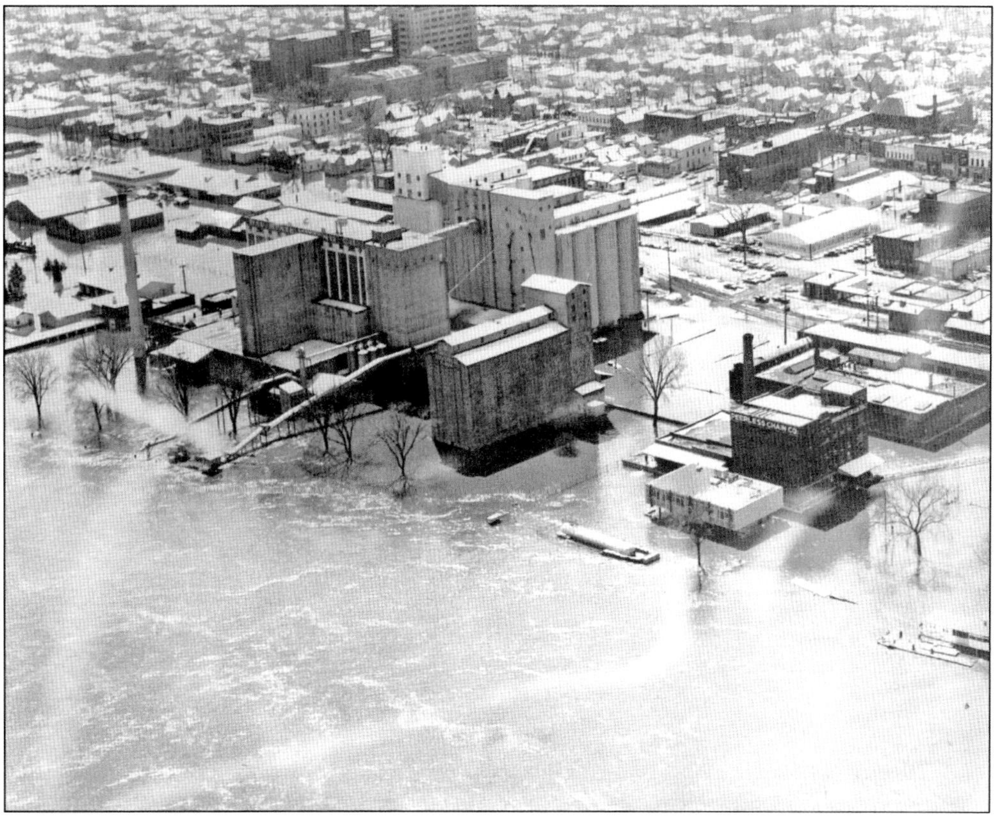

Winona appeared to be an underwater city when the Mississippi River crested on April 19, 1965, at 20.7 feet above flood stage. Peerless Chain and Bay State Milling Companies can be seen surrounded by water, along with parts of East Second Street.

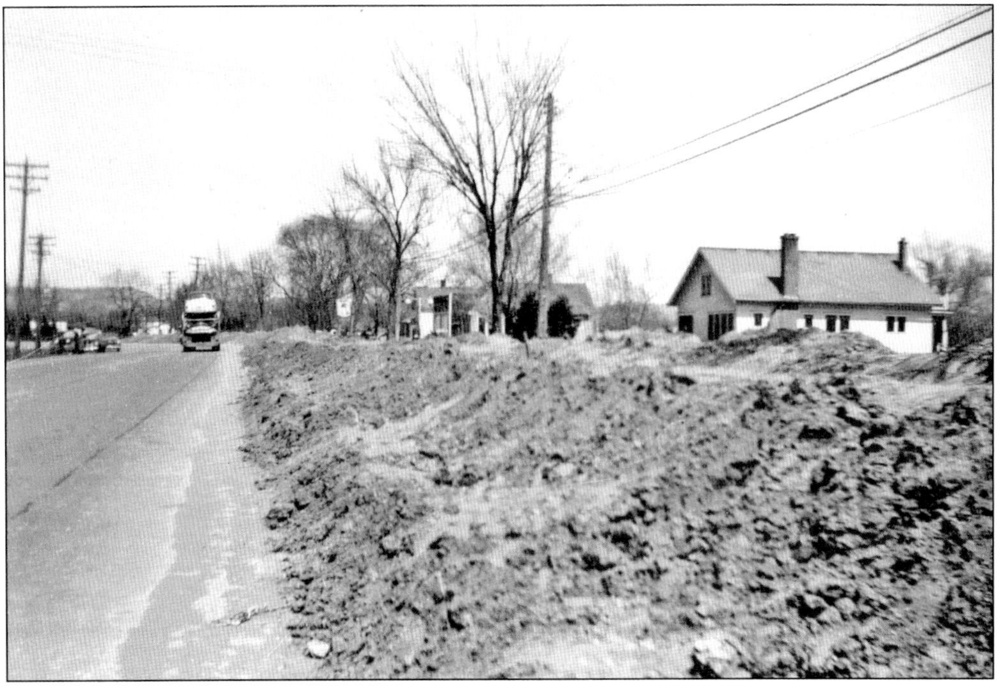

Around April 9, 1965, a 3,000-foot secondary dike was constructed along Mankato Avenue by the N.A. Roverud Company to provide for addition protection should the river rise above 24 feet. This view looks north along Mankato Avenue toward the Sarnia intersection.

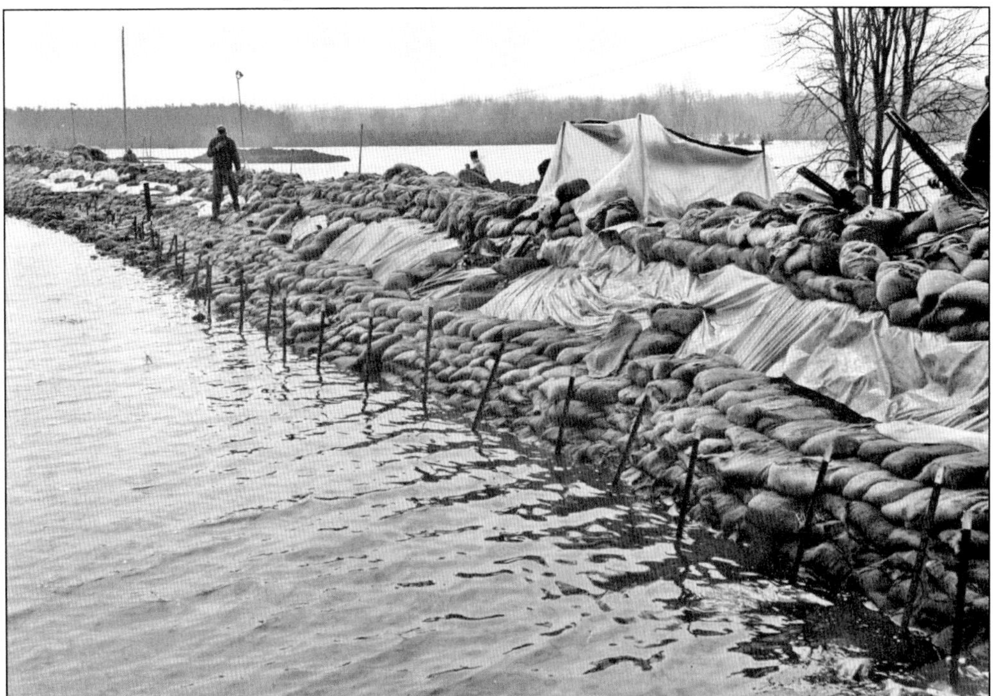

A portion of the Prairie Island dike was made of sandbags, which were reinforced with plastic sheeting and metal stakes to keep out the encroaching Mississippi River during the flood of 1965.

The Winona Paint and Glass building on West Second Street shows the depth of water that entered the city during the flood of 1965.

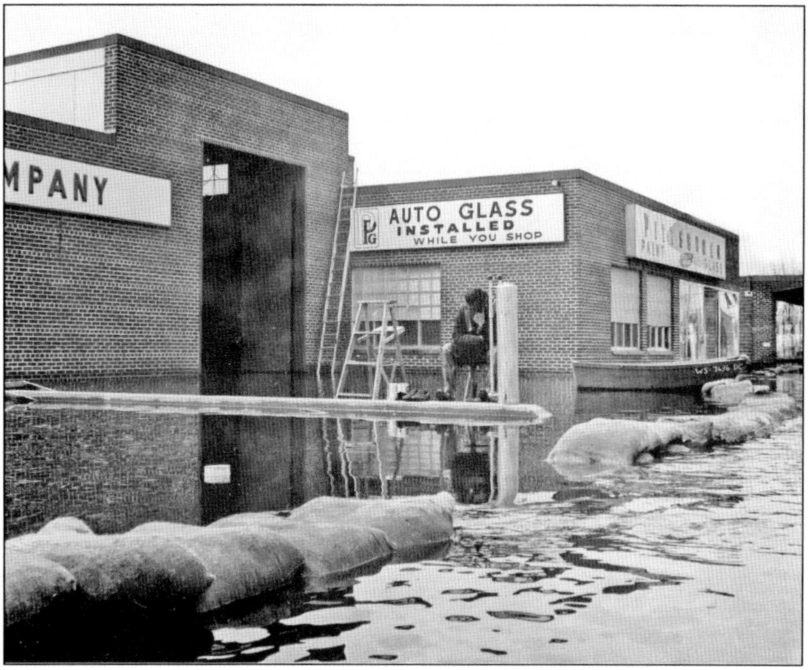

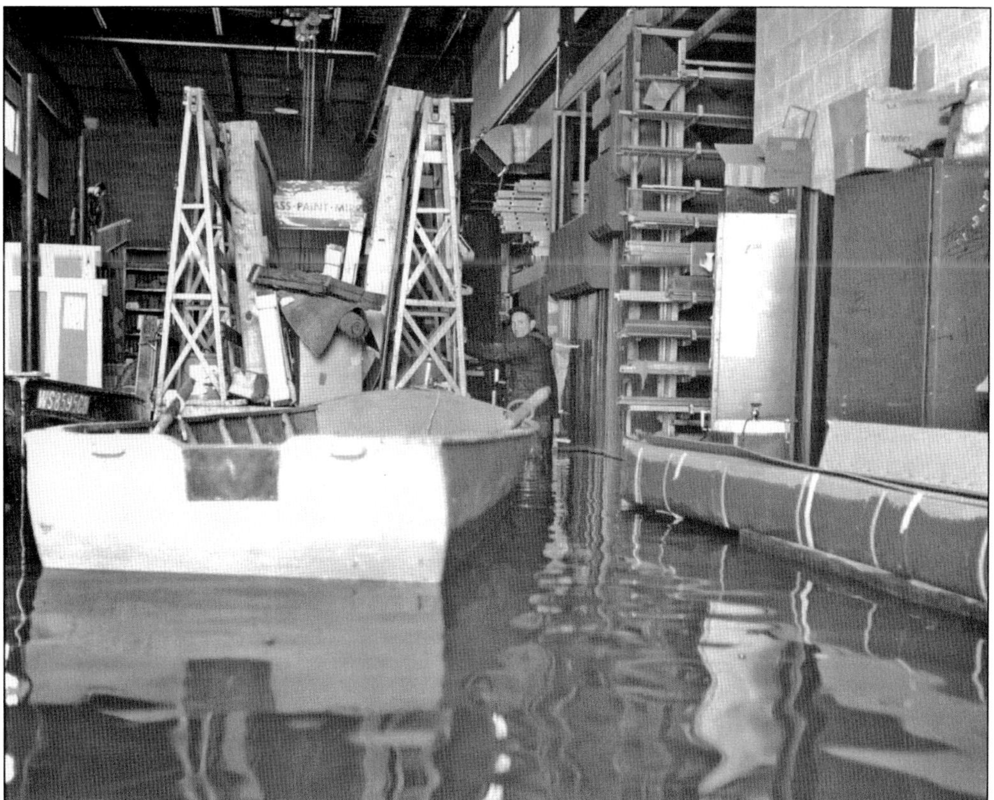

The interior of the Winona Paint and Glass building is pictured during the 1965 flood.

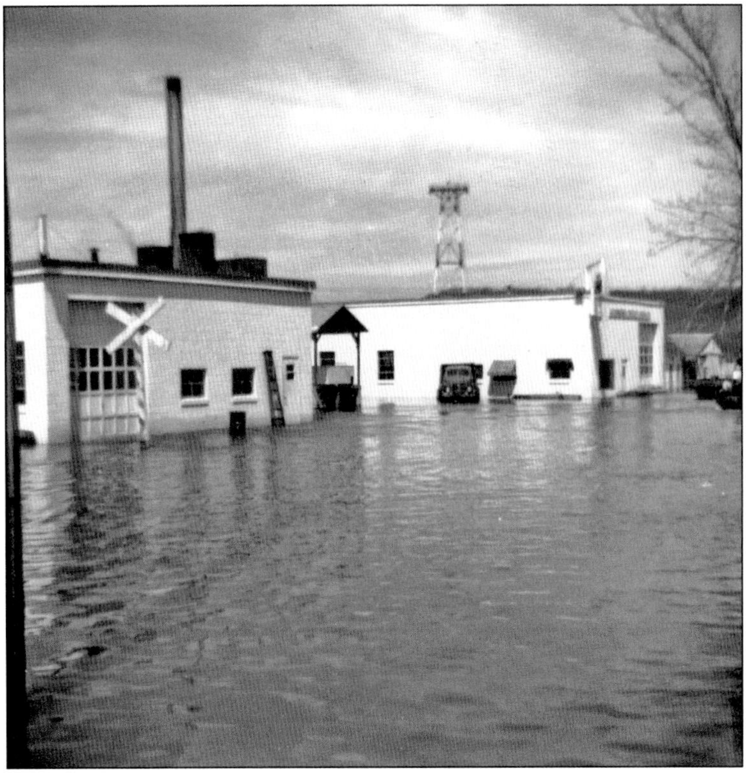

The Lake Center Switch Company buildings at Johnson and Front Streets show the extent of the impact of the 1965 floodwater.

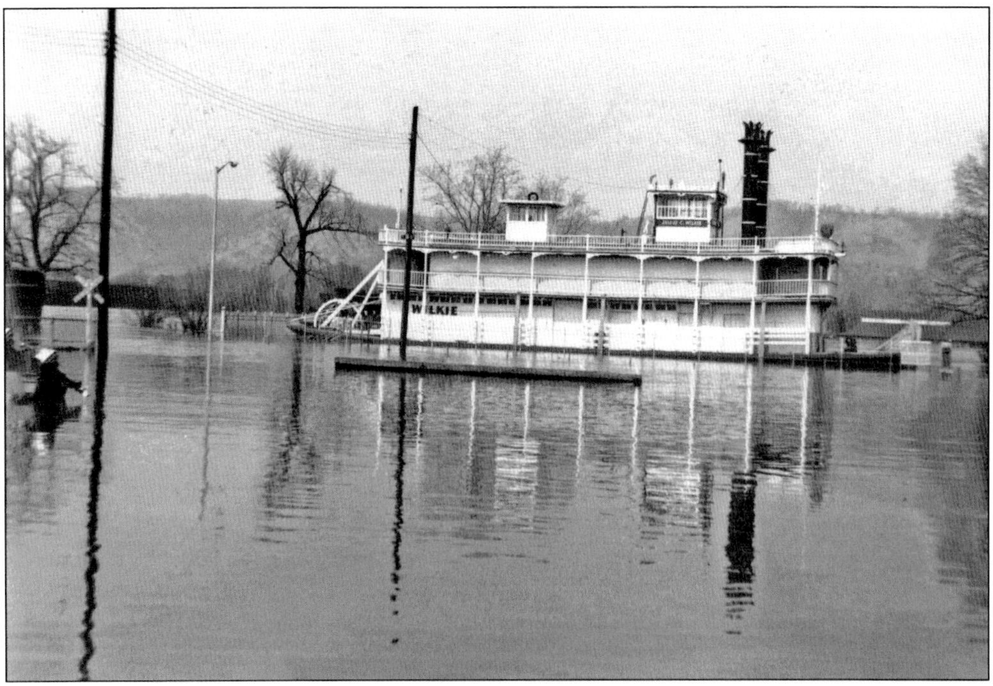

The Julius C. Wilkie Steamboat Museum, located at Levee Park, had floodwaters to the top of its hull. The *Wilkie*, a former tugboat, was placed in Levee Park in 1958 and had holes drilled into its hull to keep it from floating away.

All along Second Street, the river encroached upon buildings and dwellings.

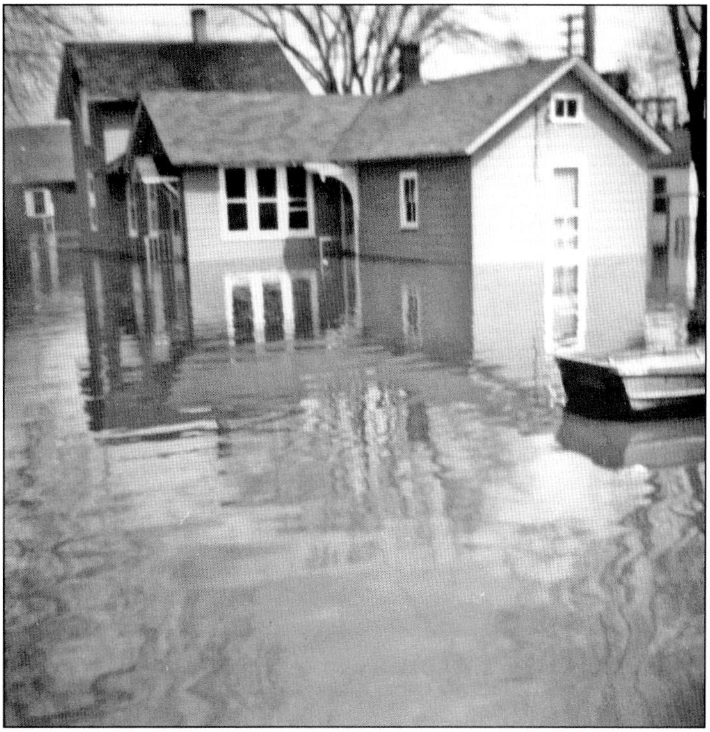

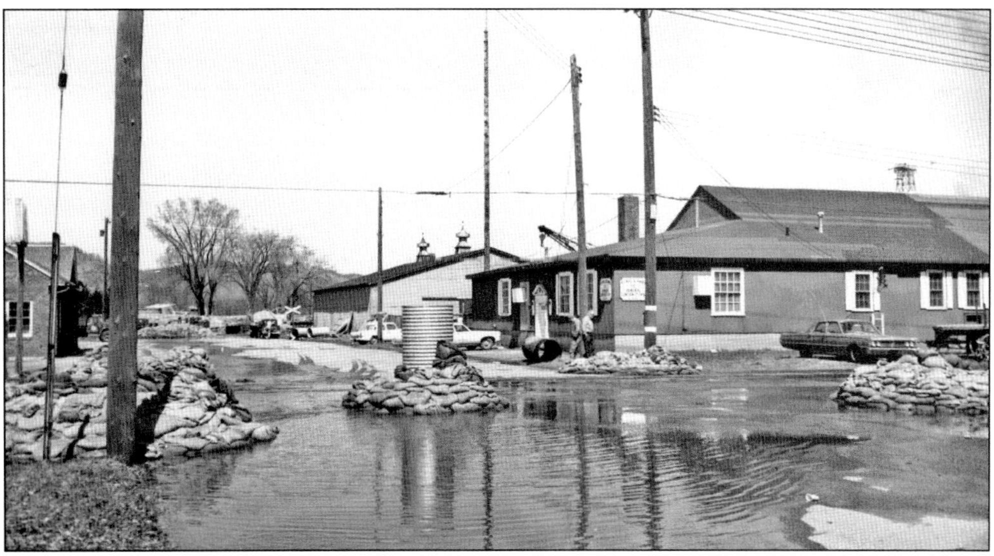

One of the many dangers in Winona was water entering the city through the sewer system. One defense was to cover manholes with sandbags to hold them down. The culvert pipe allowed for some rise with the water. This covered manhole is at East Second and Kansas Streets, and the building to the right belongs to the Schwab Construction Company.

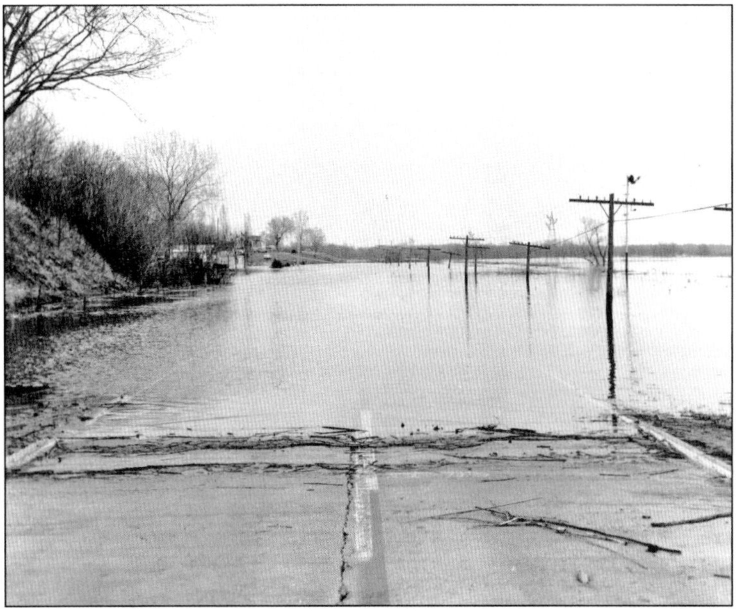

In April 1965, floodwaters covered Wisconsin Highway 35 between Fountain City, Wisconsin, and Winona to a depth of three feet. The water during the 1952 flood also covered the roadway, and after it receded, the roadway was rebuilt to withstand such waters.

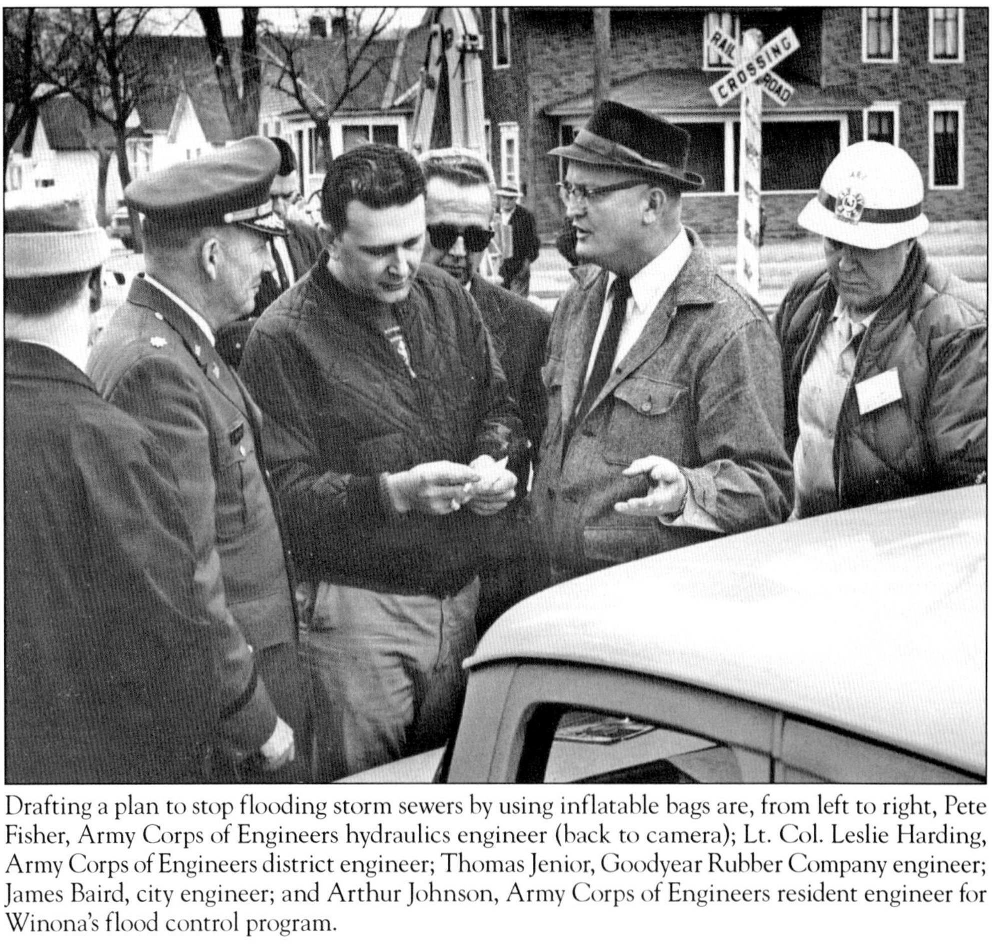

Drafting a plan to stop flooding storm sewers by using inflatable bags are, from left to right, Pete Fisher, Army Corps of Engineers hydraulics engineer (back to camera); Lt. Col. Leslie Harding, Army Corps of Engineers district engineer; Thomas Jenior, Goodyear Rubber Company engineer; James Baird, city engineer; and Arthur Johnson, Army Corps of Engineers resident engineer for Winona's flood control program.

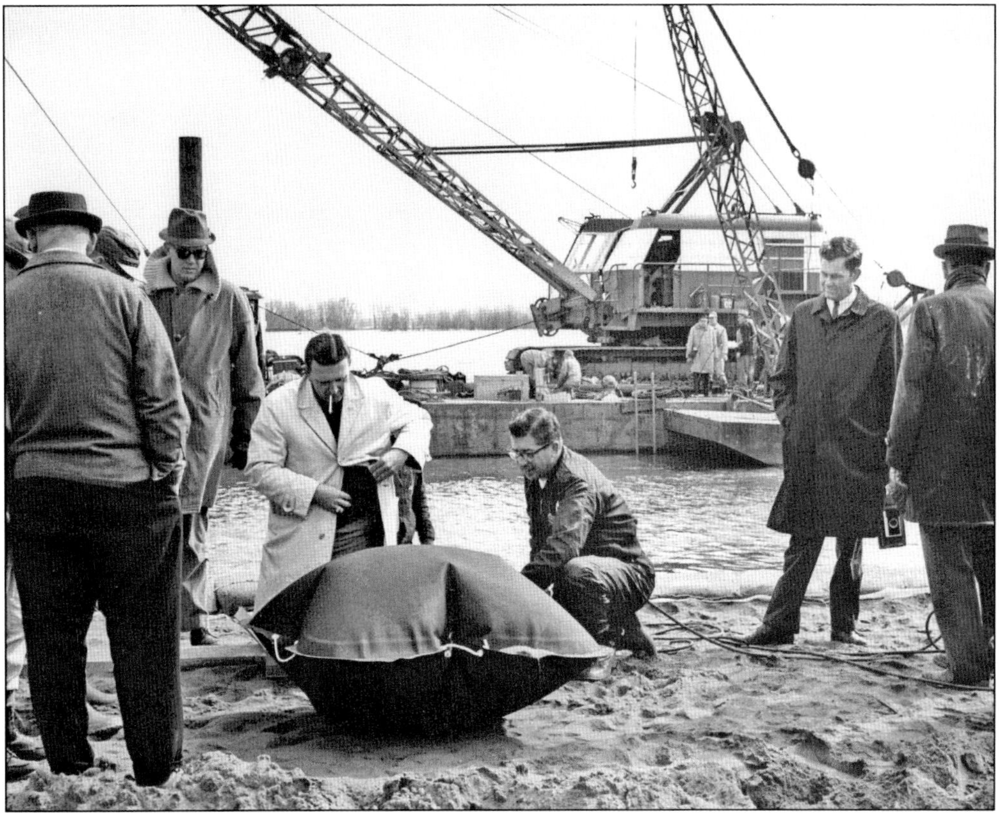

Auto dealer Tom Underdahl, with sunglasses, watches an inflation test being conducted on a dunnage bag by Goodyear engineer Tom Jenior, in the white coat, and general line salesman Jack Hafemann. Dunnage bags, used to protect goods during shipment, were obtained from Goodyear Rubber Company through the efforts of Underdahl.

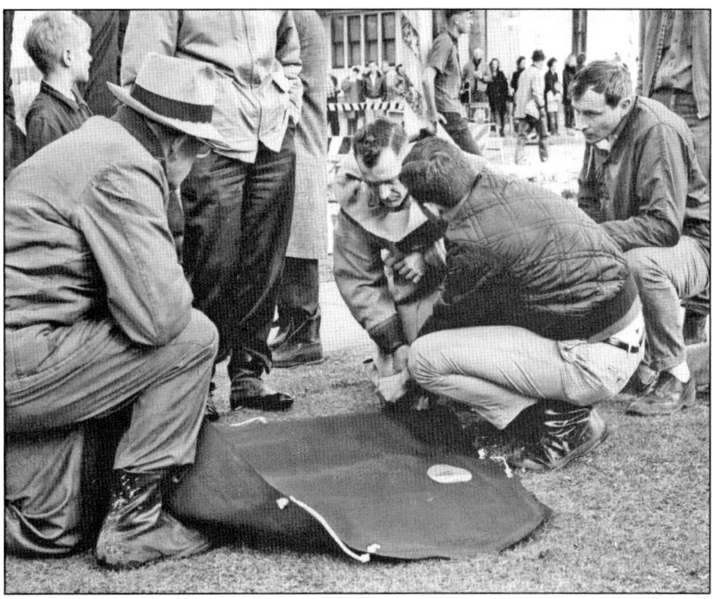

Ray Beyers, kneeling at center, receives some instruction on how the inflatable dunnage bag will work. Beyers, a former Navy diver, volunteered to help the city during the flooding crisis.

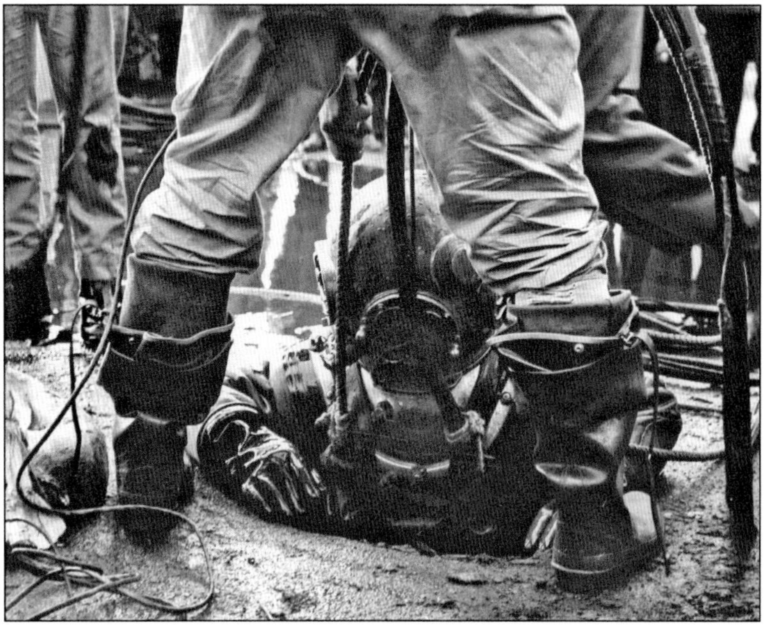

Pictured after successfully sealing off a flooded storm sewer from rising water on April 19 is former Navy diver Ray Beyers in a bulky, air-filled diving suit. Beyers descended into the flooded sewer at East Second and Chatfield Streets with a dunnage bag, which he inflated after placing it into position in the sewer line.

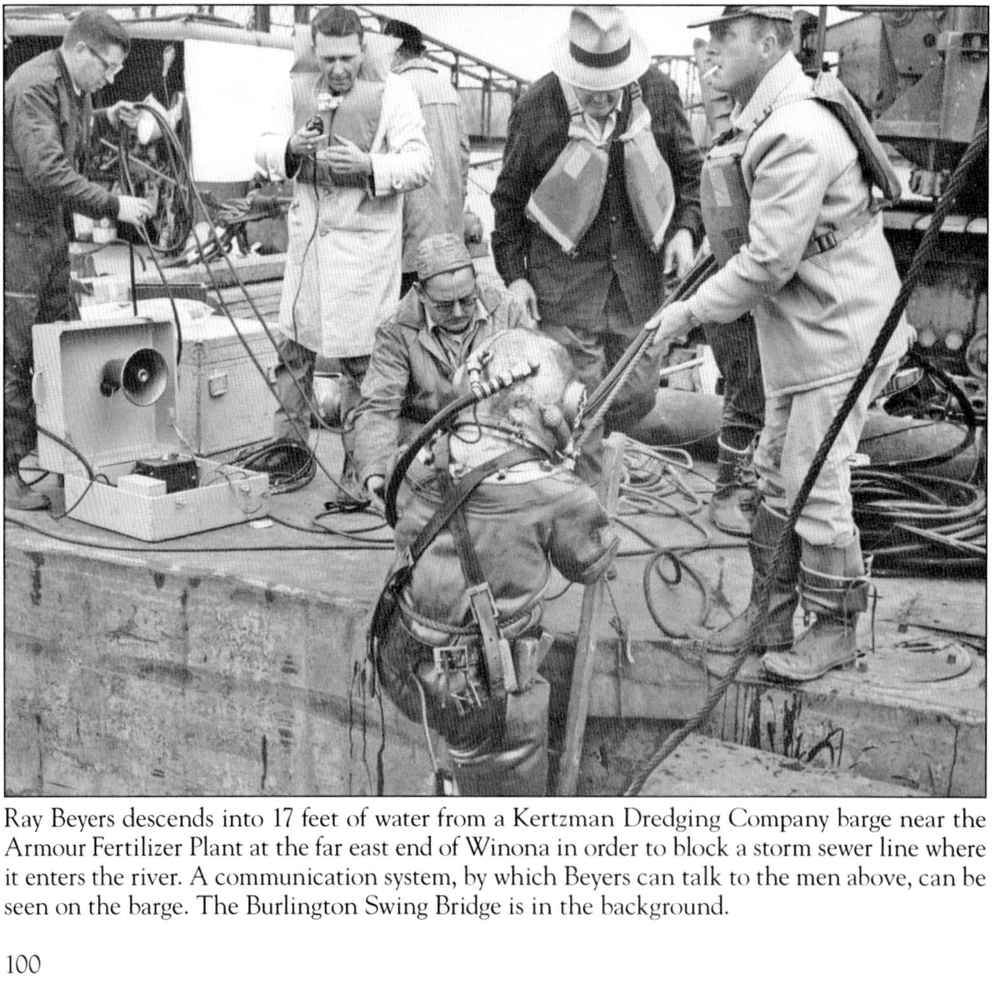

Ray Beyers descends into 17 feet of water from a Kertzman Dredging Company barge near the Armour Fertilizer Plant at the far east end of Winona in order to block a storm sewer line where it enters the river. A communication system, by which Beyers can talk to the men above, can be seen on the barge. The Burlington Swing Bridge is in the background.

Occasionally, there was time for fun along the dikes during the flood crisis. "The End" does not mean the flood is over but that the water is receding. The men pictured here on April 25 refer to their location at the end of the Prairie Island dike. The sign offers "waterfront homes, with running cold water, fish in your living room," and so on. A couple of days after this photograph was taken, Winona was deemed to be in the clear.

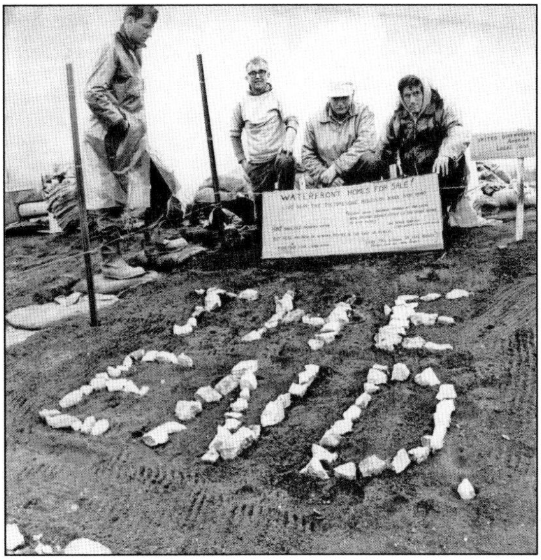

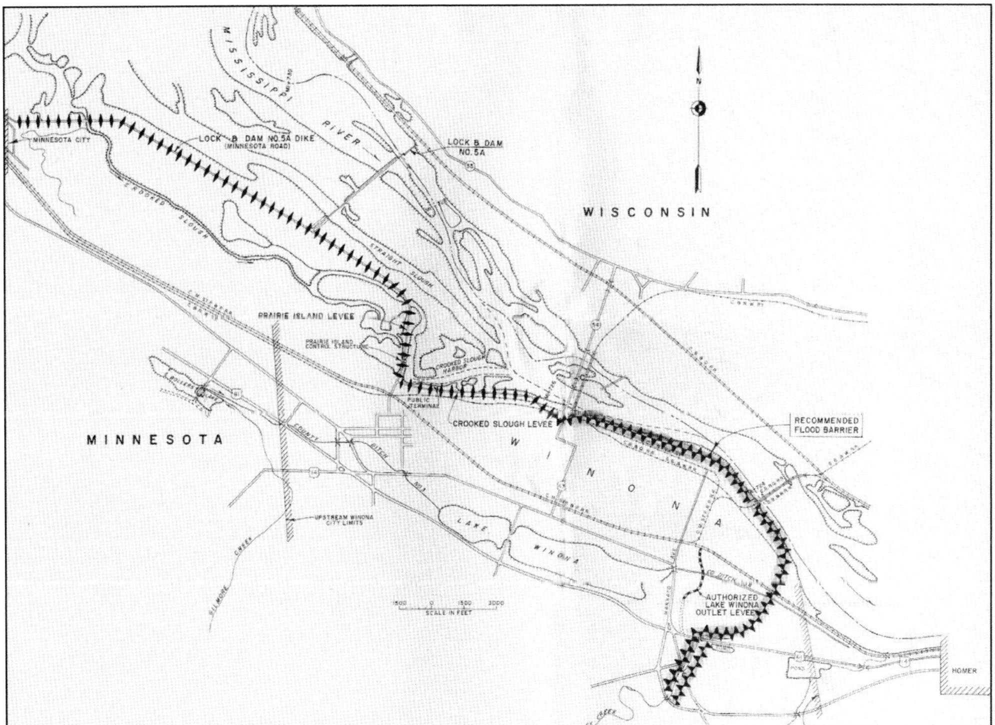

In the early 1970s, the Army Corps of Engineers proposed flood control measures for the city of Winona. The map shows both the existing dikes to the north and west of the city and proposed dikes in the eastern part of the city. Ground breaking for the $33 million project occurred on September 7, 1979. The project was completed in five sections, the first between Walnut and Vine Streets. The entire project was planned to be completed in 1984.

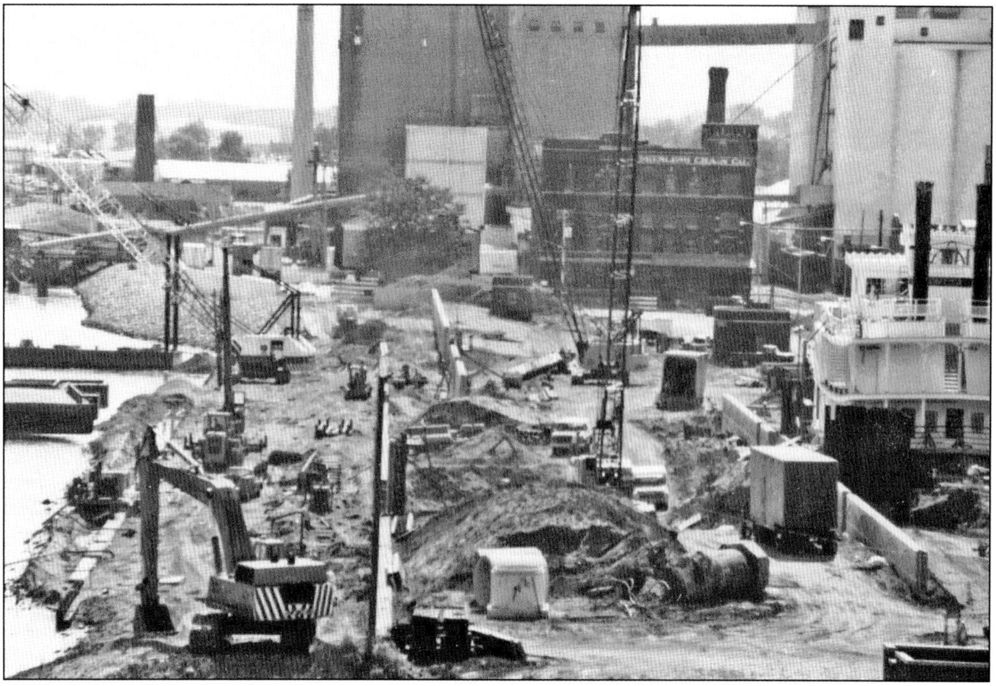

It was not until August 1979 that monies were allocated and construction began on $25 million of dikes and flood walls along the eastern side of Winona. Ground breaking at Levee Park for the installation of flood walls and other flood control dikes occurred on August 30, 1980. The construction of flood walls shown in this photograph is near Winona's main business district. The *Julius C. Wilkie* steamboat is pictured to the right, and Bay State Milling Company's elevators are in the background.

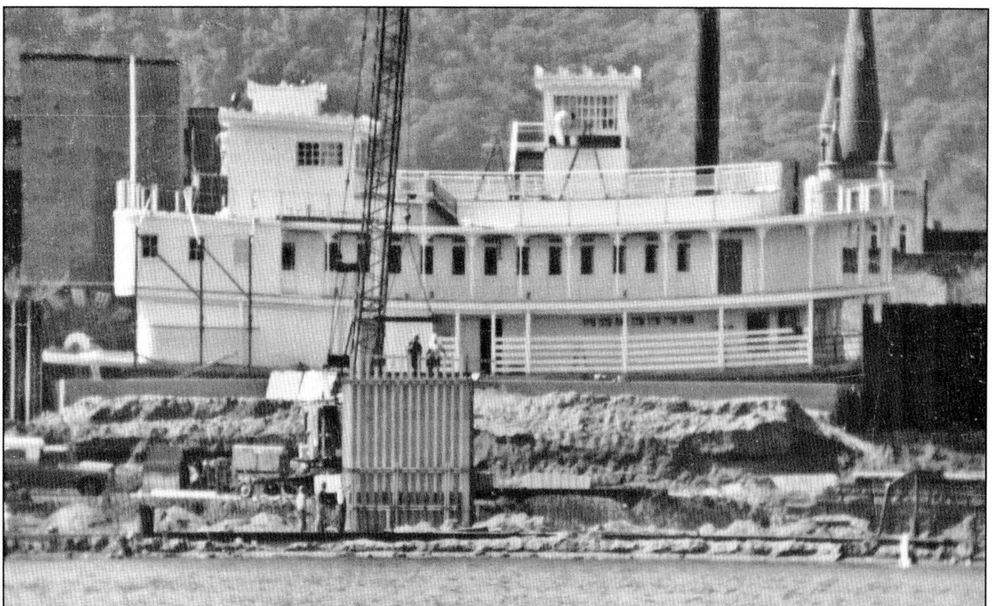

The first task to be accomplished was to move the *Julius C. Wilkie* back from the work site. This occurred in late 1980. Following its move, the installation of flood walls began along the riverbank.

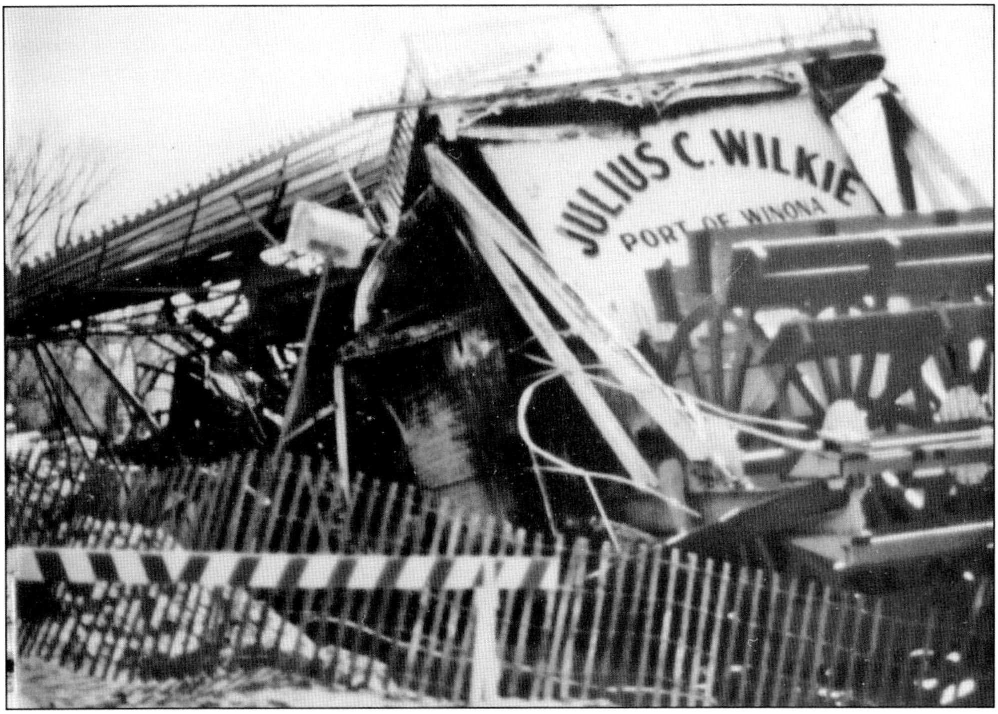

During the night of March 12, 1981, the *Julius C. Wilkie* caught fire and was completely destroyed. It was suspected that a welder's torch had thrown sparks onto the wooden steamboat.

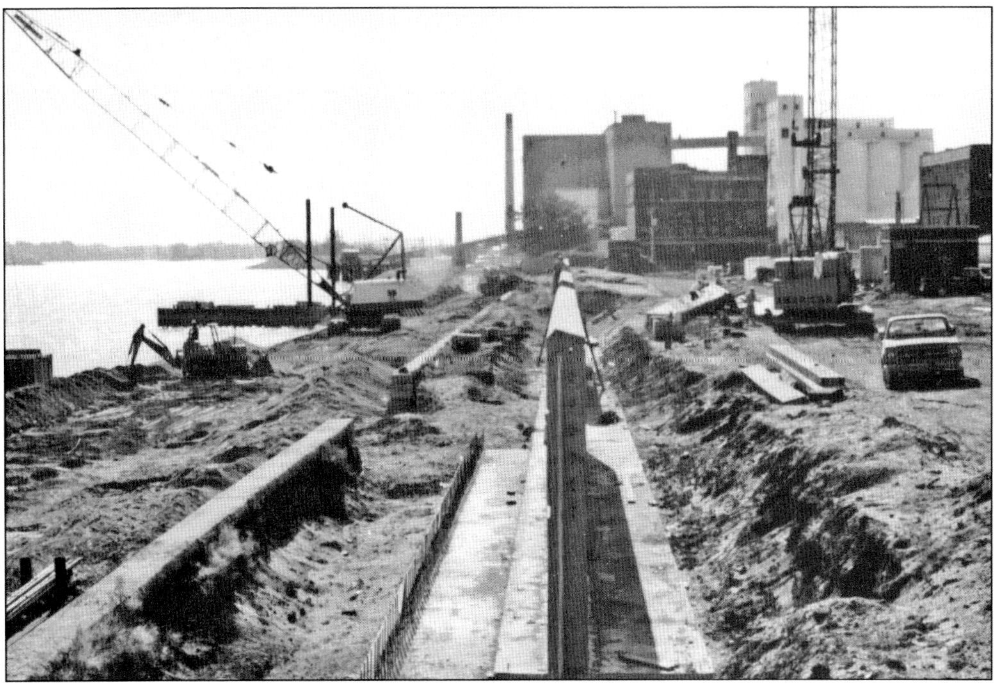

Following the burning of the *Wilkie*, progress on the flood walls continued, which changed the entire landscape of Levee Park. However, the long-term plan was to develop the park into the Upper Mississippi River Interpretive Center.

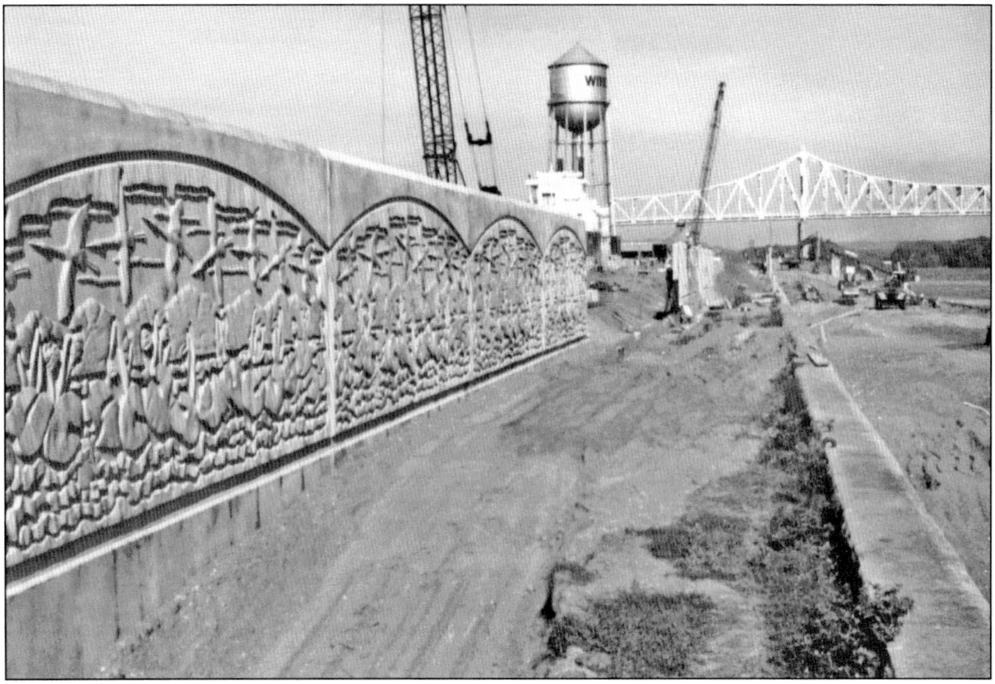

Leo Smith and Peter Shortridge designed flood wall artwork with the theme "Life on the River." Pictured is the 25-foot relief repeated 16 times to create a single long, flowing scene facing the river and stretching from Lafayette to Center Streets.

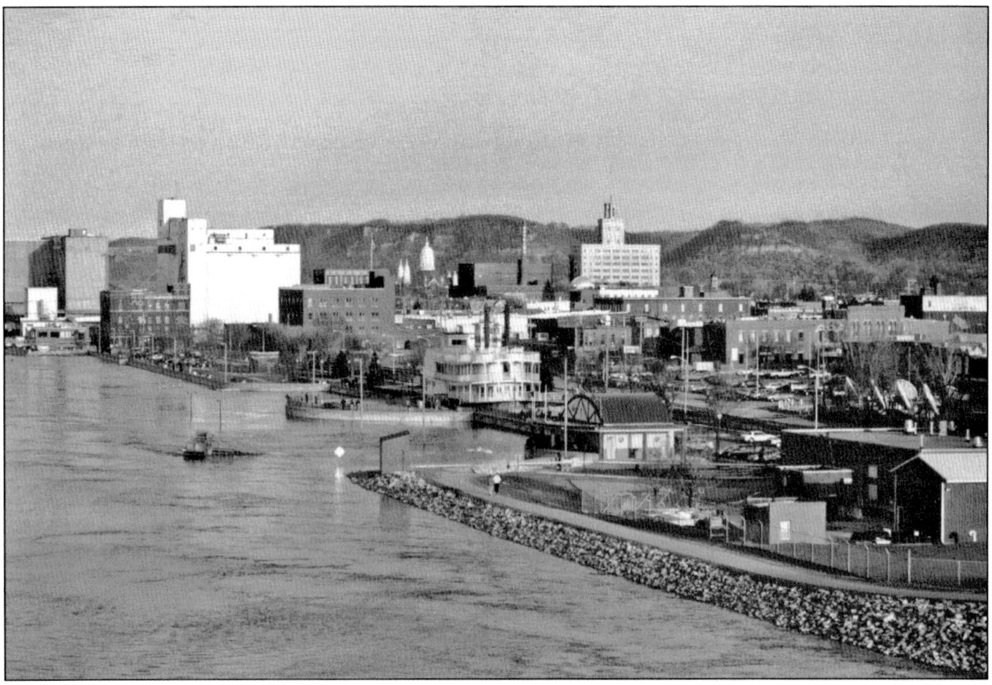

Winona was saved from the second highest flood crest in April 2001 as the levees and flood walls held back the rising water. The new *Julius C. Wilkie* can be seen in its prominent place in Levee Park. A portion of riprapped levee can be seen extending upriver from Levee Park.

Nine

Celebrating the River

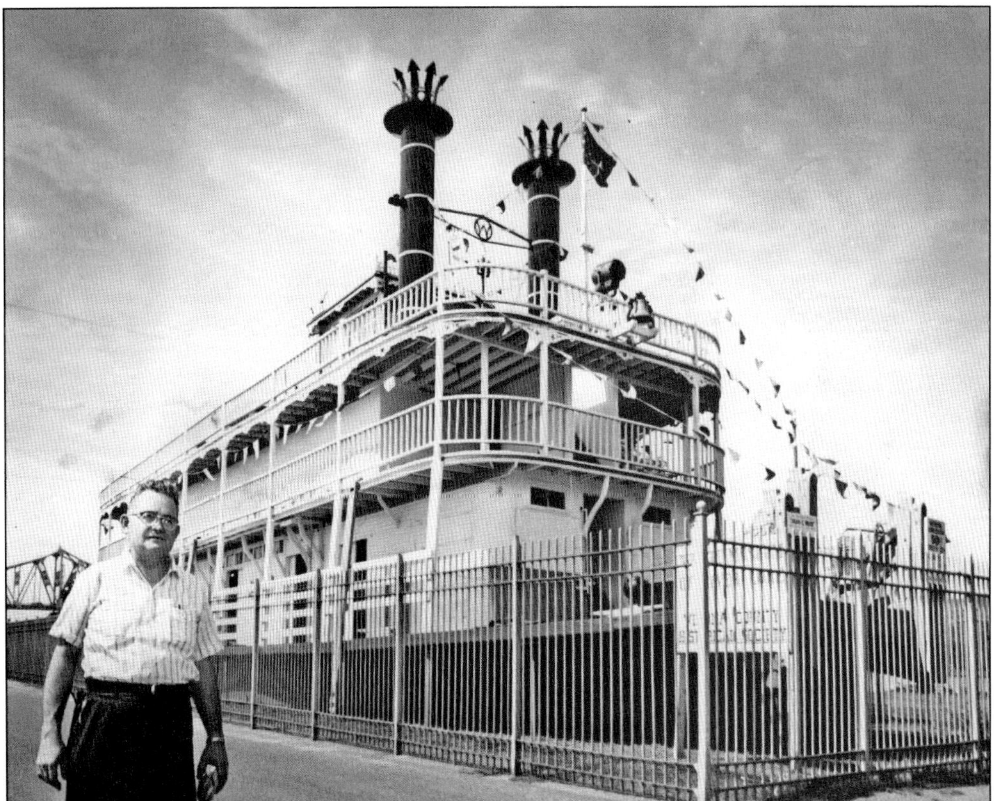

The Julius C. Wilkie Steamboat Museum at Levee Park is pictured in August 1963 with Dr. Lewis Younger, president of the Winona County Historical Society. Younger was instrumental in the purchase of the steamer *Pearson*, which was converted into the *Wilkie*.

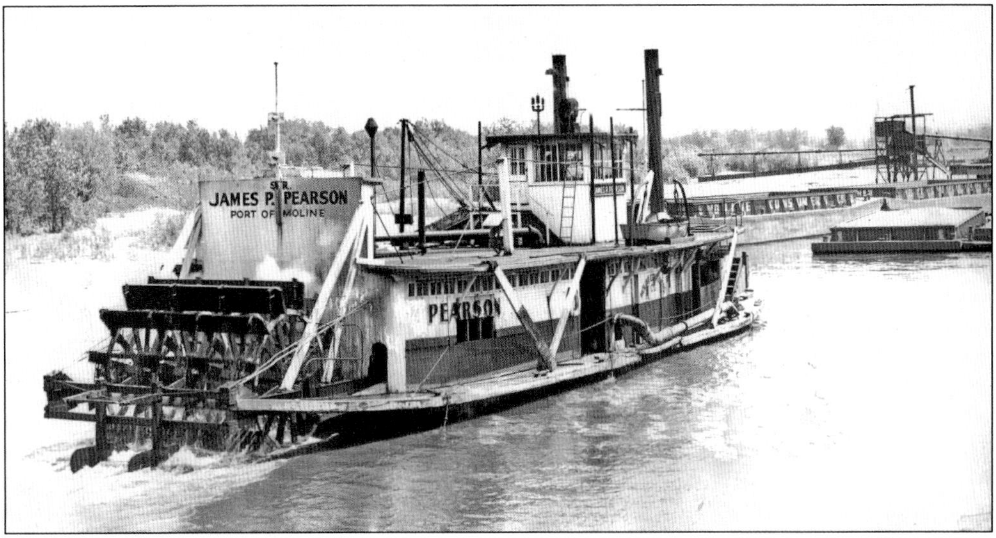

The *James P. Pearson*, a 96-foot-long stern-wheeler tugboat that worked at Moline, Illinois, was purchased by the Winona County Historical Society for $2,500. It was to be set in Levee Park as a monument to pioneer river life.

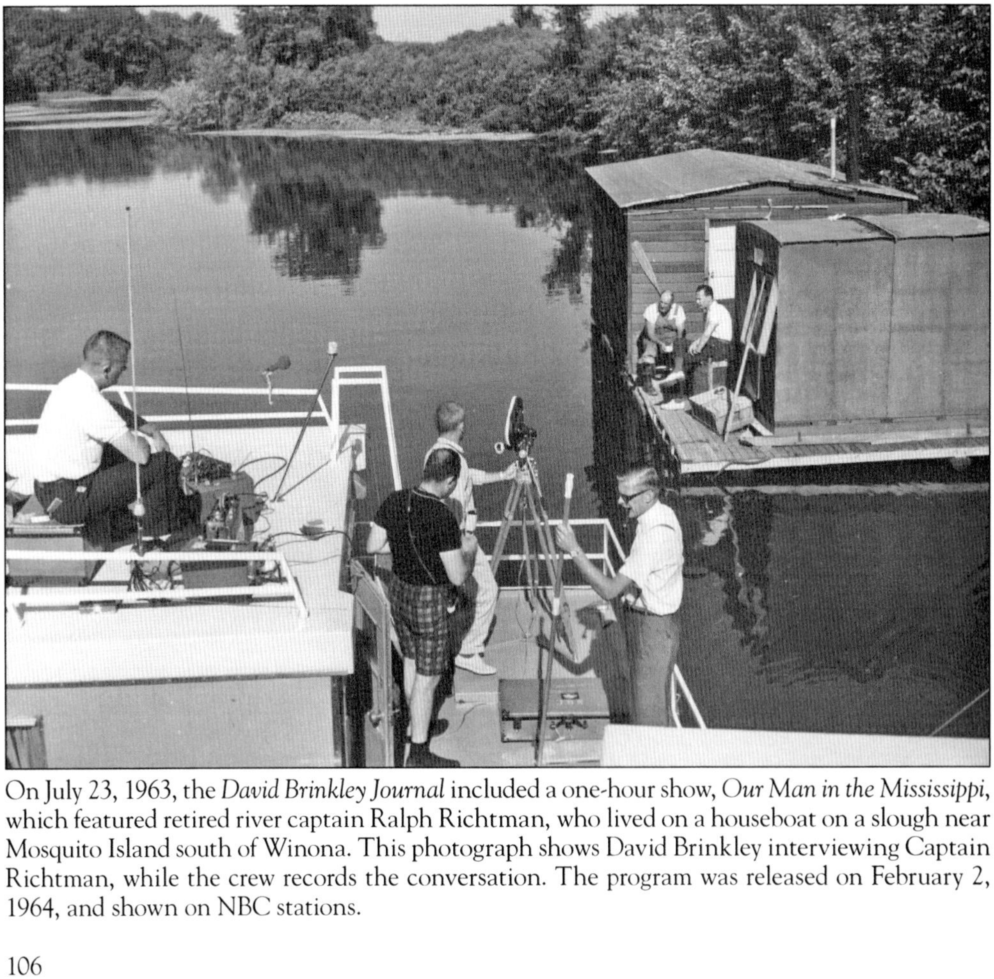

On July 23, 1963, the *David Brinkley Journal* included a one-hour show, *Our Man in the Mississippi*, which featured retired river captain Ralph Richtman, who lived on a houseboat on a slough near Mosquito Island south of Winona. This photograph shows David Brinkley interviewing Captain Richtman, while the crew records the conversation. The program was released on February 2, 1964, and shown on NBC stations.

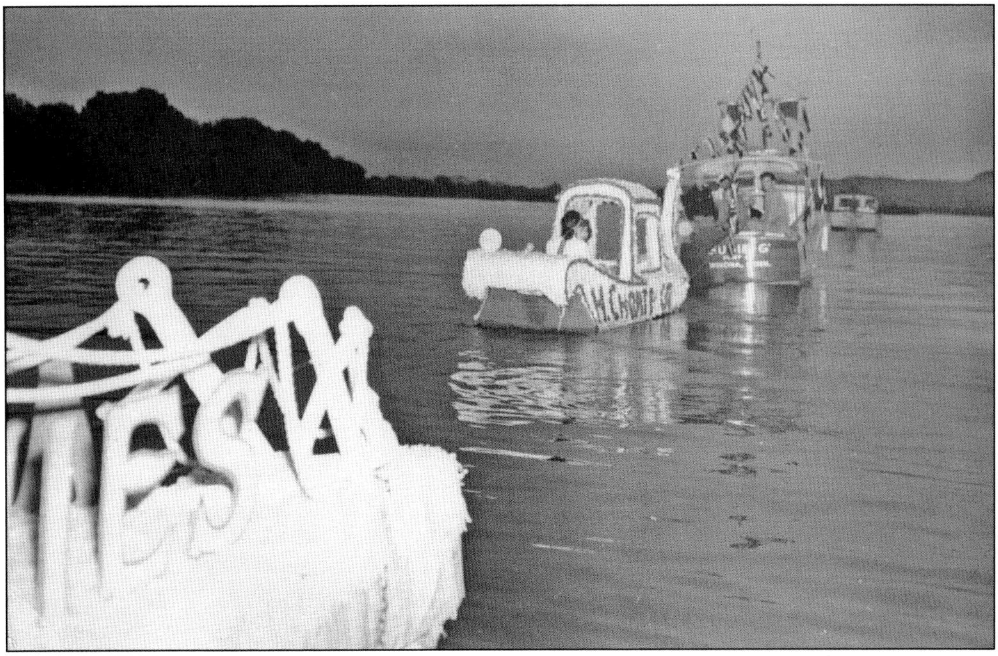

The first annual Steamboat Days Venetian Nights Regatta was held on the Mississippi River on Friday evening, July 23, 1948. In the center is the entry of an H. Choate & Company white gondola with gondolier Jeanne Ctibor and passenger Donna Riebau. The Choate gondola won first prize in the regatta. In the foreground, taking second place, is a colorful bride and groom float representing Arnie's Bar.

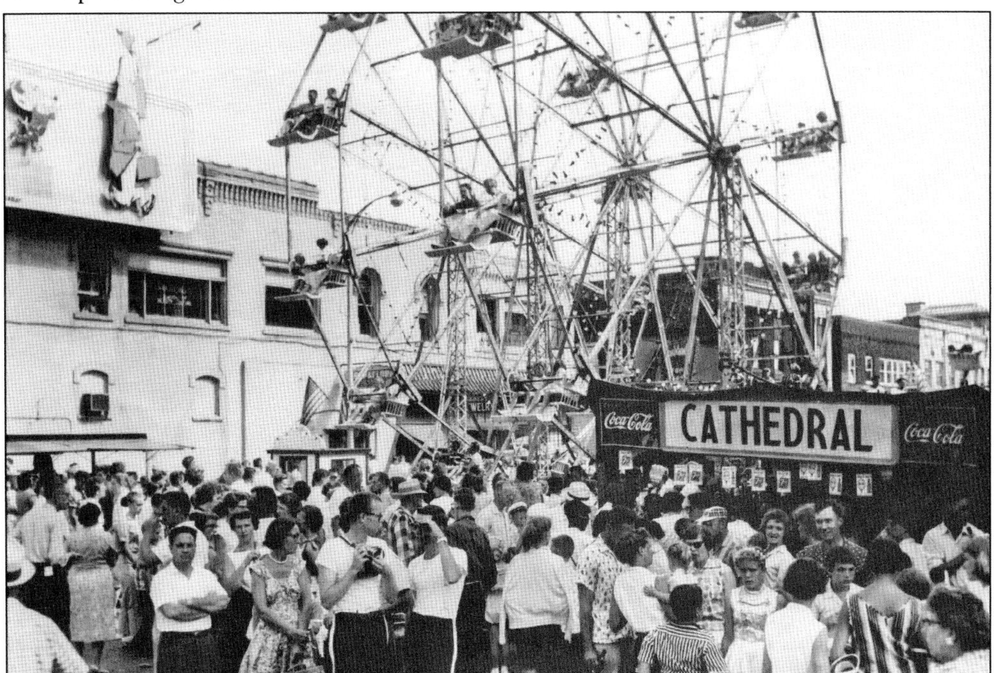

The Sunset Amusement Company's carnival was in full swing on Main Street between Third and Fourth Streets during the 1958 Steamboat Days.

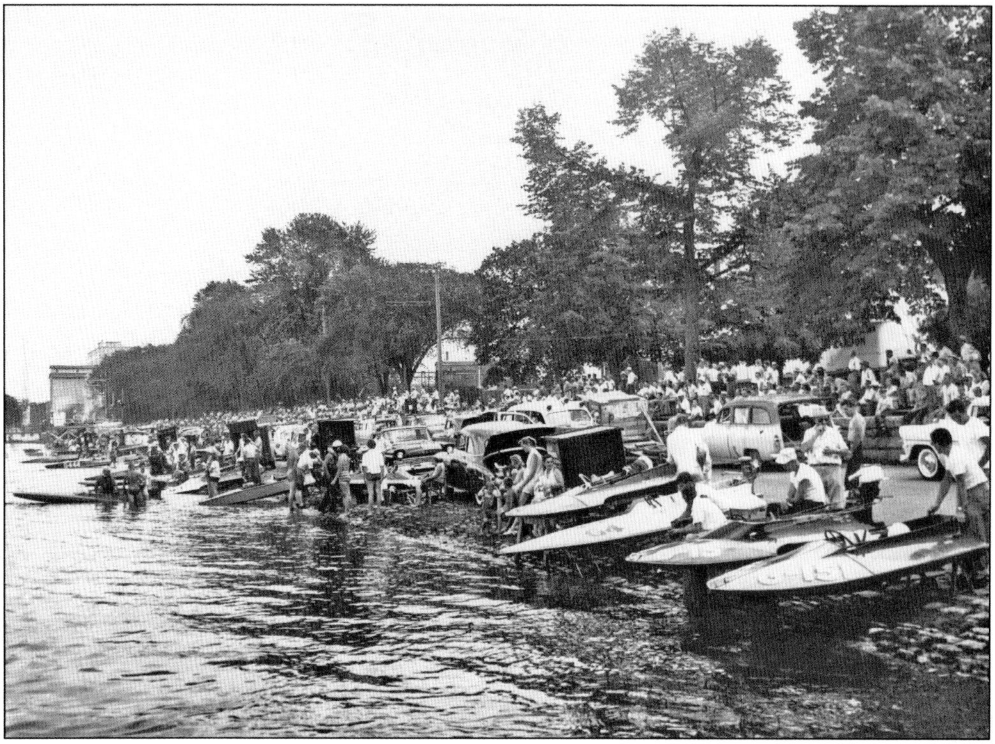

Levee Park was jammed to overflowing on Sunday afternoon, July 10, 1955, as thousands of spectators came to watch the Steamboat Days boat races. This photograph shows part of the crowd near the boat docks and repair pits in the foreground.

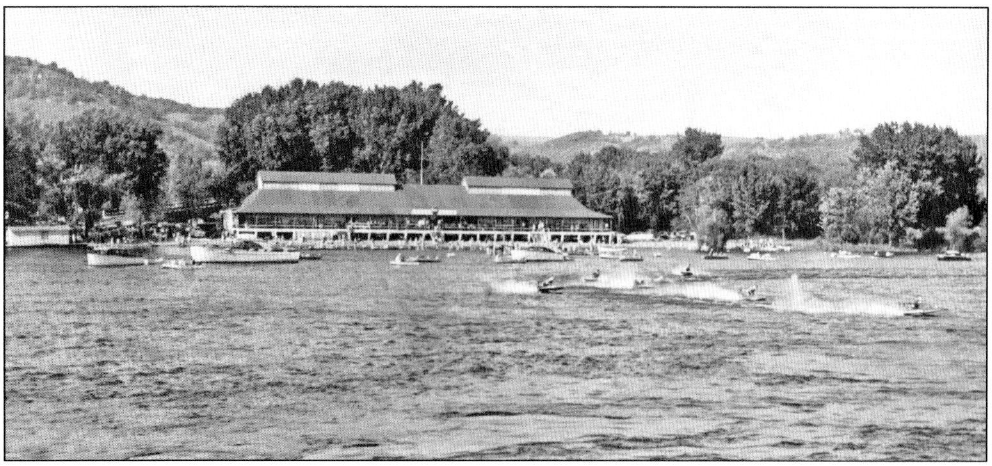

Skimming the surface of the Mississippi River on July 12, 1955, are runabouts rounding the turn in the Midwest Power Boat Association races. Over 100 racers entered this Steamboat Days sporting event. In the background are the John A. Latsch bathhouse and beach on Latsch Island.

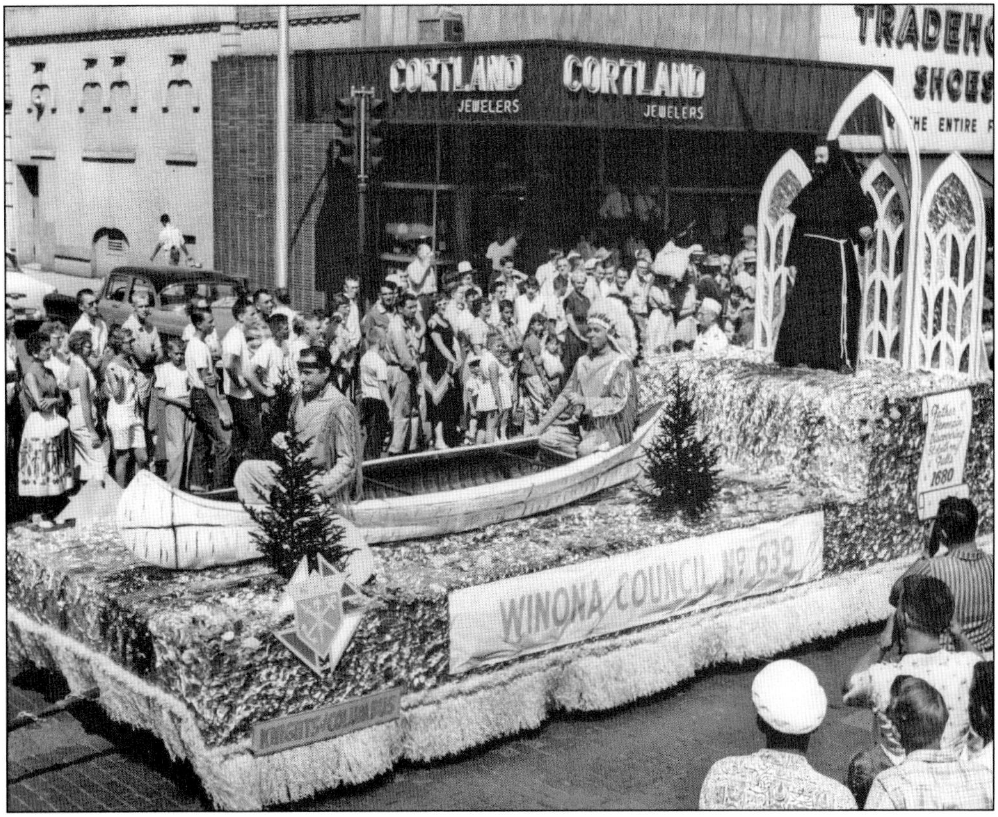

On July 13, 1958, the Knights of Columbus Winona Council No. 639 float won first place. The Steamboat Days float depicted Father Hennepin discovering the Falls of St. Anthony.

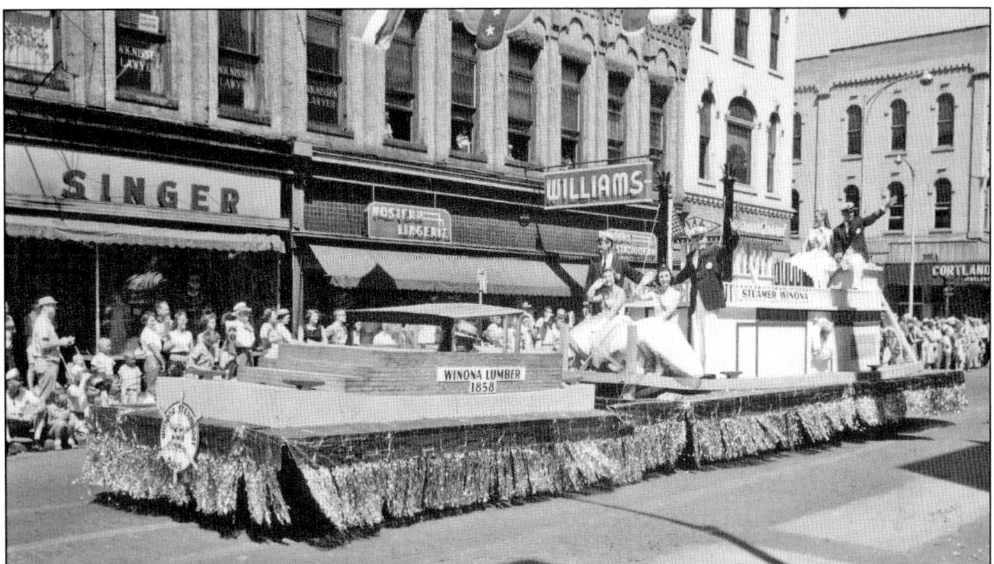

The July 13, 1958, Steamboat Days parade included the Winona County Historical Society's float depicting steamer *James P. Pearson*, which had been recently renovated into a museum of river lore.

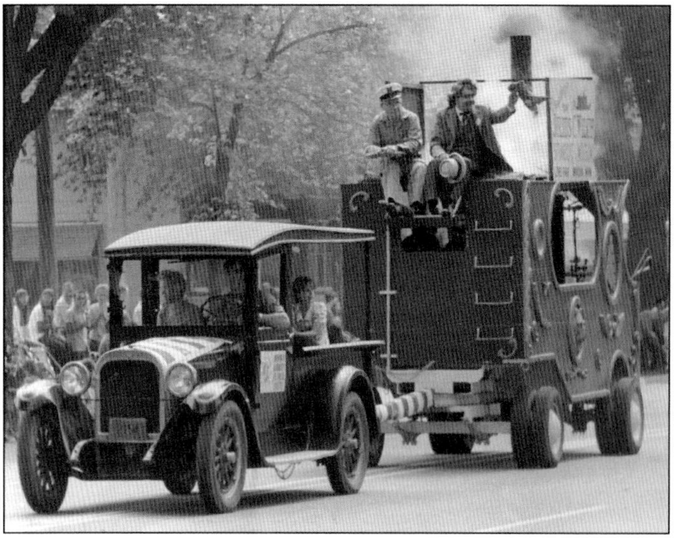

The *Julius C. Wilkie* steam calliope, donated by the Wilkie Foundation in April 1960, was mounted in a bright red circus wagon and was seen in many parades around the city. On July 5, 1974, William Ede (waving bandana), dressed as Mark Twain, rides atop the calliope along with Dr. Lewis Younger, executive director of the Winona County Historical Society.

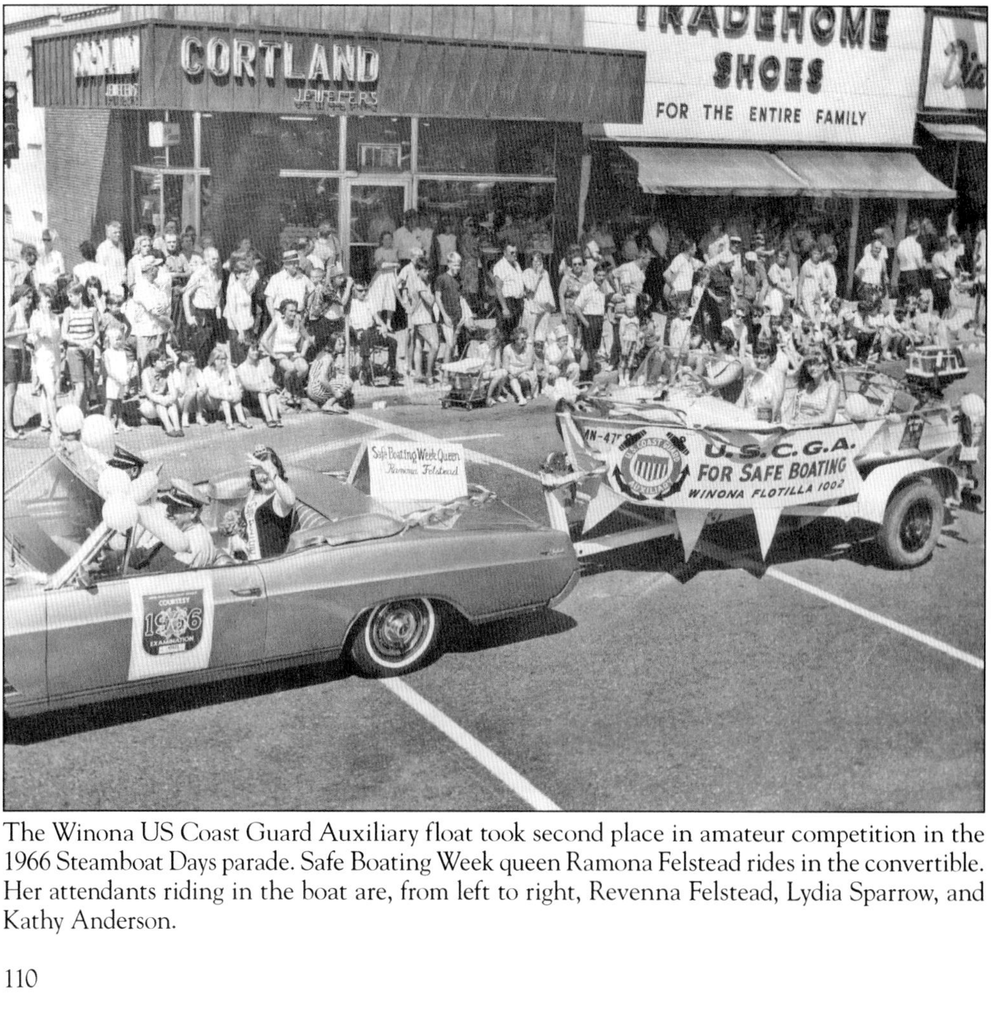

The Winona US Coast Guard Auxiliary float took second place in amateur competition in the 1966 Steamboat Days parade. Safe Boating Week queen Ramona Felstead rides in the convertible. Her attendants riding in the boat are, from left to right, Revenna Felstead, Lydia Sparrow, and Kathy Anderson.

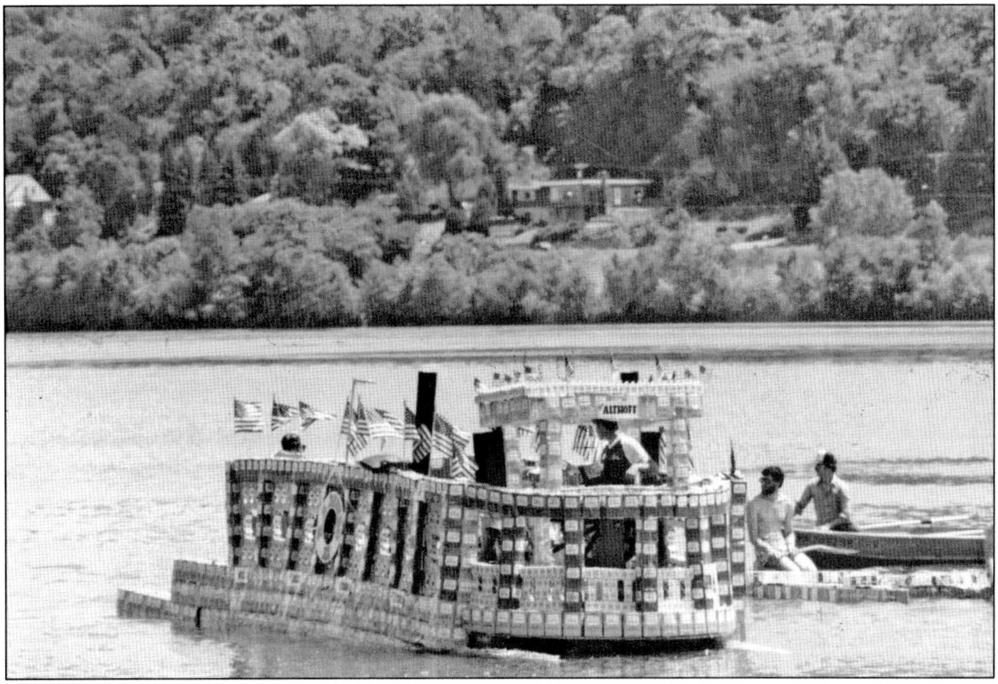

Bob Althoff's milk carton B.A. *Bimbo II* churns ahead in the 1982 Steamboat Days Rivertown Renaissance Race on Lake Winona.

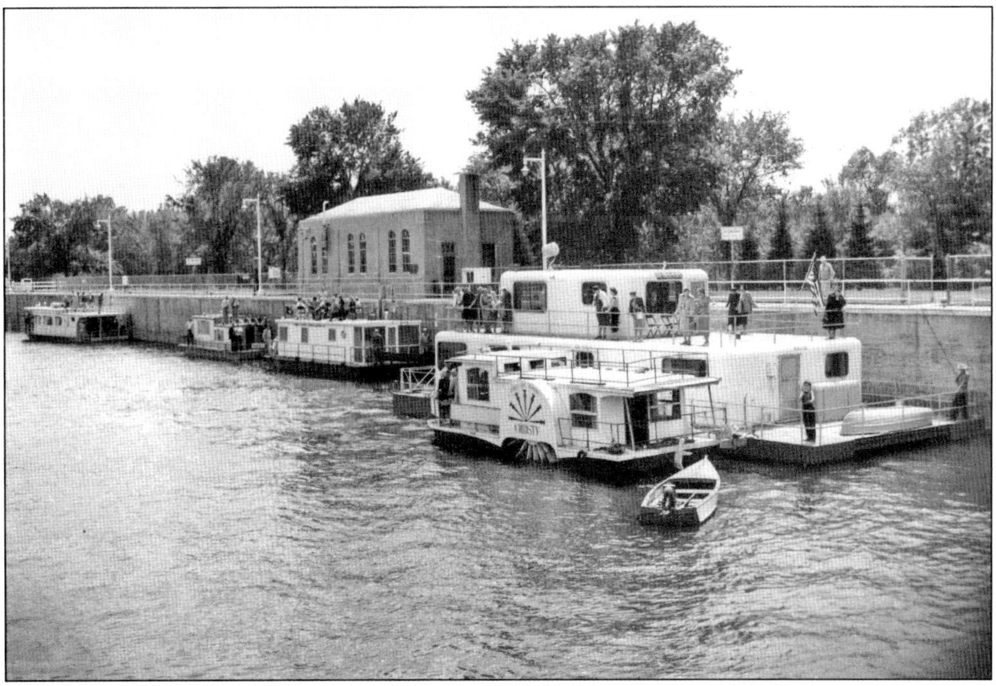

The Portia Club Riverboat Tour on June 10, 1961, was a fundraiser for the Winona Chapter of the American Field Service Foreign Students Program and included some homemade boats that were constructed of marine plywood. These boats and others on the tour are seen locking through the Whitman Dam.

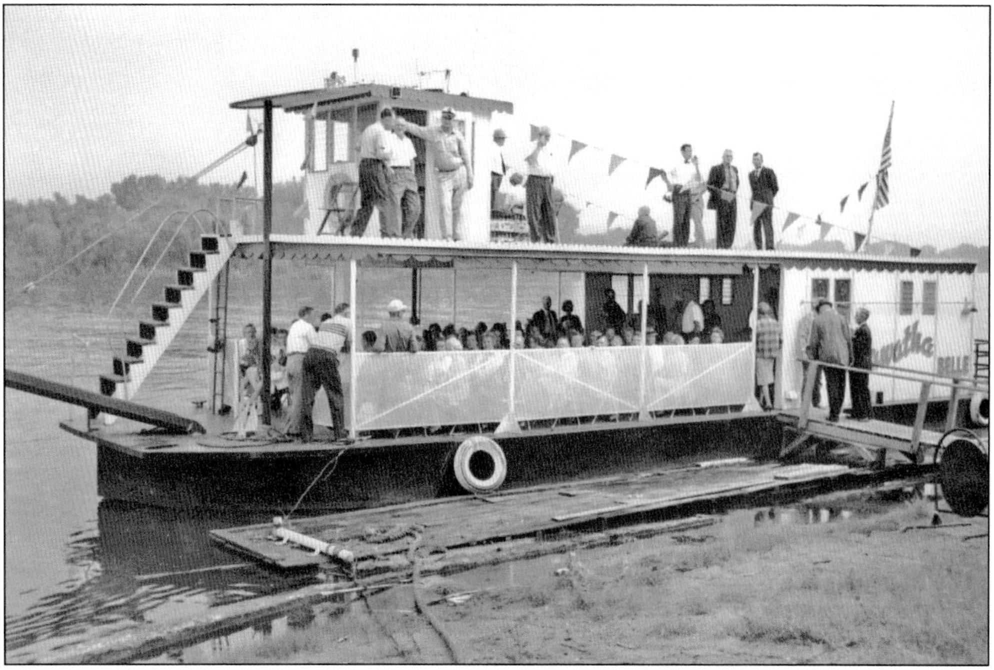

The *Hiawatha Belle*, a 55-foot excursion boat, was built by Whittaker Marine in 1959 and owned by Raymond and Milton Meyer. It was designed to resemble an old excursion boat that plied the Upper Mississippi River and was the first excursion boat to operate out of Winona in many years. It made its debut in time for the 1959 Steamboat Days and offered river cruises from Levee Park and Whittaker Marina.

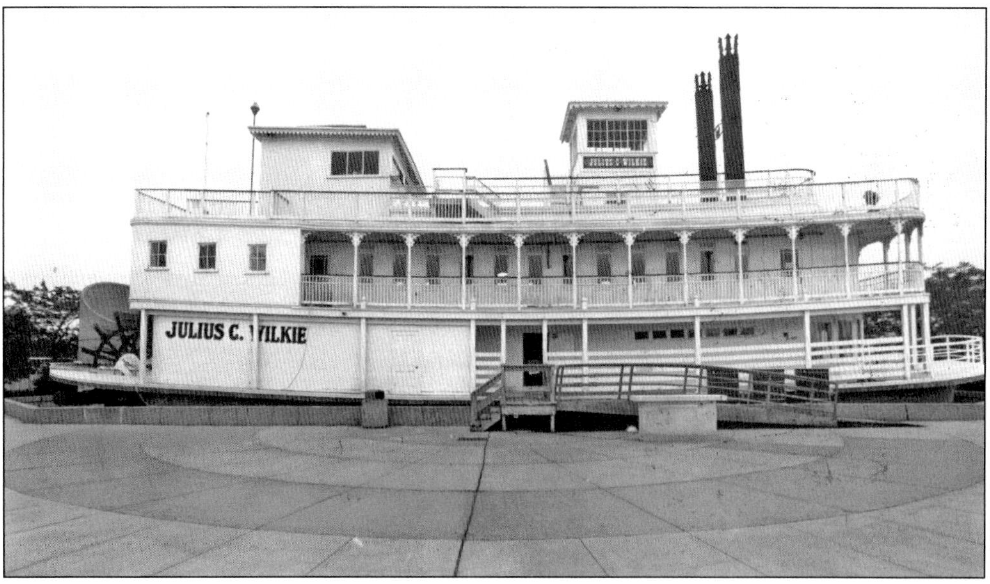

The new *Julius C. Wilkie*, centerpiece of the Winona Steamboat Center, was rebuilt in a reflecting pool on a plaza constructed as a part of the Winona flood control project. A sizable portion of the funding for the steamboat center came from Leighton Wilkie, president of the Wilkie Brothers Foundation. The center was dedicated on July 2, 1982, and opened in April 1983. Due to poor maintenance and continued financial difficulties, the structure was razed in July 2008.

Ten

MASTERS OF THE RIVER

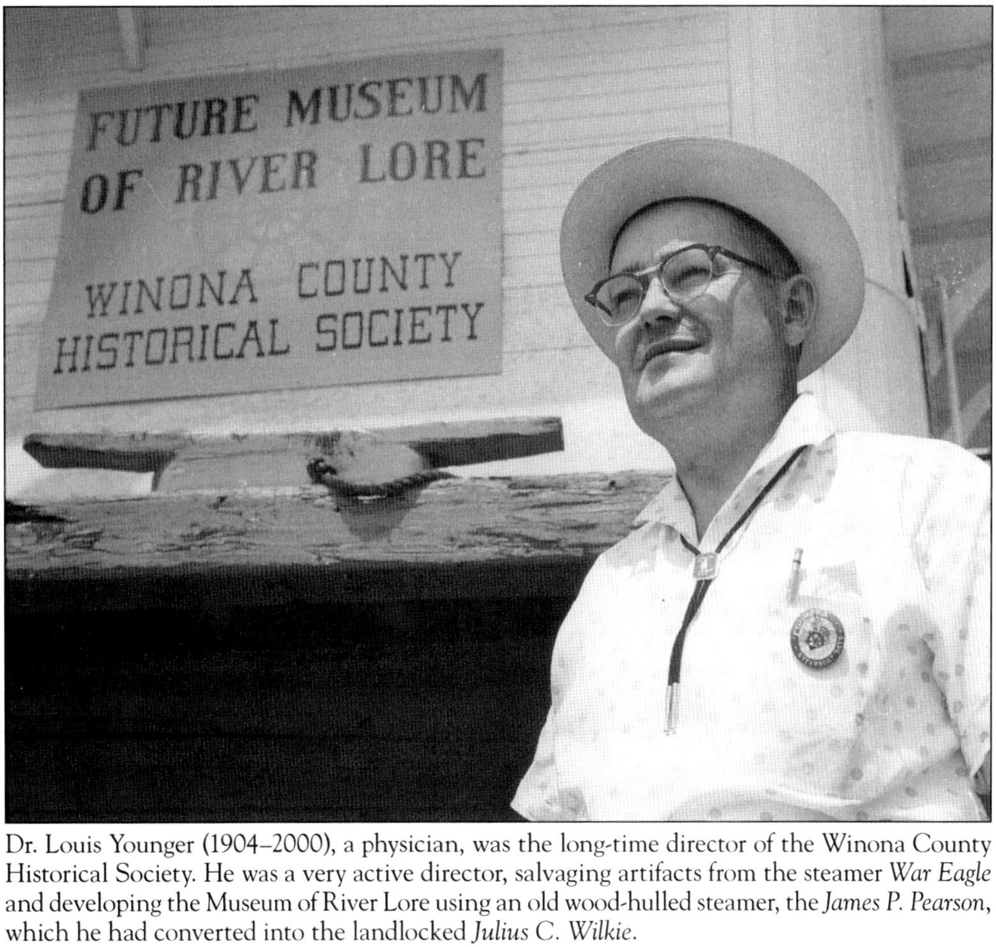

Dr. Louis Younger (1904–2000), a physician, was the long-time director of the Winona County Historical Society. He was a very active director, salvaging artifacts from the steamer *War Eagle* and developing the Museum of River Lore using an old wood-hulled steamer, the *James P. Pearson*, which he had converted into the landlocked *Julius C. Wilkie*.

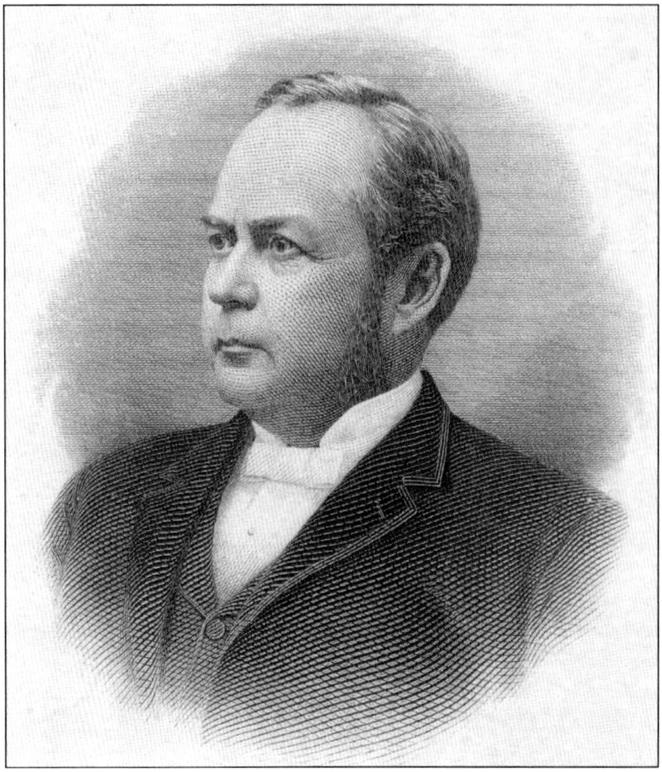

William Windom (1827–1891) was elected to the US Senate in 1871 and served until 1881, when he was nominated to Benjamin Harrison's cabinet as the secretary of the treasury. While serving in the Senate, Windom legislated for improvements to enhance navigation of the Mississippi River.

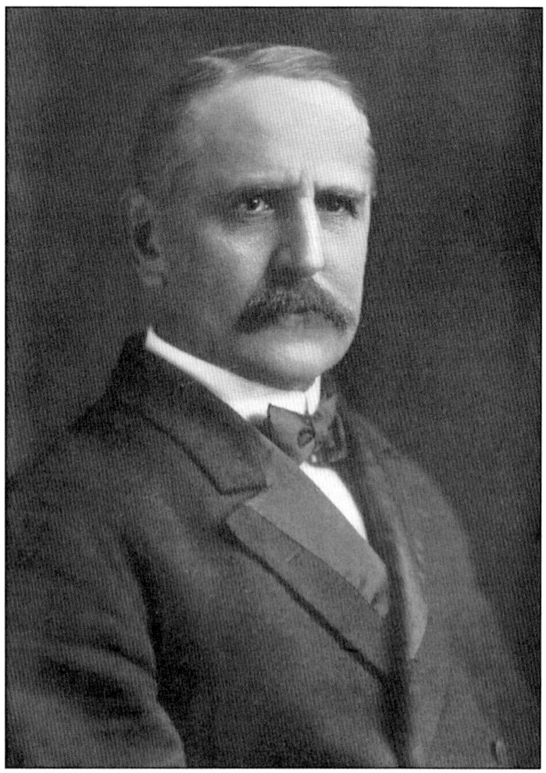

James A. Tawney (1855–1919) represented southeastern Minnesota's First District in Congress and for six years was the chairman of the House Appropriations Committee. As chairman, Tawney promoted legislation to improve navigation on the Mississippi River with a six-foot main navigation channel.

Calvin R. Fremling (1929–2010) taught biology at Winona State University for 32 years and was an active researcher in the study of aquatic ecology in the Mississippi River and in Lake Winona. He was the author or co-author of 47 publications, including a comprehensive study of Lake Winona, and his book *Immortal River: The Upper Mississippi in Ancient and Modern Times.*

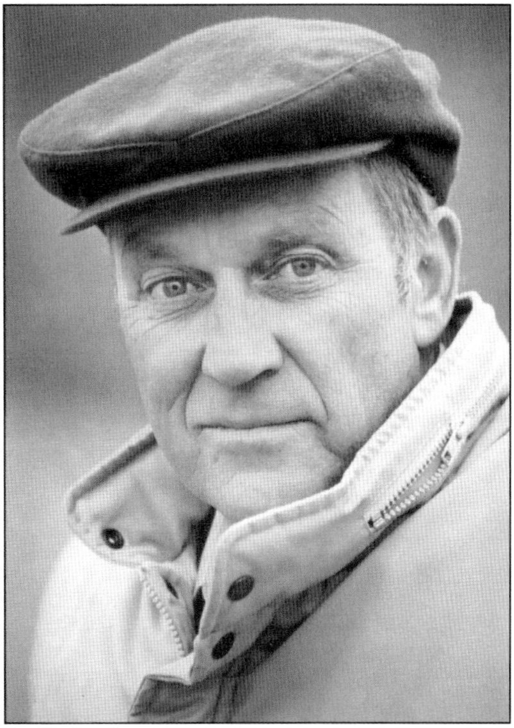

Dr. Fremling is prepared to work in his laboratory, the Mississippi River, studying aquatic life, especially the mayfly. Fremling completed his PhD at Iowa State University with the study of the mayfly at the Keokuk, Iowa, lock and dam no. 19.

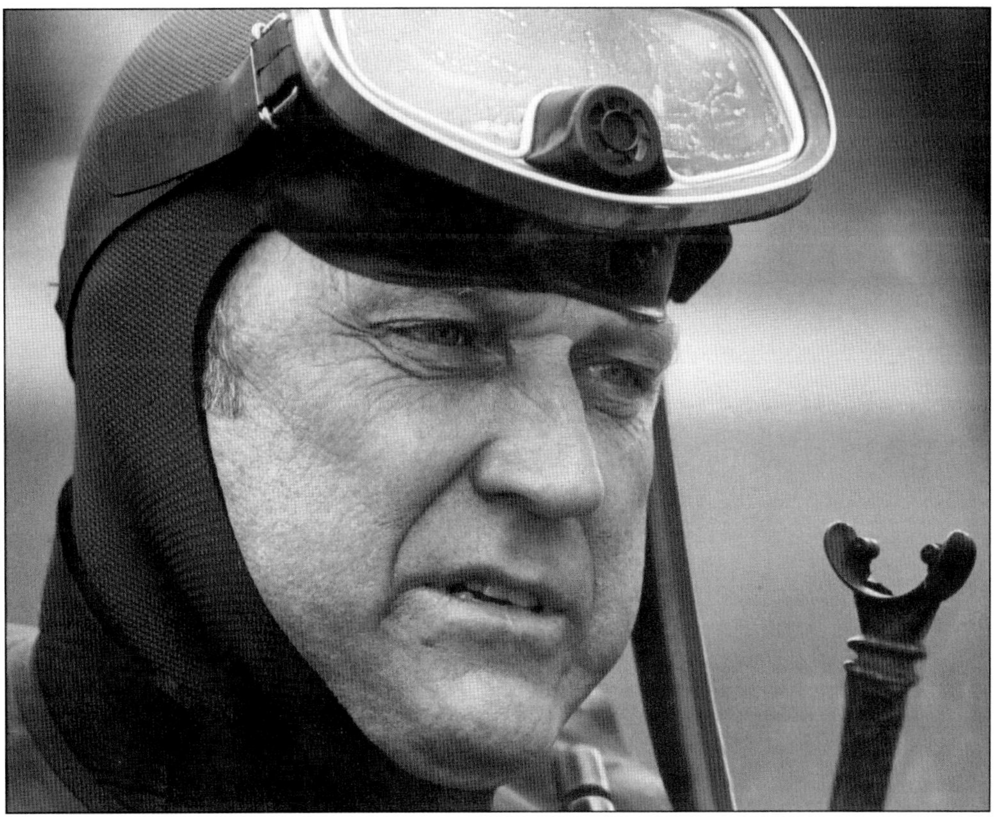

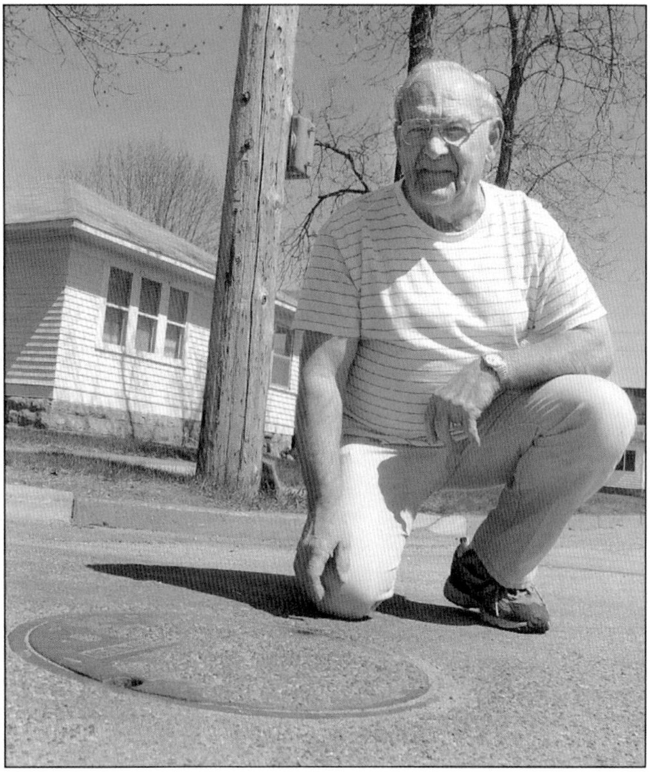

Raymond W. Beyers (1931–2009) poses at one of the storm sewers he descended to stop floodwaters from entering the city during the flood of 1965. He served in the US Navy during the Korean War. During the flood, he volunteered his diving skills he learned in the Navy to enter the storm sewers in borrowed diving gear. Beyers was a city firefighter and served as captain for 17 years, retiring in 1992.

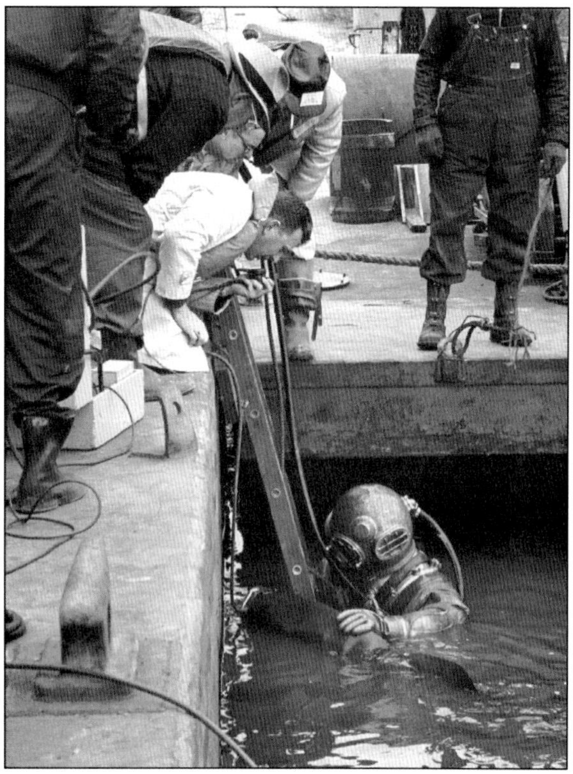

Ray Beyers is descending from a Kertzman Dredging Company barge into 17 feet of river water to stuff a dunnage bag into a storm sewer outlet near the Armour Fertilizer Plant at the foot of Jefferson Street on Winona's far east end.

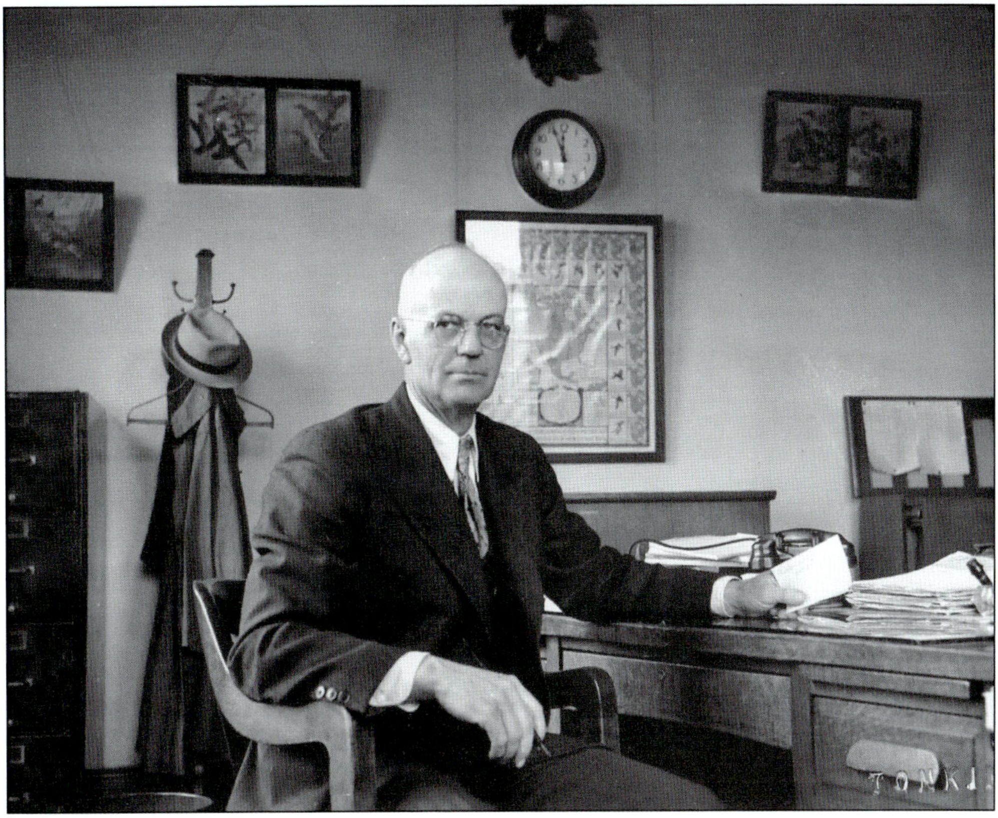

Ray C. Steele (1889–1958) was appointed superintendent of the Upper Mississippi River Wildlife and Fish Refuge in 1929 and served in that capacity for 30 years. While in charge of the refuge, he was responsible for the management and development of one of the most important wildlife refuges in the nation.

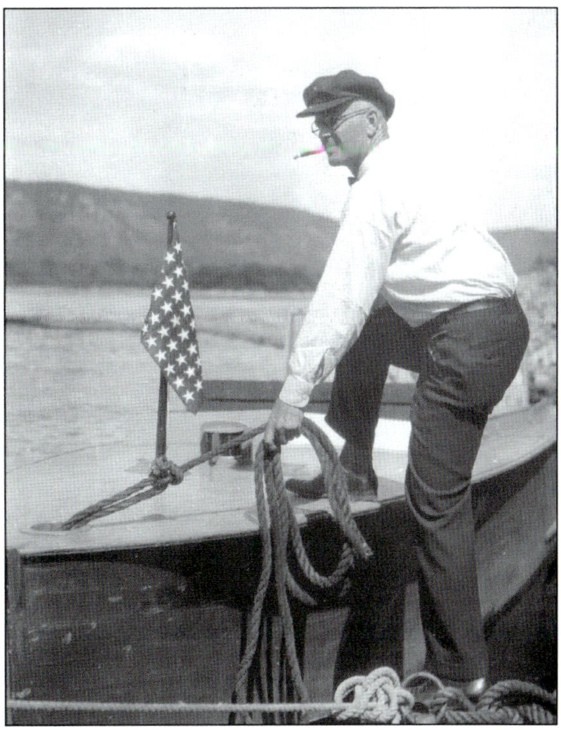

Ray Steele is boarding his personal power cruiser for a trip around the Upper Mississippi River Wildlife and Fish Refuge. Steele, a World War I veteran, had joined the US Biological Survey in 1920 as a game warden in Portland, Oregon.

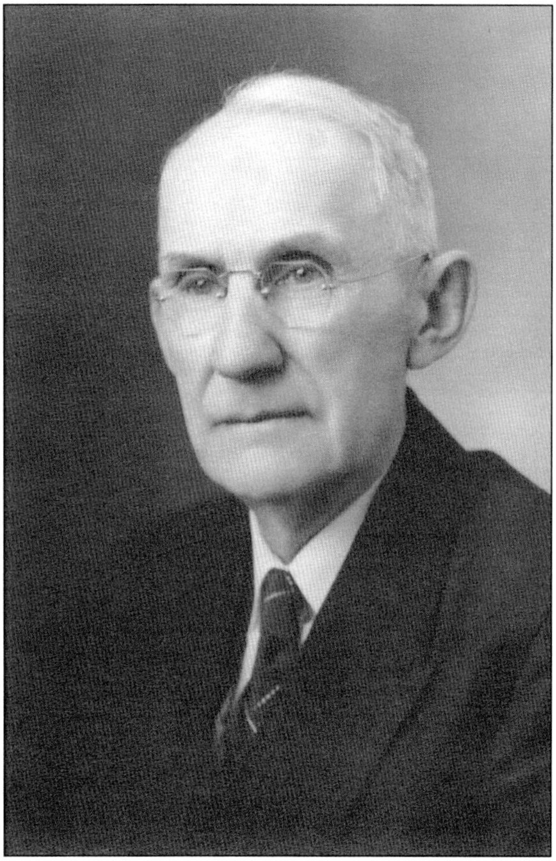

Frank Fugina (1868–1953) was one of the last of the Mississippi River's steamboat pilots, captains, and operators. His career spanned a period of 70 years, beginning when he was 15 years old. He was also an authority on the deepening and other improvements of the river channel. Captain Fugina was the author of *Lore and Lure of the Upper Mississippi River*, which was published in 1945, and wrote a column entitled "Ol' Man River" for the *Winona Daily News* beginning on April 26, 1947. After Fugina's death, the column was continued by Catharine Pletke until November 5, 1955.

The steamer *Columbia* was the first excursion boat owned by Captain Fugina, which he had purchased in 1905. It operated between Alma and La Crosse during the 1905 shipping season, carrying some 50,000 passengers. The *Columbia* was sold at the end of the 1905 season to the Florida East Coast Railway Company and replaced by a larger steamer.

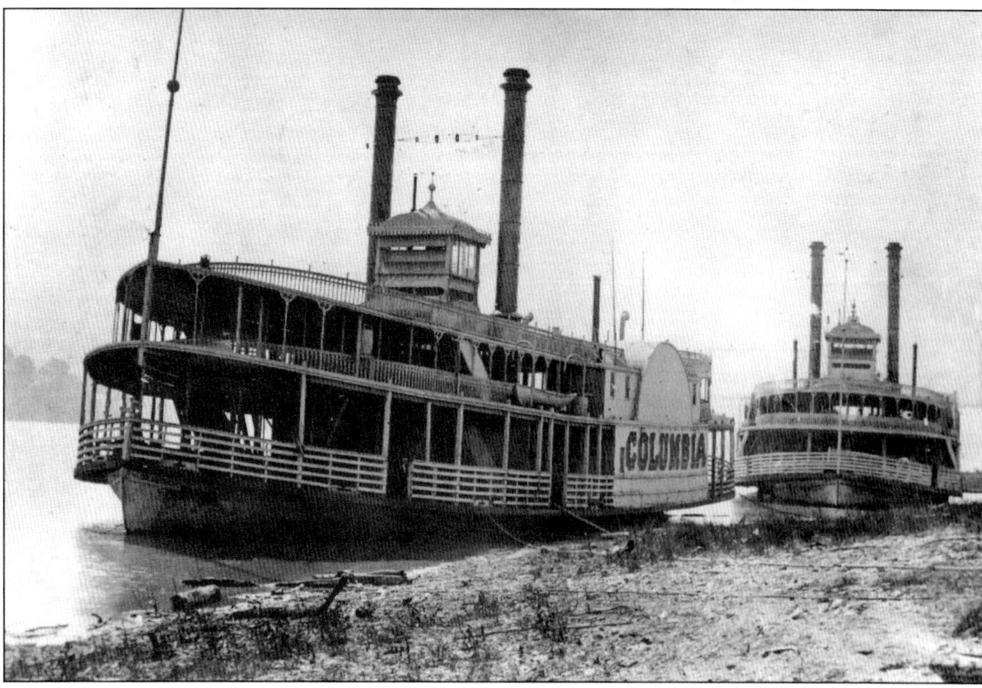

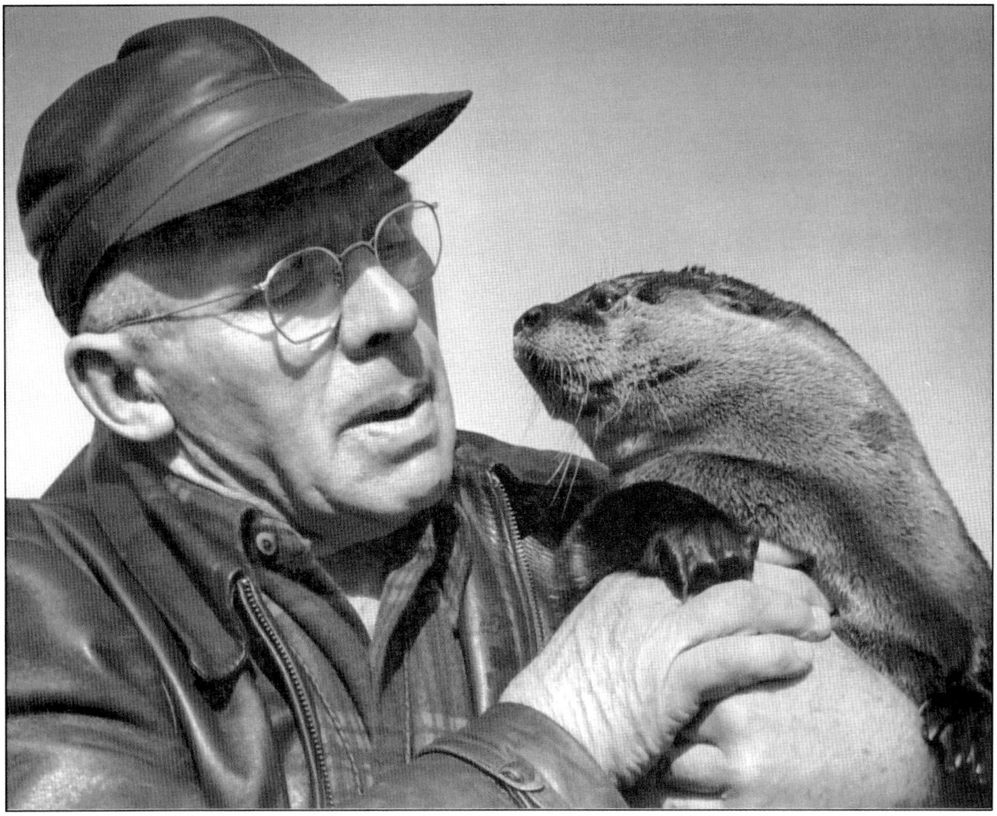

Emil E. Liers (1890–1975) is holding one of his many otters. He started his career as a trapper. While trapping an otter, he discovered her cubs, which he took home and cared for. Liers never trapped again, but rather developed a sanctuary for otters and became an expert on the animals. He wrote several children's books about wildlife and opened a sanctuary where he exhibited his otters. Liers is also seen below, playing with two otters at the sanctuary.

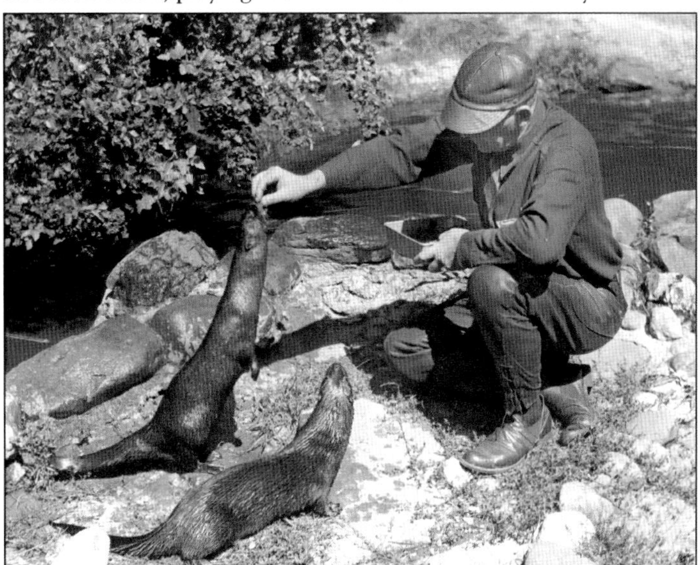

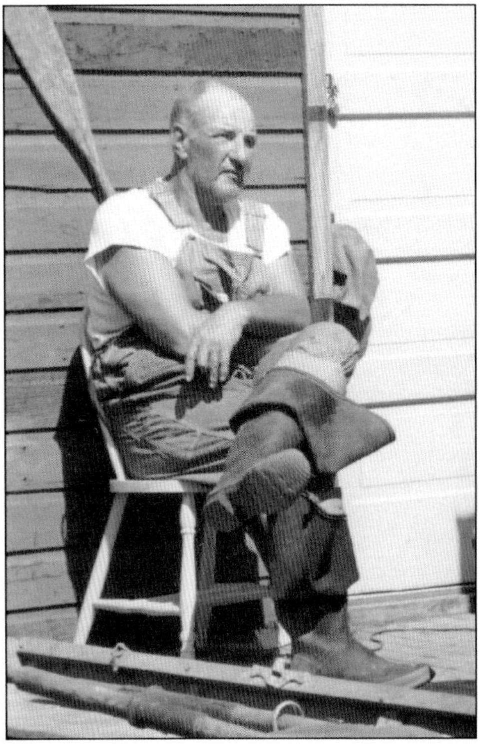

Ralph Richtman (1910–1972) is seen at left on his boat house near Winona. He was a longtime river boat captain and pilot and a commercial fisherman for over 30 years. He had tried to bring clamming back to the Upper Mississippi River after a Muscatine, Iowa, pearl button company hired him to promote their venture. Below, Richtman is pictured chatting with David Brinkley about the Mississippi River on his boat house near Mosquito Island on July 23, 1963. Brinkley was interviewing Richtman for the television documentary *Our Man on the Mississippi.* The program was much maligned by the local population as depicting the slum section of Winona.

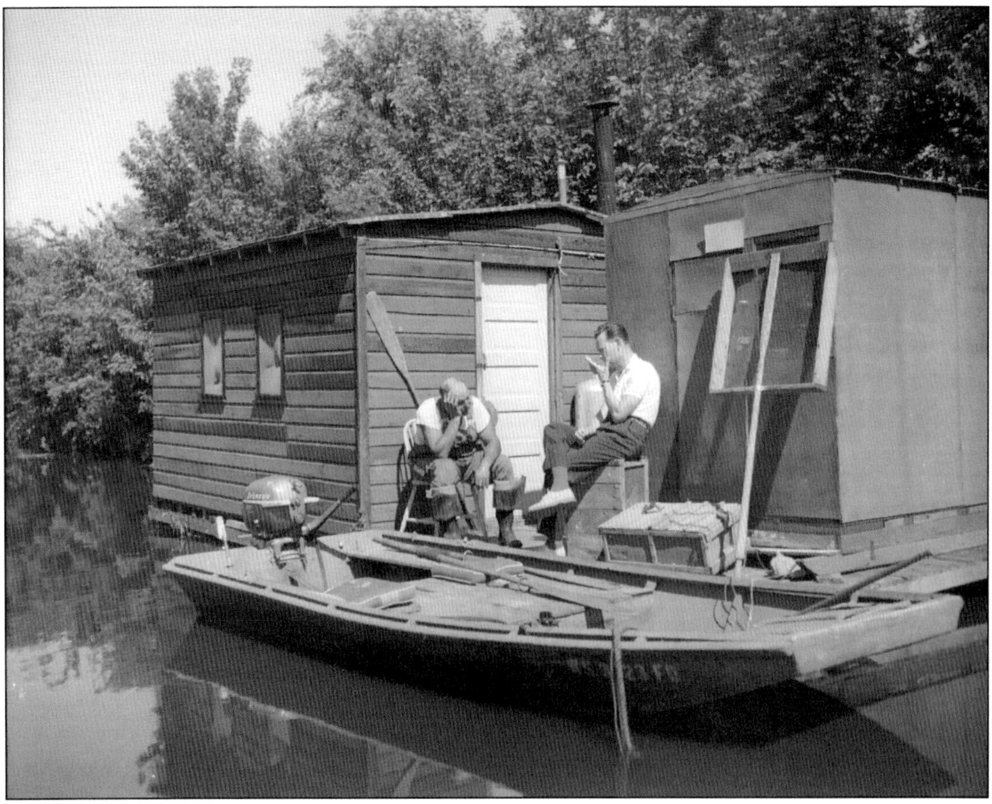

John A. Latsch (1860–1934) was in the wholesale grocery business serving steamboats and area grocers. However, his true calling was in philanthropy. He purchased land along the Mississippi River and donated it to the City of Winona and the states of Minnesota and Wisconsin to serve as parkland, recreational areas, and for conservation. His generosity also extended to hospitals, cemeteries, and other local establishments.

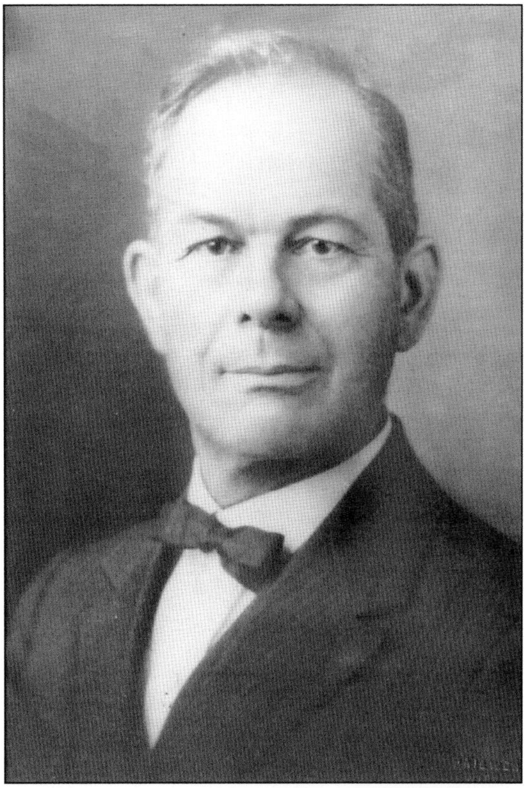

Some of the Mississippi River and valley that John Latsch canoed along, purchased, and donated to the states of Minnesota and Wisconsin to be used as park land can be seen here.

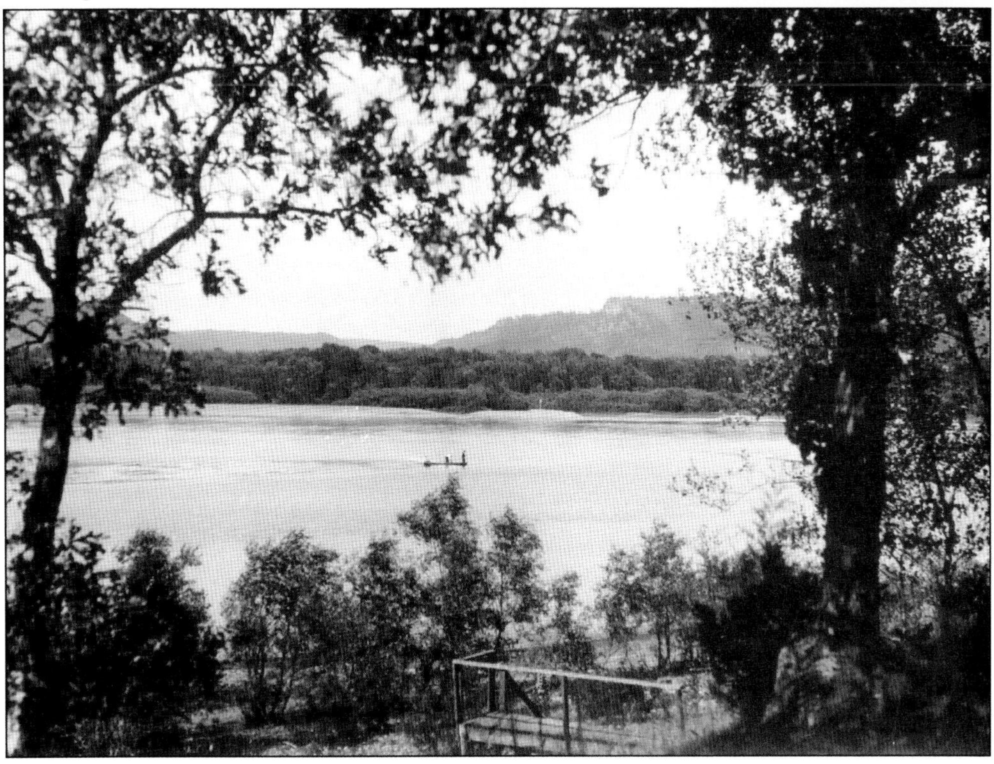

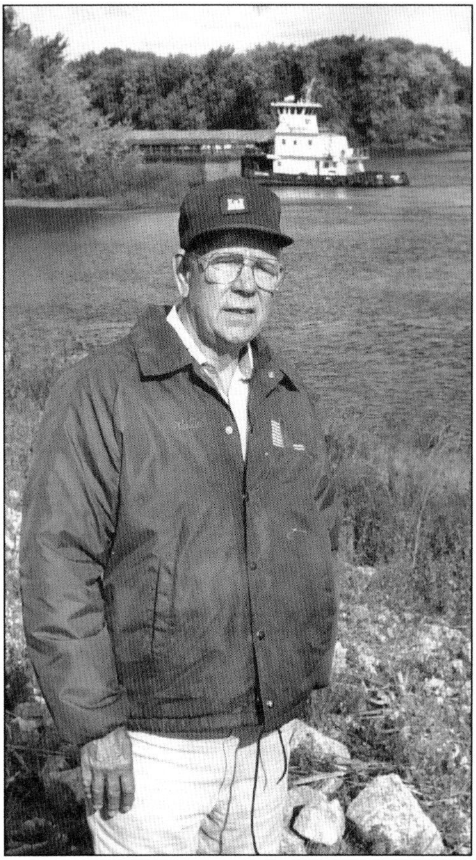

Wallace J. "Wally" Voss (1923–2010), after service in the US Navy during World War II, was employed by the Army Corps of Engineers as a lockmaster at the Mississippi River between Alma and Trempealeau. During the flood of 1965, he successfully directed corps efforts to protect Winona and the region from that devastating flood. Voss established the Corps of Engineers dive team and was later inducted into the diving hall of fame. His career with the corps spanned 37 years; the last 18 were spent at the lockmaster's house at Lock and Dam 5A in Fountain City. He retired from the corps in 1989. Below, Corps of Engineers diver Randy Piel enters the Mississippi River during renovation efforts at Lock and Dam 6 at Trempealeau in early December 1993.

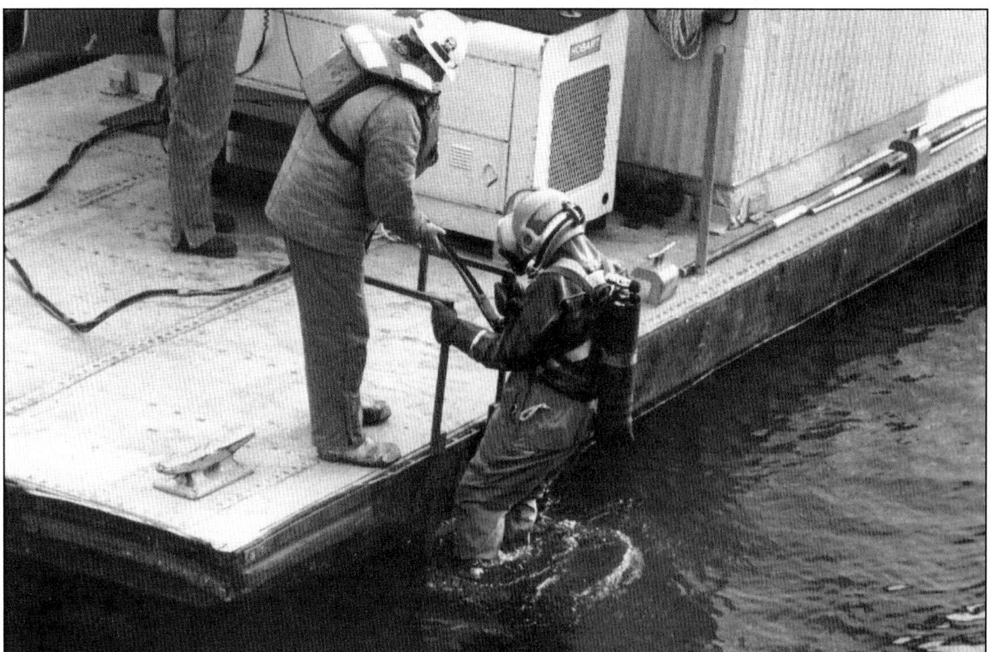

Orrin F. Smith (1854–1939), the second white male born on Wapasha Prairie, was named after Capt. Orrin Smith, Winona's founder. In 1887, Orrin was employed as the Winona agent for the Diamond Jo Packet Line, the position he held for four years, after which he moved to Chicago as an accountant for the 1893 World's Fair. He was an authority on the early history of Winona and the Upper Mississippi River.

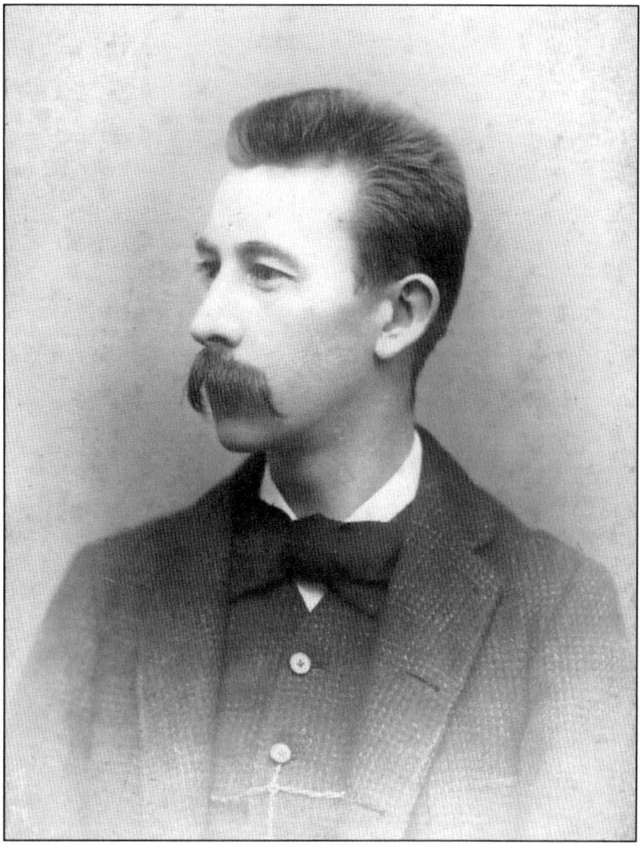

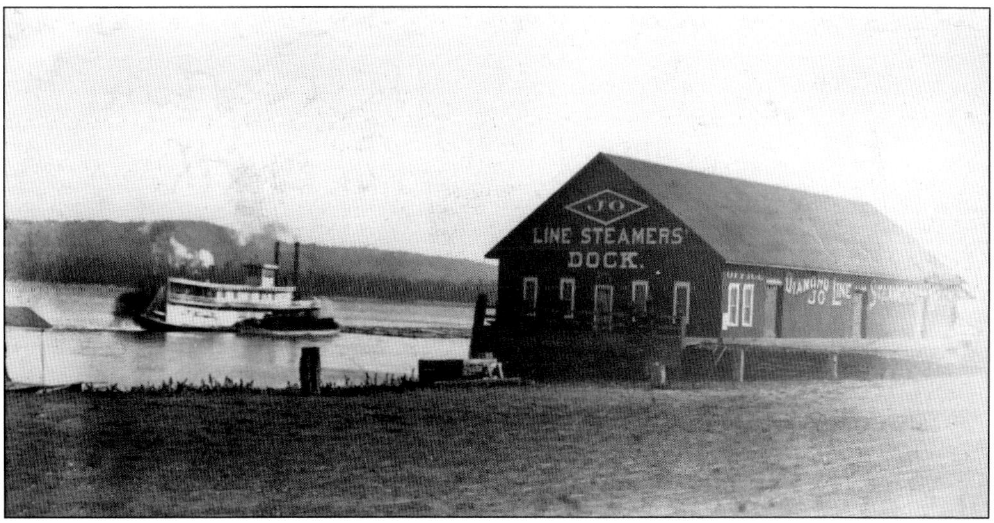

The Diamond Jo Packet Line's warehouse and dock was constructed at the foot of Lafayette Street in 1887. The dock was 290 feet by 50 feet, and the warehouse was 100 feet by 50 feet. The warehouse was encased in corrugated iron and included an office and passenger waiting area, along with much freight storage space. The company had leased space along the levee from the city for the nominal rental of $5 a year. By 1915, the warehouse became an eyesore, and the dock was mostly unusable.

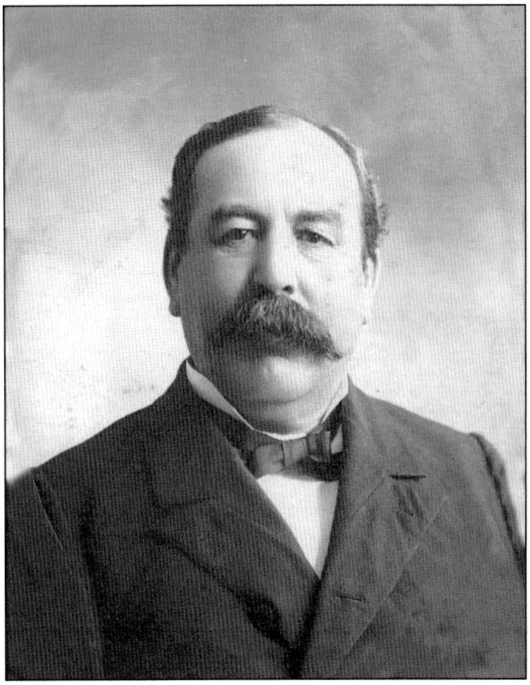

Samuel R. Van Sant (1844–1936) like his father, Sam, was a successful boat builder and by age 25 owned his own boatyard. He designed a new steamboat to move large rafts of timber down the Mississippi River to the saw mill. He moved his business to Winona in 1883, and in 1892 entered state politics and represented Winona in the legislature and also served as Minnesota's 15th governor.

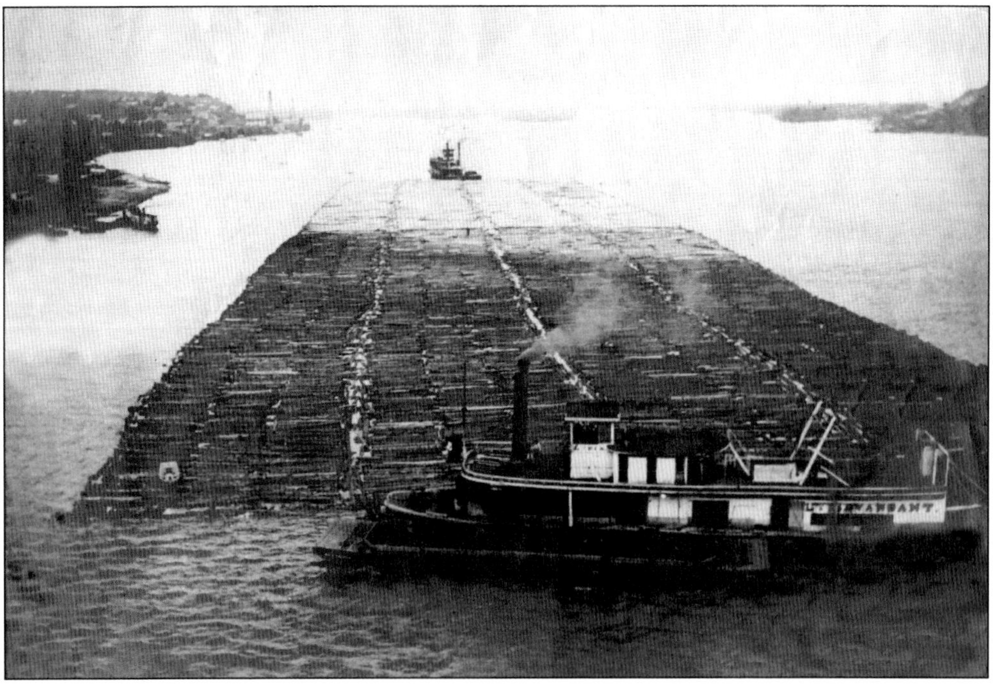

The steamer *J.W. Van Sant* and her bowboat *Lydia Van Sant* are towing a double-decked raft to a downriver sawmill. The logs are being rafted two deep; the smaller logs are placed crosswise on top of the larger logs. The *J.W. Van Sant* was the first stern-wheel raft boat with a large power plant that was purposely constructed around 1885 for the rafting business on the Mississippi River. The *Lydia Van Sant* was built in 1897 and was especially designed as a bow boat. Both were operated by Sam Van Sant.

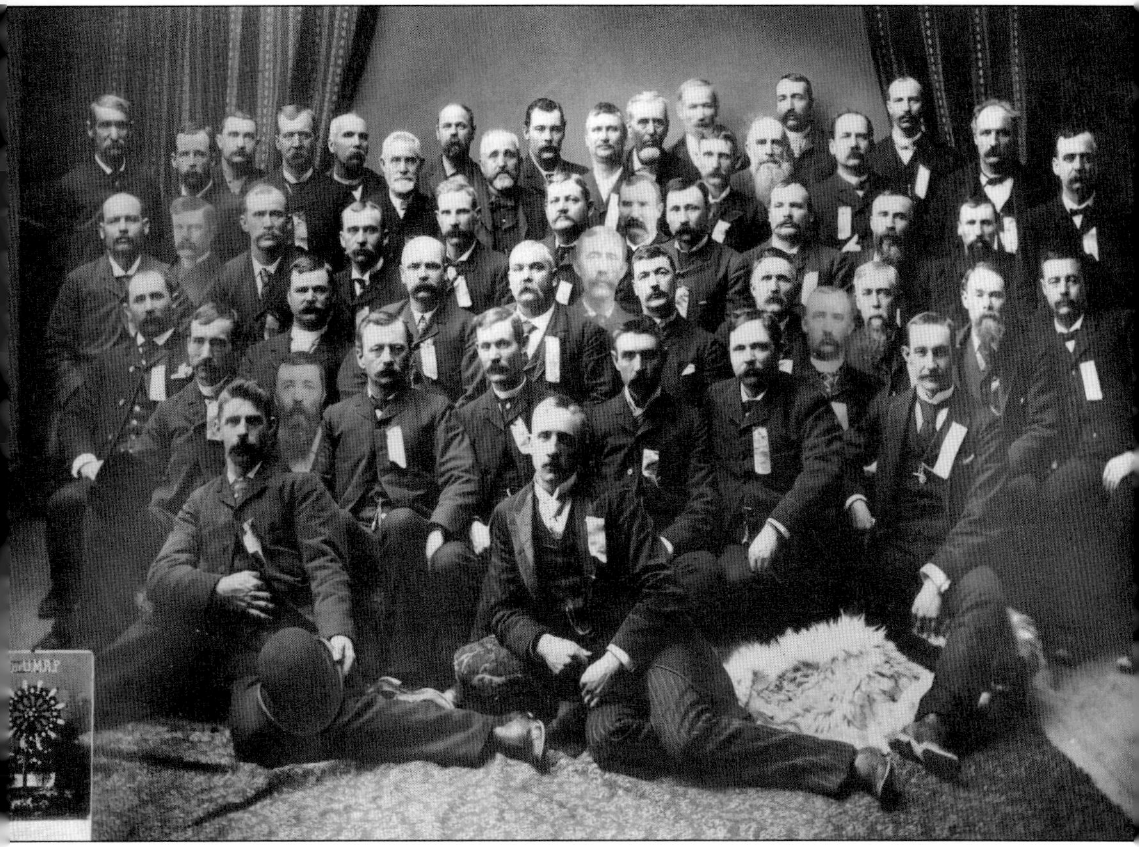

The Upper Mississippi River Pilots' Association held its annual meeting in La Crosse on December 4, 1890. The day was spent in discussing matters relating directly to the raft-towing business. The only thing of interest to the public was the adoption of a resolution directing the board of directors to enter into correspondence with owners and contractors in regard to working on Sunday. Pilots in attendance were, from left to right, (first row) J.B. Jenks and Harry Hugunin; (second row) James Newcomb, James Follmer, Henry Slocumb, John Hugunin, John O'Connor, A.P. Lambert, John H. Wooders, Russell Baldwin, Albert J. Hill, and Thomas Dolson; (third row) A.F. Case, George Nichols, J.E. Short, Wm. McCaffrery, T.C. Withrow, Vol. A. Biglow, Peter O'Rourke, James Hugunin, Ira Fuller, J.M Hawthorne, and Thomas Duncan; (fourth row) John Monore, Frank Looney, W.S. Mitchell, Abe Mitchell, M.M. Looney, J.W. Rabbo, Henry Fuller, Joseph Buisson, William York, W.W. Gordon, William Kratka, Jacob Ressor, and Wm. H. Whistler; (fifth row) John Langford, Frank Wetenhall, Hiram Bersie, James Whisler, A.R. Withrow, Dan Davison, Al. F. Hollinshead, J.W. Turner, Peter Hire, R.W. Cassidy, Chas. Rhodes, G.L. Short, Ithe Chacey, and Gara Denberg.

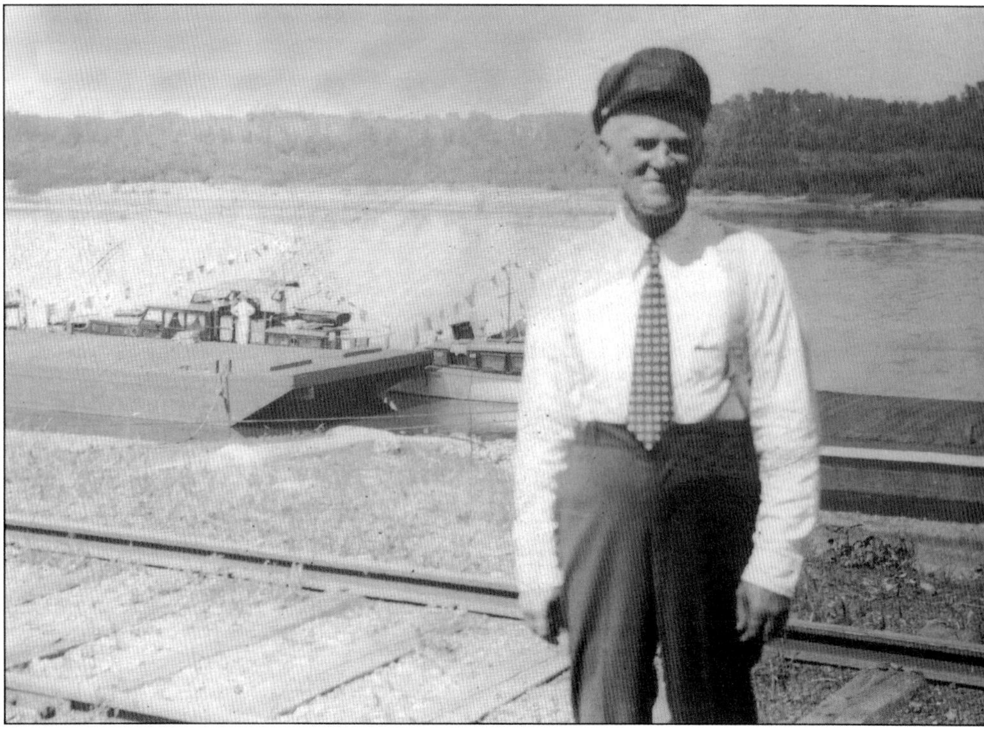

William Henning (1874–1968) was a 50-year veteran of the Army Corps of Engineers and between 1937 and 1943 served as the master of the dredge *William A. Thompson*. Henning began working on the river as a deck hand and fireman on board the *Robert Harris* and started his government service as a pilot on the towboats *Emily* and *Fury*. He also partnered with Frank Fugina in the excursion business on the steamer *Columbia*, the *H.L.*, and the *Fountain City*.

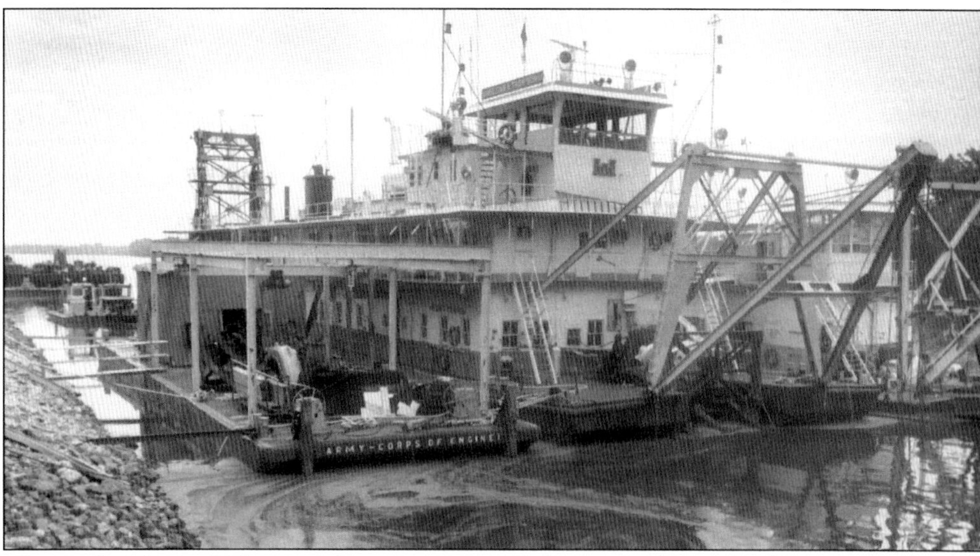

The 260-foot dredge *William A. Thompson* is at rest at the Corps of Engineers boat yard in Fountain City. The dredge, a part of the Army Corps of Engineers' heavy artillery for the maintenance of the Upper Mississippi's navigational channel, plays many roles on many parts of the Upper Mississippi River.

BIBLIOGRAPHY

Bennick, Walter. *Winona*. Charleston, SC: Arcadia Publishing, 2012.

Bunnell, Lafayette Houghton. *Winona and its Environs on the Mississippi in Ancient and Modern Days*. Winona, MN: Jones & Kroeger, 1897.

Curtis-Wedge, Franklyn, ed. *The History of Winona County Minnesota*, Volumes I and II. Chicago, IL: H.C. Cooper Jr. & Company, 1913.

Fremling, Calvin Rollins. *Immortal River: the Upper Mississippi in Ancient and Modern Times*. Madison, WI: University of Wisconsin Press, 2005.

————. "Biology and Possible Control of Economically Important Trichoptera and Ephemeroptera of the Upper Mississippi River." Ames, IA: Iowa State University Retrospective Theses and Dissertations, 1959.

Fugina, Frank J. *Lore and Lure of the Upper Mississippi River*. Winona, MN: Self published, 1945.

History of Winona County: Together with Biographical Matter, Statistics, Etc. Chicago, IL: H.H. Hill and Company, 1883.

Larson, Ron. *Upper Mississippi River History: Fact, Fiction, Legend*. Winona, MN: Steamboat Press, 1994.

Phillips, Martha Greene. *The Floating Boathouses on the Upper Mississippi River: Their History, Their Stories*. Self published, 2009.

Upham, Warren. *Minnesota in Three Centuries, 1655–1908*, Volume I: Description and Explorations, Semicentennial Edition. Mankato, MN: Publishing Society of Minnesota, 1908.

Winona County Historical Society and Winona Radio, ed. *Winona Memories: Historic Photo Album 1851–Today*. Pediment Publishing, 2001.